JOHN RIGG was born and raised in Leeds, Yorkshire. He graduated from the University of Cambridge with a degree in economics, later completing a PhD. He has worked as an economic consultant in London and in the Senior Civil Service in Scotland.

His sporting career principally comprised playing rugby league at primary school, rugby union at secondary school and college and cricket to a reasonable club standard.

John's first book on sport, *An Ordinary Spectator: 50 Years of Watching Sport*, was published in 2012. He has also written sport-related articles for *Backspin*, the *Rugby League Journal* and (co-authored with Richard Lewney) the *International Review of the Sociology of Sport*.

John's non-sporting articles have included those on economics and statistics for the *Scottish Economic Bulletin* and *Scottish Economic Statistics* and family history for the *Cleveland Family History Society Journal*.

He is married with two children and lives in Scotland.

Find out more about John and his writing at www.anordinaryspectator.com

Also by John Rigg

An Ordinary Spectator: 50 Years of Watching Sport

STILL AN ORDINARY SPECTATOR
Five More Years of Watching Sport

John Rigg

SilverWood

Published in 2017 by SilverWood Books

SilverWood Books Ltd
14 Small Street, Bristol, BS1 1DE, United Kingdom
www.silverwoodbooks.co.uk

Copyright © John Rigg 2017
Cover images © Dary423, Lance Bellers, Neil Wigmore @Dreamstime | Brocreative, zsolt_uveges, Mark Herried, fotoinfot, Pavel L Photo and Video @Shutterstock | Jaco Janse van Rensburg, flairmicro, nmint @123RF

If any copyright holder believes that their material has been used without due credit, the author will make reasonable efforts to correct omissions in any future re-printing.

The right of John Rigg to be identified as the author of this work has been asserted in accordance with the Copyright, Designs and Patents Act 1988 Sections 77 and 78.

All rights reserved. No part of this publication may be reproduced, stored in a retrieval system, or transmitted in any form or by any means, electronic, mechanical, photocopying, recording or otherwise, without prior permission of the copyright holder.

ISBN 978-1-78132-650-3 (paperback)
ISBN 978-1-78132-651-0 (ebook)

British Library Cataloguing in Publication Data
A CIP catalogue record for this book is available from the British Library

Page design and typesetting by SilverWood Books
Printed on responsibly sourced paper

This book is dedicated to my mother, Peggie Rigg

Contents

	Preface	xi
Football	An Echo at Rangers	1
Cricket	Don Wilson	3
Football	Olympic Games Football...	5
Rugby League	No Trains to Featherstone	7
Rugby Union	A Longevity Record at West of Scotland	9
Cricket/Memory	A Philosophical Query...	11
Cricket	The "Nano-Drama"...	13
Cricket	The Future of Test Match Cricket	16
Cricket	The Future of Test Match Cricket...	20
Football	Under the Rock	22
Rugby League	The Elderly, Frail-looking Figure...	25
Rugby League...	Martin Offiah...	27
Rugby League...	Scores and Values	30
Cricket	The Western Terrace	33
Cricket	Proper Cricket	35
Rugby League...	A New Season	38
Cricket	"He's a Player"	41
Rugby League	Professional Sport: A Microcosm	44
Football	Killing Time(s)	46
Sport/General	"It Makes Me Realise..."	48
Cricket	The End of an Era	52
Rugby League	50th Anniversary of a Torrid Ashes Battle...	54
Football	Into The Valley	59
Rugby Union	A Weekend in Bristol	62
Rugby Union	Bragging Rights	64
Rugby League	Match Programmes...	66
Football	Hoardings and Plaques	71
Sport on Television	Television Lines	74
Football	A Polish Masterclass and "Our Club"	78
Cricket...	"Hit For Four"	81
Gaelic Football	"Hard but Fair From Gun to Tape"	84
Football	Outcomes and Hopes	88
Cricket...	Casual Conversations of a Sport Tourist	90

Rugby League	The Shay and Mrs Simpson	95
Swimming	We "Gie It Laldy" at Tollcross	98
Gymnastics	The Pommel Horse and Darth Vader	101
Cricket…	Test Match Special	104
Rugby League	Gateshead Thunder…	108
Rugby Union	Return to Scotstoun	111
Rugby League	The Garden Gate	113
Cricket	Suspended Animation	116
First World War	Ruhleben	118
Football	A Stramash in Paisley	121
Rugby Union	Stade Toulousain	124
Rugby League	Boxing Day Repeats	127
Football	The Chances of Success	130
Football	Internazionale	133
Rugby League	A Close Rivalry of Half a Century ago	144
Ice Hockey	The Clan and the Capitals	150
Rugby Union	The Case for Sharing	153
Cricket	Yorkshire CCC…	156
Hockey	I'll Go To The End Of Our Street	161
Football	3rd Versus 17th	164
Rugby League	An Afternoon in Whitehaven	167
Cricket	The Unorthodox and the Traditional	171
Rugby League	The Battle for Fourth Place	174
Cricket	The Past and the Present in Roberts Park	177
Speedway	The Eye of the Tiger	181
Cricket	"Match Drawn (Pitch Violated)"…	185
Rugby League	The Spectacular and Thrilling "Boy Hero"	189
Cricket	Headingley and Hove	193
Football	Legends	196
American Football	Friday Night Lights	199
American Football	The Alamodome	203
Cricket	"Death of a Gentleman"	207
Rugby Union	What's in a Name?	210
Cycling…	Seeing and Believing	213
Rugby Union	No New Kitchen	216
Football	Allegiances	218
Rugby Union…	Overlaps and Skills	220
Rugby League	Two Cumbrias	224
Cycling	Cycling Nun Raises Irish Hopes…	227
Football	The View from the Milburn Stand	229
Football	The Bully Wee	233

Rugby League	Humiliation, Tactical Offside…	236
Cricket	Bank Holiday Monday	241
Cricket	Six and Out	245
Golf…	Income Levels	248
Rugby League	Eights	252
Rugby League	Mr Jepson	256
Football	Blue Ribbons and a Talented Sportsman	258
Rugby League	Elite Sportsmen at the Top of Their Game	262
	Notes	265
	Acknowledgements	269
	Bibliography	270
	Index	273

Preface

When writing *An Ordinary Spectator: 50 Years of Watching Sport*, which was published in July 2012, I structured the book around what I labelled as "My Seven Ages" of sports spectating. This variant on the Shakespearean theme began with my status (from the age of 6) as an Awestruck Novice, in which I entered "a strange new world of allegiances and rivalries, of history and tradition, and of the emotional highs and lows of sports spectating."

At the book's conclusion (when I was 56), I had reached my penultimate Age – the Affluent Reflective – when, with the security of a comfortable middle-class lifestyle, I had become more selective in my choice of sports events and, occasionally, more willing to move up the price range for some that I attended. At that point, the last of my Seven Ages – the Childlike Sage, characterised by the Bard's "second childishness and mere oblivion" of inevitable mental and physical deterioration – had not been reached.

This follow-up book takes the story on a further five years by bringing together the various pieces of sports writing that I have published since 2012. Most of these have taken the form of occasional blogs released on www.anordinaryspectator.com/news-blog/, though I have also drawn on articles published in *Backspin* and the *Rugby League Journal* and a contribution to the (then) online Members Forum of Yorkshire CCC.

As with *An Ordinary Spectator*, the main constituents of what follows relate to the sports of rugby (union and league), cricket and football. However, whilst some of the venues will be familiar – Scarborough Cricket Ground, South Leeds Stadium, Scotstoun Stadium *et al* – others (large and small) are visited for the first time: football at Newcastle United and Clyde, rugby league in Barrow and the Olympic Stadium in London, for example. The overseas locations include the playing fields of Germany, Texas and Ireland. In addition, there are also a number of sports that did not feature in the original book: ice-hockey, field hockey, Gaelic football, speedway, swimming and gymnastics. The eclecticism of this list is something of a virtue, I think. It means that, by definition, there are perspectives and nuances of sports spectating presented in this volume that were not examined the first time round.

This book differs from its predecessor in another significant respect. Where a piece describes and/or reflects on a sporting event that had just taken place (usually a couple of days or so beforehand), there is an immediacy to my interpretation of events that was obviously not present in most of *An Ordinary Spectator*, where the relevant actions had occurred years – if not decades – earlier.

This is both an advantage and disadvantage: on the one hand, it generates the freshness of a contemporary perspective that has not been distorted by the passage of time; on the other, it disallows the possibility for more considered reflection and analysis of what I had seen. In some cases, the piece prompts an obvious question – "What happened next?" – that I have generally attempted to answer through the use of selective Notes presented at the end of the book.

By contrast, in other pieces – usually, though not exclusively, when not reporting on a contemporary sporting event – there was just this opportunity to provide a more reflective interpretation in the article or blog. In some instances, this was prompted by the anniversary (often the fiftieth) of an episode of sports spectating that had been deeply personal to me: for example, seeing the great Brian Bevan playing for Blackpool Borough in 1963 or recalling my first visit to Headingley Cricket Ground for the Roses Match of 1966. On other occasions, the article has sought to express my views on a specific issue within the contemporary sporting environment – examples range from the use of points differentials to determine the winners of rugby union's Six Nations Championship through to the impact of technological developments in cricket bat manufacture on the prevalence of six-hitting.

The book therefore represents a combination of the past and the present with – I would argue – each informing the other. Of course, at its most straightforward, the recollection of sport as it used to be played (or presented or watched) can provide a sense of poignant reminiscence. It is this objective – combined with what are sometimes forthright descriptions of their respective sports in times past – which is met by high-quality magazines such as *Backpass* (football) and *Backspin* (cricket). In addition, however, the nostalgic examination of a sport's past can also provide insight on the virtues and faults of its present-day equivalents. The contents of the *Rugby League Journal* consistently provide excellent examples of how, by drawing on an informed knowledge-base covering the sport over the long period since the Second World War, there is a credibility underpinning the arguments about how the modern version of rugby league could be improved.

Looking through the collection of pieces presented in this book, I am struck again by three themes which emerged strongly in *An Ordinary Spectator*. The first is a key characteristic of spectating life: that of echoes and repeats. In the first book, I introduced this concept as being analogous to the well-established dramatic technique whereby there is a "low key introductory reference to a character – or, alternatively, an incident or a place or a particular set of circumstances – that is later revealed to be of some significance." (An illustration presented there was the rugby player, Andy Farrell: a teenage league international representing Great Britain against New Zealand at Headingley in 1993; a 30-something playing in the union code for Saracens against Glasgow fifteen years later). One variation on this theme that I like in this volume concerns a police sergeant with whom I chatted outside the Ibrox Stadium in Glasgow before a football match in 2012, who mentioned that he had been on duty for the famous Rangers-Leeds United European Cup tie at the same venue almost twenty years earlier.

Second, there is my continued admiration for the skill, dedication and/or courage of the sportsmen and women I have observed. In *An Ordinary Spectator*, I highlighted this through the identification of my "First XI" of sporting "nano-dramas" of the previous half-century: the split-seconds of action that I had seen that had made the hairs on the back of the neck stand on end. (One of these was Gary McAllister's first-minute volleyed goal for Leeds United – which silenced the stadium – in the match at Ibrox noted above). In this volume, I simply note – with a combination of awe and respect – the examples of sporting excellence: a masterclass in centre-forward play by Robert Lewandowski; a superb display of full-back skills by Clement Poitrenaud; an exquisite Bubba Watson chip out of a Troon bunker; an exhibition of all-round brilliance by the Australian rugby league team. And so on.

The third recurrent theme is sport's innate ability to act as a barometer of the society around it. I emphasise again that this is not an original thought, but it has been striking how the point is repeated in the pieces that follow. In *An Ordinary Spectator*, I referred to several commentators who had eloquently remarked on these lines, including Mike Brearley, CLR James, WF Deedes and Simon Barnes. Accordingly, I draw again on

Tony Collins's introduction to his authoritative *Rugby's Great Split: Class, Culture and the Origins of Rugby League Football*: "Sporting culture reflects the society in which it is rooted and can offer us a window through which to study that society." Examples are given in the pages that follow, ranging from the role of high school American Football in San Antonio, Texas, through to the staging of the Homeless World Cup in Glasgow's George Square.

There is an extension to this argument. It concerns the extent to which the development of a particular sporting thread – an idea, perhaps, or a memory – can lead one down some apparently unrelated paths. Hence, in this volume, I find myself covering, amongst other things: the First World War internment camp at Ruhleben, Berlin; the religious wars in Scotland in the 1680s, known as "The Killing Times"; and the tourist attractions of Grasmere in Cumbria. Unrelated paths perhaps, but interesting ones nonetheless.

The articles and blogs presented in this book are more or less unchanged from their original publication. The principal editing that I have undertaken, where appropriate, has been to shift some of the quotations taken from *An Ordinary Spectator* (abbreviated to *OS*) to the beginning of the article; I hope that this has assisted in establishing the general context to the piece before allowing the relevant theme to be explored. (I have retained the present tense in which many of these pieces were written). I have also removed some of the direct references to *An Ordinary Spectator* itself. A couple of blogs have not been included because they added very little to the material already given in the original book. In addition, as noted, a limited amount of post-event updating has been presented (in the End Notes to the book), though hopefully this does not distract from the contemporary feel of the pieces.

As in *An Ordinary Spectator*, my status at the sporting events I have reported in this volume has been that of observer – usually detached and independent. Accordingly, I was particularly struck by a photograph – reproduced here – taken of me by Llyr James when we attended a football match at the Stadion an der Alten Försterei in Berlin in 2014. With hindsight (and with due apologies for any perceived pretentiousness), it is evident that the compositional device is appropriately that of the *Rückenfigur* – a foreground figure, seen from behind, contemplating the view in front of him – as frequently used by the great nineteenth century German landscape artist, Caspar David Friedrich. More relevantly, however, the photograph perfectly captures what I take to be my spectating persona: attentive and reflective and, whilst part of the overall picture, also separated from it in my own space.

*

A final thought by way of introduction. I stated in *An Ordinary Spectator* that the use of the "Seven Ages of Watching Sport" concept was more than simply a literary conceit. It also partly reflected the obvious (but important) point that one's perspective inevitably changes as one gets older: "Put simply, the 6 year-old's analysis of what he sees in front of him will be different to that of the 16 year-old; likewise the 16 year-old and the 56-year old. These differences will be determined not only by age and experience – though these factors are clearly significant – but also by circumstances and context."

I wonder if this principle also allows for differences between the 56 year-old and the 61 year-old. At the time of completing *An Ordinary Spectator* (in 2011 for publication in 2012), I had newly retired from the Senior Civil Service in Scotland and I was coming to terms with the removal of the everyday contact and social interaction that full-time employment had brought. In the articles and blogs of the last five years, it is revealing how many references there are to casual conversations that I have had with complete strangers: a behavioural trait that, until this period, would not perhaps have been associated with me. (The policeman outside Ibrox Stadium I have already mentioned; a later example – late one evening, next to a bus-stop in San Antonio, Texas – extracted me from potentially serious difficulty). In one blog, I use the phrase "[t]he honesty and intimacy imparted in the conversations with strangers" in connection with a brief (but revealing) chat I had with someone at a County Championship cricket match. I do think that – in my case at least – the increased incidence of such behaviour can be attributed to a combination of the passage of time and the change in personal circumstances.

But is it also associated with entry into the seventh and final Age – the Childlike Sage? Not necessarily, I trust. I realise that that time might one day come – perhaps it is inevitable – but it is not here yet.

Football

An Echo at Rangers

In *An Ordinary Spectator: 50 Years of Watching Sport*, I report on how, after first moving up to Scotland in 1992, I took the opportunity to watch matches at both Celtic and Rangers that year. For the former, in April, a home match against Dunfermline Athletic produced a lacklustre end-of-season win in front of a modest crowd in a run-down stadium. By contrast, for Rangers, playing Leeds United in a European Cup qualifying round in October, there was a vibrant victory for their vociferous supporters to celebrate in a packed stadium. I describe that noise at Ibrox that night as the loudest that I have ever heard in a sporting arena.

How times change.

Following the completion of the book, I re-visited both clubs for fixtures at the end of the 2011-12 season: Celtic vs Motherwell and Rangers vs Dundee United. There was a home victory in each case – 1-0 and 5-0, respectively – but the context has, of course, shifted dramatically. For Celtic, the match was part of the long celebratory climax to the season as their huge lead in the Scottish Premier League table – aided, but far from dependent on, the 10 point penalty incurred by Rangers for going into administration – was maintained. For Rangers, at that time, there was only huge uncertainty about the future – survival? liquidation? a possible American purchaser (unwanted by some)? – which the short-term euphoria provided by the evening's comfortable win could not assuage.[1]

In the book, I include Gary McAllister's goal for Leeds in the 1992 encounter as one of my First XI of outstanding "nano-dramas." Following a corner in the first minute of the game, the ball was headed out to the edge of the Rangers penalty area and then expertly volleyed by McAllister into the Rangers net. I recall that the crowd – in theory, all Rangers fans, as a ban had been placed on visiting supporters – fell deathly silent, apart from a handful of Leeds followers down to my right, who had somehow managed to breach the embargo but whose cover was now betrayed by their own celebrations.

As I had arrived for the Dundee United match well before kick-off time, I took a slow walk around the outside of the Ibrox stadium. In front of the imposing main entrance, I fell into conversation with a sturdy middle-aged policeman who was on duty for the game. I mentioned that it was my first visit to the ground for almost 20 years – since the Leeds game, in fact. He responded that he had been on duty on that night also, on the half way line, and he promptly described the McAllister goal precisely as I had remembered it, complete with the reaction of the small knot of Leeds fans and the hostile intensity of the counter-reaction by the surrounding Rangers support.

The years fell away as he spoke. It was two decades ago. And it was yesterday.

www.anordinaryspectator.com/news-blog July 2012

Cricket

Don Wilson

> *I followed [the ball] on its full trajectory, as it nearly disappeared into the sky and then, as gravity took its toll, plummeted to land somewhere between us and the refreshment tents. It was a magnificent strike, characteristic of Wilson's potential for dangerous hitting, when, as a tall left-hander, he would plant his right leg down the wicket and look to free his arms in a full swing. [OS, page 76]*

In recent years, I have had regular occasion to note the passing of those former sportsmen (in their 70s or 80s) who had been in their peak or veteran years during the period of my earliest interest in sport.

Don Wilson, who died at the weekend at the age of 74, played for Yorkshire CCC between 1957 and 1974 and for England in 6 test matches. He was already firmly established in the county side, therefore, when my father and my Uncle Vic took me to see Yorkshire play, for the first time, against Lancashire in the Headingley Roses Match of 1966. Wilson was a tall, slim, angular left-arm bowler and it did not take me long to work out that he was the ideal complement to the off-spinning wiles of Ray Illingworth.

The principal references to Wilson in *An Ordinary Spectator* are in relation to the Gillette Cup semi-final of 1969. I was 14. My friend Brian Stevens and I, having caught an early morning bus from Leeds, took two of the last remaining places in the packed Scarborough ground and watched an enthralling battle between Yorkshire and Nottinghamshire. I describe the accuracy of Wilson's bowling to the great Gary Sobers as Yorkshire successfully defended the reasonable, but not overwhelming, score they had registered in the first innings.

But, if I were restricted to identifying a single memory of Wilson, it would be of that huge six that he struck when Yorkshire sought quick runs towards the end of their innings.

I read the short paragraph reporting Don Wilson's death in yesterday's Sunday newspaper and, in my mind's eye, it was a warm summer's day in my early teenage years and I was craning my head back to watch the path of a cricket ball against a blue sky.

www.anordinaryspectator.com/news-blog July 2012

Football

Olympic Games Football: What Do I Know?

I have visited the Olympic Stadiums in Munich, Barcelona and Moscow – though none of these trips were for the Games themselves. Two were to watch football matches and for the third (Moscow) I simply walked in off the street and sat alone (and untroubled) in a seat in one of the open stands.

Last week, I became an Olympian spectator for the first time.

I must start by admitting that I do not think that football should be in the Olympics. (Nor tennis and golf for that matter). It has its own cycle of major tournaments that already provide more than adequate opportunities for global recognition and acclaim. However, having somehow failed in my bid to obtain tickets for the men's 100 metres sprint final, I settled for attendance at two of the matches in the London 2012 Olympics played at Hampden Park: Belarus vs Egypt (men) and France vs Sweden (women).

The final round of men's group matches began with Belarus probably only needing a draw (unless New Zealand were to obtain an unlikely win against Brazil); Egypt needed to win. The game took some time to get going – 10 minutes until the first foul, 25 minutes until the first shot on target – which prompted my neighbour in the stand to remark that it was like watching Scotland. However, once Egypt got into their stride, it was clear that they would be comfortable winners: 3-1 as it turned out. I was impressed by the speedy Mohammed Salah on the right wing and the commanding defenders, Ahmed Hegazi and Saadeldin Saad. Egypt were now quarter-finalists and looking promising, I thought later in a central Glasgow branch of Ladbrokes, particularly at the second longest odds of 20 to 1.

The French women were also good value for their quarter-final win, coming from behind to beat Sweden 2-1. The Swedes were physically strong and well organised, but France had the guile in midfield (Louisa Necib and Elise Bussaglia), a commanding goalkeeper (Sarah Bouhaddi) and pace and athleticism in the forward line. Another good bet, I wondered.

The attendances for the two games – 8,000 and 12,000, respectively – were well below the Hampden capacity, of course. But these were not the usual football crowds in any case. At each game, the neutral majority applauded both sides, respected the referees (both excellent, I should note) and indulged in their Mexican waves. There were families with young children who, thankfully, were not subjected to the usual aggression and language of male-dominated terraces. I enjoyed both matches, and I enjoyed the occasions – of being part of the London 2012 Olympics, albeit at some distance.

A recurrent theme in the book is the self-directed question: what do I know? In their subsequent quarter-final, Egypt were convincingly beaten by Japan: Mohammed Salah was substituted, Ahmed Hegazi went off injured and Saadeldin Saad was red-carded. For their part, despite dominating the second half, France lost the women's semi-final to their Japanese counterparts after a goalkeeping error by Bouhaddi led to the first Japanese goal and Bussaglia missed a late penalty.

What do I know – other than that you don't see many poor bookmakers.

www.anordinaryspectator.com/news-blog August 2012

Rugby League

No Trains to Featherstone

A weekend in Leeds presented the opportunity to visit one of the traditional rugby league grounds I had not been to before. Featherstone Rovers have played at Post Office Road – in modern parlance, the Big Fellas Stadium – since their admission into the Northern Rugby League in 1921. There are no trains from Leeds to Featherstone on a Sunday, but Arriva Buses filled the gap – changing at Castleford on the way out and Pontefract on the way back – on schedule and for a reasonable price.

Featherstone needed to win this last league game of the season to secure the Championship's league leader's shield for the third season in a row. There is no automatic promotion to the Super League and, in any case, the capacity of the compact Post Office Road ground falls well below the top division's designated requirements. It is to the club's credit, therefore, that the high levels of its ambition and playing standards have been consistently maintained, when the opportunity to progress further up the league hierarchy is denied.

Within a few minutes of the game starting, there was little doubt that Featherstone would achieve the afternoon's objective. Their opponents, Keighley Cougars, had done well to qualify for the league's play-offs after promotion at the end of last season, but they seemed to be shaken by the aggression of Featherstone's early tackling and the home side stretched out to an 18 point lead within the first quarter. Keighley rallied before half time and a scored a try of their own, but after the break, with the famous Post Office Road slope in their favour, Featherstone ran in another five tries to win 46-4. I was impressed with the skilful prompting of the half-backs, Andy Kain and Liam Finn, though they benefited from the imposing lead given by the Featherstone forwards.

It was a pleasant afternoon in the late summer sunshine. I had a good seat in the Community Club Stand on the half way line. The home support – the vast majority of the 2,800 attendance – was enthusiastic, but fair, enjoying the thrill of a long run down the right hand touchline by the local favourite, Tangi Ropati, but also recognising the bravery of the last-ditch tackle near the corner flag by the covering Richie Barnett.

At half-time, there were well received laps of honour by the club's Under 23 team, which had won its own Championship Grand Final, and the Featherstone Rovers Ladies' team, which had had Challenge Cup final success. However, it is clear that in Featherstone – as elsewhere – the opportunities to indulge in an element of *schadenfreude* are not to be missed: the biggest cheers of the afternoon were for the progress reports on Castleford's comprehensive Super League defeat at the hands of the Catalan Dragons.

Towards the end of the match, I left my seat in the stand and walked round behind the goalposts at the Railway End of the ground. A few dozen Keighley supporters straddled the terrace – some sitting down in the sunshine – having waited in vain throughout the second half for their side to reach this end of the pitch. As I did so, somewhat quirkily, Keighley enjoyed a short period of sustained attack close to the Featherstone line. They went through their planned moves and ran strongly in the attempt to secure a second try, urged on by their loyal support. But it was to no avail. The Featherstone defence maintained the resilience and commitment that it had shown in the opening minutes, based now not so much on concern for the outcome of the match as on professional pride and respect for the opposition.

I reflected on this short passage of play on my bus journey back to Leeds. It had been a vignette not only of the match as a whole but also, more generally, of rugby league at this level. Hard, committed, skilful, respectful – with, on both sides of the supporters' divide, the local community paying close attention to every detail.

www.anordinaryspectator.com/news-blog September 2012

Rugby Union

A Longevity Record at West of Scotland

> *[The] teenage hooker…impressed more or less from the outset, apparently able to handle the physical challenges of the front row and possessing an impressive turn of speed, and West's tactic of launching their new tyro from a line out peel to run at the opposing stand off began to bear fruit very quickly. [OS, page 253]*

Recently, a bright autumnal afternoon brought my first visit of the season to the West of Scotland rugby club for their fixture with Ardrossan Academicals. After two successive seasons of relegation, West are now in the western section of RBS Championship – effectively the joint third division of Scottish club rugby's hierarchy – and no longer sharing a stage with the likes of Melrose and Boroughmuir. Moreover, with only one win in the first 6 fixtures of the current season, they lay joint bottom of the league, so further demotion could not be ruled out.

Ardrossan started purposefully, with a clear dominance in the scrum, and quickly moved into a 14-3 lead. Things did not look too promising for West. But they kept their heads up and, from 22-36 down midway through the second half, pulled away to win 53-36. This suggests that the front-line defence of both sides could do with some improvement – and this is certainly the case – but I could not fault the enterprise and commitment of both sides' efforts in producing an entertaining game. At the end of the match, the players lined up to shake hands in the traditional manner.

One of the West replacements was Gordon Bulloch, a former captain not only of the club but of the Glasgow professional team and, indeed, of Scotland. (He won 75 caps for his country and was a British Lion on the tour to New Zealand in 2005). Bulloch operated as a flank forward in this game, though the position he played throughout his career was hooker.

As noted above, I was impressed with the young Bulloch from his early games for West, beginning in October 1994. He played for the club for 4 years before moving into the full-time professional ranks; he later returned to lead the club to successive promotions from 2006 before (apparently temporarily) going into retirement.

After the West-Ardrossan match, I reflected on the fact that it had been 18 years – to the month – that I had first seen Gordon Bulloch play. At present, I cannot think of any rugby player – in either union or league – whom I have seen in action over so long a playing span (in terms of first and, to date, last sightings) within my spectating career. It is quite a record: a testimony to his fitness, durability and enthusiasm.

Later, in an exercise of anorakian proportions, I gave some thought as to whether Bulloch holds the corresponding record for all the sports that I have watched. Not quite is the answer. I saw my cricketing contemporary Jim Love play professionally for Yorkshire against Lancashire at Old Trafford in August 1976 and for Scotland against Yorkshire in Glasgow in May 1995: a span of 18 years and 9 months.

Of course, for Gordon Bulloch, the meter is still running…

www.anordinaryspectator.com/news-blog October 2012

Cricket/Memory

A Philosophical Query: Can a False Memory Also be the Truth?

One of consistent features of the feedback to *An Ordinary Spectator* has been the recognition of its attention to detail. For me, this has been very gratifying, given the efforts that went in to ensuring the accuracy of the book's content.

Of course, it would have been unrealistic to expect that the book would be totally error-free, and I dutifully note in the Acknowledgements that the responsibility for any errors that remain is mine.

I have stumbled across one such mistake in the course of undertaking some further research on Yorkshire cricket in the 1960s. In itself, the error is not serious – no-one is falsely accused or misrepresented – but I find it interesting that it has occurred and, accordingly, I have been reflecting on its significance.

In *An Ordinary Spectator,* I state that, on the occasion of my first visit to a county cricket match – the Roses encounter at Headingley in 1966 – my father and uncle took me to the second day's play. The match situation was that "[a]t the beginning of the day's play, Yorkshire were in a strong position, having bowled Lancashire out cheaply on the first day and moved into a first innings lead, with Geoff Boycott still at the crease…" I describe how, before setting out for the ground, we learned that Boycott had been dismissed early in the day's play and that that had prompted a serious discussion on whether we should go at all. We did, of course, for which I have been grateful ever since.

The error in the above passage – now discovered – is that Boycott had been dismissed on the first day. The excellent www.stats.cricketworld.com website confirms that Yorkshire were 165 for 6 overnight with Brian Close and Jimmy Binks at the crease. And yet my memory of the "should we/shouldn't we go?" question in the light of Boycott's dismissal remains crystal clear.

The solution is relatively easy to find. Between 1965 and 1969 Yorkshire played Lancashire on only one other occasion in the championship at Headingley. (The other home Roses fixtures were held at Bramall Lane, Sheffield). This was the 1968 fixture, which I also attended and which I also recollect – with particular reference to the all-round excellence of Ray Illingworth – in *An Ordinary Spectator*.

The latter game followed a similar pattern to the 1966 fixture. Lancashire were bowled out relatively quickly, Yorkshire started their first inning on the first day and then built up a sizeable first innings lead on the second before dismissing Lancashire again to win convincingly. Crucially, www.stats.cricketworld.com reveals that Boycott was 35 not out at the end of the first day but quickly dismissed by Brian Statham on the following morning, having added only one run to his overnight score.

Clearly, in my recollections of attending the 1966 and 1968 Headingley Roses matches, I have mixed up one of the details. And it is only a detail – that of a brief conversation with my father and uncle – with no great significance in the wider scheme of things.

And yet, the corrected version does seem to take something away from the overall story. For my purposes, the narrative is stronger when the decision on whether to go and watch Yorkshire for the very first time overcomes the hurdle of Boycott's premature dismissal. When I composed *An Ordinary Spectator*, that was how – in good faith – I recalled the chronology of events. And with the reader's permission – notwithstanding the overwhelming new evidence – that is how I will continue to recall them.

The interpretation of falsehood as truth. One for the philosophers, I think.

www.anordinaryspectator.com/news-blog November 2012

Cricket

The "Nano-Drama" I Would Most Like to have Witnessed

In *An Ordinary Spectator*, I list a "First XI" of sporting "nano-dramas" that I have witnessed over the last half-century. I refer to these as "the drama of the moment – of the micro-second – in which a defining characteristic of the sporting contest is revealed... It is in these moments that sport really makes the heart pound and causes the sharp intake of breath to be made." The book's examples cover incidents from rugby league, rugby union, cricket, football and golf and they involve, amongst others, Geoff Boycott, Martin Offiah and Payne Stewart.

An obvious question to ask, given the contents of the list, is: "Which sporting nano-drama would I most like to have seen, live and in the flesh, either during my period of sports spectating or in earlier times?"

There is a long list of possible candidates, of course: Jesse Owens crossing the line to win gold at the Berlin Olympics of 1936, Don Bradman's duck in his final test match innings at The Oval in 1948, Roger Bannister breasting the tape for the first sub-four minute mile in 1954, Geoff Hurst's controversial goal in the World Cup final of 1966, Johnny Wilkinson's winning drop goal in the Rugby World Cup final of 2003... An impossible task to select only one, perhaps.

And yet I have a clear favourite. I would go back to Saturday 26th July 1947: the first day of the Fourth Test Match between England and South Africa at Headingley.

This was the first post-war test match to be played at Yorkshire's headquarters, the previous game having been against Australia in 1938 when Bradman had made a mere 103 to follow his Headingley triple centuries of 1930 and 1934. The series stood at 2-0 to England with two matches to play. Norman Yardley, a Yorkshireman, captained the England team.

South Africa batted first and were bowled out for 175 allowing the England openers – Len Hutton and Cyril Washbrook – to begin the home side's innings with an hour to play on the first evening. The scene is beautifully described in John Marshall's *Headingley*, published in 1970:

Hutton and Washbrook walked, apparently quite unconcerned, to the wicket. The crowd gave them all the encouragement of which a fervent Yorkshire crowd is capable, and that is plenty. After applauding the pair all the way to the wicket, there was a very special burst, taken up all round the ground, as Hutton took guard.

The nano-drama I would most like to have witnessed is that moment when Len Hutton takes guard and the applause rings out from all corners of Headingley. 65 years on, I find it both immensely moving and hugely symbolic.

At one level, it was about Len Hutton and Yorkshire cricket. Although he had made his record test match score of 364 as long ago as 1938, the Second World War had of course severely interrupted Hutton's career and the 1947 South Africa game was his first test match at Headingley. The Yorkshire crowd had come to cheer on their own son, much as they would do in a slightly different way when Geoff Boycott made his 100th first class century on the same ground against Australia in 1977.

But there was more to it, I think. It was also about a sporting occasion reflecting the society around it. By July 1947, the war in Europe had been over for over two years, but, for the British, there was now a stark realisation about the long economic struggle ahead. It was a time of austerity and rationing. The heavy rain that interrupted that year's Headingley test match was an apt reflection of the greyness of the times.

However, it was also a period of hope. Hitler's Germany had been defeated. Families had been re-united. A baby boom was underway. People could look forward to peaceful times. The policies being enacted by the post-war Labour Government – including the nationalisation of key industries and the creation of a National Health Service – would lead, it was believed, to the New Jerusalem.

Marshall's "special burst" of applause, as Hutton was taking guard, reflected all these aspects of the Headingley crowd's psyche: the pride in the local hero, the gratitude that they had survived the long ordeal of war, the desire that things revert to what they had once been, the hope for the future…

This particular nano-drama dates from some seven years before

I was born, so I have some excuse for not being present. However, the writings of another readily create a poignant mental image of the occasion and its central character.

Postscript

Len Hutton was dismissed for exactly 100 on the following Monday. (Sunday was a rest day). John Marshall states that, when Hutton reached his century, "[t]he noise of [an earlier] thunderstorm was a gentle rumble compared with Yorkshire's tribute to the Pudsey lad." England won by 10 wickets on the third day.

www.anordinaryspectator.com/news-blog December 2012

Cricket

The Future of Test Match Cricket

I thoroughly enjoyed the recent India/England test match series (albeit via the Sky Sports evening highlights package) and noted – with some parochial satisfaction – that three Yorkshire CCC players contributed to the England cause, including the highly impressive Joe Root.

I wonder, therefore, if I am being unduly pessimistic in having major concerns for the future of this form of the game.

For the first half century of test match cricket – from the first Australia/England match in Melbourne in 1877 through to the England/West Indies series of 1928 – only 3 countries contested test matches. My nagging fear is that within a relatively short time – and 10-15 years is relatively short in the grand scheme of things – it will be the same sides (Australia, England and South Africa), and these sides only, that seriously participate at this level.

The death knell for test cricket has been rung before, of course. In the post-war period, any number of reasons have been conjured up for its eventual demise – slow over rates, pedestrian scoring, the threat of one-day cricket, and so on – and yet the game has survived. So why this current round of pessimism?

I think that there are four factors that, in combination, not only provide particular grounds for concern at the present time but will threaten test match cricket in the years to come. Three of these factors affect the spectator demand for test matches; the other relates to the response by the cricket authorities.

First – and most obviously – there is the impact of the Indian Premier League (IPL) and its rich imitators (current and future) on the playing strength of those test nations whose cricket authorities are not wealthy or determined enough to contract their star players for the longer form of the game. For many of these cricketers, the riches presented by the global one-day travelling circus already provide an overwhelming incentive either to curtail their test match careers when they are still good enough to represent their countries (Lasith Malinga) or, at the extreme, to bypass a test match career completely (Kieron Pollard).

The outcome is that several test sides – especially the West Indies, New Zealand and Sri Lanka – will not be as strong as they could be, with the obvious implications for results (see below) and spectator/media interest. If I am attending a test match, I want to know that the players in front of me are the very best that those countries could field. If not, why should I bother?

Second, there are the effects of information overload on the modern spectator. This is a relatively new phenomenon, which can be illustrated through a straightforward contrast of the "then and now." When England hosted Australia in 1975 and the West Indies in 1976, we were captivated not only because of the drama of the series themselves but because many of the opposition's star players had the exotic combination of being both brilliant and unfamiliar. We had seen Jeff Thomson terrorise England during the previous winter only through the painful viewing of the BBC's half-hour highlights programme; Viv Richards had had a low-key season and a half on the county circuit with Somerset; Michael Holding was virtually unknown in England. Moreover, many of the supporting casts of tourists (Ashley Mallett, Collis King *et al*) had also been rarely seen. They had a mystery to them that we were keen to explore.

Contrast that with the plethora of detail relayed to us in today's television coverage: wherever he/she might be in the world, the global viewer is now bombarded not only with a player's career average and highest score but also his favourite pop group and, seemingly, inside leg measurement. I am certain that, in the future, we will still want to see the next generation of genuine stars. But, I'm not so sure about the supporting cast. Some of the mystery has gone and, as a result, some of the incentive to check out those players in the flesh.

Third, there is the polarisation of test match results. My sense is that Australia, England and South Africa are moving further away from the other test-playing nations and that this gap will not be closed in the foreseeable future. To give one set of fairly damning statistics, between 2008 and the end of 2012 – a period that includes the temporary ranking of India at the top of the test match standings – these 3 countries (A/E/SA) played host to the others (India, Pakistan, Sri Lanka, New Zealand, West Indies, Zimbabwe, Bangladesh) in a total of 45 test matches. The home sides won 35 of these games and 6 were drawn. The visitors won exactly

4: a meagre 9 per cent. (Update: 4 out of 46, following New Zealand's embarrassment in Cape Town in the first test match of 2013).

These results create a vicious circle, in which even in England – where the gates for test matches are generally the most healthy – there will be a spectator backlash. Indeed, we have already seen this in the low attendances at Cardiff and Southampton in 2011. If New Zealand or the West Indies are to be permanently relegated to an early summer two-match series – to make way for the more attractive fare of South Africa or Pakistan or a concocted one-day series – who is going to pay £60 or more per ticket to watch them (devoid of some of their key players) on a cold May day in Manchester or Durham?

Likewise elsewhere. How long will the Australian public put up with the mediocre efforts of visiting sides other than England and South Africa? The lamentable performance by Sri Lanka in the Boxing Day Melbourne test (defeat by an innings and 201 runs) is only the latest in a series of weak challenges by visiting teams: Pakistan have lost their last 9 tests in Australia, Sri Lanka their last 5 (to the end of 2012), India their last 4 and the West Indies 10 of their last 11. Perhaps the Australian cricket public enjoys shooting fish in a barrel, but I suspect that, after next winter's Ashes series, even their attention might begin to wander.

There is a counter-argument to this point, of course. It is reasonable to acknowledge that, throughout the post-war period, there have always been one or two sides well ahead of the pack. Usually, these have been A/E/SA, but, at other times, India, Pakistan and the West Indies have successfully challenged this hegemony before retreating back into the middle order. Moreover, the "meagre 9 per cent" noted above (for wins by the others in A/E/SA in 2008-12) is little different from the corresponding outcomes between 2003-08 (10 per cent) or 1998-2003 (11 per cent). Furthermore – to draw on evidence from another sport – that fact that Scotland has never beaten New Zealand at rugby union does not prevent 65,000 turning up at Murrayfield hoping for a miracle.

Nonetheless, the central case holds, I think. Test match spectators will want their side to win, of course. However – against a background of increases in ticket prices that continually outstrip the general rate of inflation – they will also demand that the opposition provides genuine and sustained competition, wherever the game is played. For A/E/SA, playing Sri Lanka in Sri Lanka or India in India will always be difficult assignments. But that will be irrelevant if the challenge of the latter countries is chronically absent in Melbourne and Old Trafford and Cape Town. If it is not going to be a proper contest – again – why should I bother attending?

Finally, there are the clearly revealed preferences of the international cricket authorities. No detailed exposition is required here, as the recent test match schedules have been discussed at length elsewhere. Enough has surely been said or written about England and South Africa – the two highest ranked test playing countries going head-to-head – being given a desultory 3 test match series in 2012, so as to accommodate an inconsequential series of England/Australia one-day matches. The case rests, your honour. As an aside, here's a question: without looking it up, what was the outcome of the E/A series?

So where does this leave us? West Indies, New Zealand and, to a lesser extent, Sri Lanka under pressure from the pull on their star players of the global one-day circus; security concerns ruling out any realistic prospect of test match cricket being played in Pakistan in the foreseeable future; Bangladesh and Zimbabwe well below anything like the required standard.

This leaves India. In my view, the reaction of the BCCI (and the Indian selectors) to their decline over the last 18 months from being the top-rated test match nation – incorporating the recent series defeat by England – will be of paramount importance not only for India's own position in the test match hierarchy but for the future of test cricket as a whole. Will Duncan Fletcher be given a completely free hand to mould a properly competitive test match team? Will the next generation of Tendulkars and Dravids be identified to complement Kohli and Pujara? Will they seek to unearth any match-winning mystery spinners? Or will the Indian authorities be content to rest on the laurels of one-day success and wealth? Will they allow their test match status to drift in the middle-rankings, thereby sending a clear signal to their sub-continental cricketing neighbours that ordinariness will suffice in this form of the game? India's forthcoming series with Australia will tell us a great deal.

Finally, what of the relevance of this to English county cricket – and Yorkshire CCC in particular. Quite simply this: it is highly unlikely that the 3 test nation model hypothesised earlier would be sustainable. England could not play South Africa or Australia every year without the novelty quickly wearing off. In turn, without the test match revenues, county cricket in anything like its present format would fold.

And, in 15 years time, instead of chasing whatever test match batting records Alastair Cook leaves behind, the veteran Joe Root would be ending his career playing for the Sheffield Steelers against the Leeds Loiners in the regional play-off of the Global 20-over Big Slog.

www.anordinaryspectator.com/news-blog January 2013

Cricket

The Future of Test Match Cricket: Feedback

The previous blog was also posted on the Members' Forum of the Yorkshire CCC, where I asked whether a general pessimism about the future of test match cricket was warranted. In the 6 week period since then, there has been a healthy response – a dozen replies and over 500 views – with some very interesting contributions.

The original blog suggested four reasons for concern: the pull of highly-paid one-day cricket on the best players' commitment and availability; the diminished "mystery" attached to international cricketers; the poor results obtained in recent series played in Australia/England/South Africa by the other test playing countries; and the apparently ambivalent status being given to test match cricket by some of the national or international authorities.

In general, the responses on the Forum have indicated that these (and other) concerns are felt by other Yorkshire members, although there is also some optimism. It is also recognised that, whilst some members are much more interested in the county side's fortunes than those of England, it is the international game that generates the revenue to support the rest of the domestic first class programme.

At first sight, the more detailed responses covered a wide range of disparate subjects – from West Indian sprinters and the challenges facing Irish cricket through to recent FA Cup replays and the demise of HMV. However, in practice, they related to a single and powerful theme of critical importance to the future of test cricket: the role of the consumer. One contributor referred to the impact on well-known high street names of poor service, inappropriate pricing and inadequate responses to technological change, whilst another, based overseas, outlined the profound effects of economic and social change in India on the cricket follower and the type of cricket that he/she wishes to watch. Both lead to the same conclusion: if the consumers of test match cricket do not like what is on offer, they will look elsewhere for their entertainment and engagement.

All is not yet lost, however. The Forum's thread has included a number of the imaginative options – a Test Match World Cup, day/night test cricket, realistic ticket pricing – that are open to the bold administrator. But it has also reinforced the view expressed in the initial blog that, if the international cricket authorities complacently drift along with the current arrangements, there will be tears at bedtime.

Let us hope that any debate about the future of test match cricket lasts for many years to come as that, by definition, will mean there is something to argue about. More immediately, there are two potentially cracking series – South Africa versus Pakistan and India versus Australia – in prospect.

www.anordinaryspectator.com/news-blog February 2013

Football

Under the Rock

In the Spring of 2009 I undertook a mini-tour of football grounds in the west of Scotland: Partick Thistle, Queen's Park, Motherwell, Albion Rovers. These were some of the famous teams, whose names had jumped off the football pages of the newspapers and magazines of my sporting childhood and adolescence and whose fortunes I had followed on Saturday evening radio and television when carrying out the weekly ritual of the "classified check" on my mother's pools coupon.

Last weekend, I added to the list: Dumbarton versus Falkirk at the Bet Butler Stadium in the Irn Bru Scottish League Division One. Having been promoted at the end of last season, Dumbarton had initially struggled in the higher league, but a run of good results from the turn of the year had raised hopes that an immediate relegation might be avoided. By contrast, at this two-thirds mark of the season, the visitors seemed to have secured a mid-table respectability.

At the start of the game, therefore, Falkirk were ranked 15th in the hierarchy of Scottish club football and Dumbarton ranked 19th. The dominant first-placed club – Celtic – had recently played a home Champions League fixture with Juventus in front of over 50,000 spectators. The attendance at this Dumbarton-Falkirk fixture was officially reported as 997.

It was an enjoyable game. Falkirk were the stronger side and their two neat goals mid-way through the first half were due reward for their swifter movement of the ball and their greater threat in attack. Indeed, only some brave and athletic goalkeeping prevented their half time lead from being double the 2-0 margin that also turned out to be the final score.

I sat towards one end of the stand amongst the clusters of Falkirk supporters. They cheered their team enthusiastically and repeated the pattern that I had previously observed in the crowd at Motherwell – kicking every ball and making every tackle. The most prolonged outburst of industrial language occurred when one of the Falkirk central defenders lambasted his colleague at full back for a piece of sloppy play; the invective carried across the pitch into the hearing of the supporters around me, some of whom responded with their own thoughts.

The Dumbarton home ground is now at the foot of the Dumbarton Rock, the previous venue at Boghead – appropriately named by all accounts – having been sold off for housing in 2000. Apart from the stand side, the ground is only shielded from the outside world by rows of metal fencing along the other three sides. For the players, this means the awkwardness of trying to see the ball when it comes out of a low sun on a bright clear day such as this.

For the spectator, however, it means a panoramic view into the middle and far distance. What type of view is a matter of opinion. One respected *Sunday Herald* commentator recently referred to "...a scene of decay more post-apocalyptic than post-industrial in nature...[a] view of almost unremitting dereliction..."

I took a somewhat wider perspective. On the left, the River Leven and the landmarks of a proud town, dominated by the remaining tower of the former grain distillery; over to the right, the attractive sweep of the Kilpatrick Hills. And, directly in front of me and about 20 miles distant, the snow-covered upper reaches of Ben Lomond. I found that my eyeline was continually drawn to the mountain, its presence both reassuring and mesmeric, as if it were a Caledonian Mount Fuji.

I realise what it is that I like about attending these types of sporting encounter. At one level, I know that I was watching a routine football match. I am also aware that, in the immediate term, the result of the match mattered and the respective supporters would either take heart or be concerned about the outcome. (On seeing that I was reading the match programme on the way home, the ticket inspector on my train – obviously alert to Dumbarton's relegation fears – anxiously asked what the score had been).

But there is a bigger picture of time and place. First, time. Wikipedia tells me that Dumbarton FC is the fourth oldest football club in Scotland, founded in 1872 and Scottish Football League champions in the first two seasons of the competition, and that its 121-year tenure at Boghead is currently the longest a senior British club has stayed at the same ground. I have noted previously how I am drawn to the longevity of sporting institutions. This was no exception.

And then, place. The Rock, the river, the town, the tower, the hills, the distant peak. All contribute to a topographical and geographical uniqueness. I was sitting in the stand at Dumbarton FC and I couldn't have been anywhere else.

www.anordinaryspectator.com/news-blog March 2013

Rugby League

The Elderly, Frail-looking Figure on the Blackpool Right Wing

[T]he elderly, frail-looking figure on the Blackpool right wing received very few passes. When he did get hold of the ball, he was either easily swamped by the Hunslet defence or crowded out into touch, on one occasion in front of us to the mocking cheers of the home support. However, I noticed that my father, whilst naturally content at his team's supremacy, did not share in the disrespect shown to this particular opponent. The winger was Brian Bevan, in the respected opinion of some... the greatest winger ever to play the game. [OS, page 22]

Dad knew better than to mock this great player. And so did I. By now, I had more than a passing familiarity with the major rugby league records. I shared my dad's pleasure at the Hunslet victory, of course. But I spent a large proportion of the match looking at the lonely figure on the Blackpool wing and making a mental note that I was watching the one and only Brian Bevan. [OS, page 23]

In his acclaimed BBC television series America, broadcast in 1973, the late Alistair Cooke remarked how he found it hard to believe that, earlier in his life, he had once met a man who had been wounded in the American Civil War (1861-65). As Cooke never seemed too reluctant to indulge in some moderate name-dropping, it was no surprise to learn that the former soldier turned out to be Justice Oliver Wendell Holmes, described by Cooke as "the most distinguished jurist, in his old age, in the English-speaking world."

In an idle moment, I wondered who, of all the sportsmen and women referred to in *An Ordinary Spectator,* had the earliest date of birth. The answer is almost certainly George Pope of Derbyshire and England, whom I saw playing a charity cricket match – The Lords Taverners versus An Old England XI – at Headingley in July 1969. Pope had been long retired by this time, of course: he was 58 when he took part in that match, having been born in January 1911. (He died at the age of 82 in 1993).

I remember the day very clearly, partly because of the rich haul of signatures that I captured for my autograph book after the game had finished, but also because of events later that night. In the early hours of the Monday morning, my mother woke me up to tell me that the television pictures were about to come through of the Apollo 11 space capsule on the surface of the moon, in which Neil Armstrong was preparing his small step and giant leap. As I report in the book, "I was 14 years of age and the world was full of wonder."

George Pope's participation was in a friendly cricket match. What about the competitive arena? Which player, of all those I have seen in the more combative mode, had the earliest date of birth?

The answer is again to be found in *An Ordinary Spectator*, in which I describe how, at the age of 8 in March 1963, I watched the Hunslet rugby league team play Blackpool Borough in a league fixture at the Parkside ground in south Leeds. Brian Bevan was 38 years old at the time, having been born in Sydney in June 1924.

Bevan had always looked elderly and frail – even in the sprightliness of his youth – but his speed and agility and devastating sidestep and swerve made him the most prolific try scorer in rugby history. He scored 740 tries for Warrington between 1946 and 1962. Adding in his scores for Blackpool and in various representative matches took his career total to 796.

It is a source of some pride that I followed my father's lead in showing due respect to this great player.

Next Saturday – 30 March 2013 – it will be 50 years to the day since that Hunslet versus Blackpool Borough fixture. After all these years, I can confirm that the mental note was indeed taken and registered. If I close my eyes, I can recall Brian Bevan playing in front of me on the pitch at Parkside.

www.anordinaryspectator.com/news-blog March 2013

Rugby League/Motor Sport

Martin Offiah, Ayrton Senna and the Eurovision Song Contest

> *Although playing on the left wing, [Martin] Offiah took a pass as first receiver, running to his right, when Wigan were under severe pressure close to their own line... Once he had broken the initial tackle, I knew instantly that he would score in the corner at the other end of the field. It was as if my mind had time-shifted forward.*
>
> *Having evaded the first line of defence, Offiah was obviously going to run clear of the covering tacklers. That left him in open field with only the Leeds full back, Alan Tait, to beat. For most wingers in this position, this would be a difficult challenge, given Tait's renowned defensive qualities. Tait's problem, however, was that he was in the middle of the pitch and could not use his invisible ally – the touch line – to his advantage... [T]he winger ran around him on the wide outside and touched down near the corner flag. It was exactly as I had envisaged less than ten seconds earlier. [OS, page 280]*

It might be argued that *An Ordinary Spectator* is – at least in part – an exercise in nostalgia. I hope that it is more than this, of course – that the book contributes to an understanding of why I (or we) watch the live sporting event now and will continue to do so in the future – but, clearly, much of its content is deliberately backward-looking and retrospective.

I have been reflecting on this because later this month – on 18th May in Malmo, Sweden – Bonnie Tyler will represent the United Kingdom in the Eurovision Song Contest. Allow me to explain.

On the last day of April 1994, I saw Ms Tyler perform live at the half-time show of the Rugby League Challenge Cup Final at Wembley. As my spectating career in the pop/rock music fields had been rather less extensive than its sporting counterpart – the Rolling Stones at Wembley in 1982 and Bob Dylan at Blackbushe Airport in 1978 were the main highlights to that point – I was pleased to add the Welsh singer to my limited back catalogue, albeit for a performance of only a few minutes.

Bonnie Tyler was duly referenced in the book as achieving (in my opinion) the top marks for the supporting cabaret at the many Challenge Cup Finals that I attended with my father and uncle from the mid 1980s onwards, narrowly defeating the efforts of Tony Hadley (Murrayfield 2000). Hear'Say (Twickenham 2001) and Atomic Kitten (Murrayfield 2002) lagged some way behind.

The 1994 final was contested by Leeds and Wigan. As noted above, the match contained one of the outstanding "nano-dramas" of my sports spectating career: Martin Offiah's wonderful try from deep in his own half – and my time-shifting anticipation of what was going to happen once he had evaded the first tackle.

The following evening, when I had returned to my home in Glasgow, I telephoned my father in Leeds. We agreed that it had been a great weekend and that we would repeat the venture the following year. (We did, as also did Leeds and Wigan). As we were completing the conversation, dad mentioned that there had been an accident at the San Marino Grand Prix involving Ayrton Senna. "Has he been injured?" I asked. There was a short silence. "Dead," my father replied.

It was a JFK moment: I can clearly recall standing in the hallway of my house, telephone in hand, stunned. It was 19 years ago today.

The word "nostalgia" is derived from the Greek *nostos*: a return home. In his excellent *Museum Without Walls*, the author and critic Jonathan Meades points out that it literally means the yearning for a long-lost place we once knew and also, implicitly, the yearning for the self we were when we inhabited that place.

In this context, "place" can be defined broadly, I think. It encompasses not only a physical space – Wembley Stadium on a hot early summer's afternoon two decades ago and the immediate sporting action taking place within it – but the full circumstances of the occasion as they related to that particular "self": the companionship of my ageing father and uncle; the current issues being dealt with at work; the uncertainty about future career; the responsibility for a wife and two young children; the following day's telephone call.

It is the "yearning" aspect of nostalgia that presents the difficulty. It requires that the time/place/self being called forth are pleasant or tranquil or unthreatening. That is entirely appropriate for some – probably most – of my sports spectating career. But not all. For other parts of the narrative – the racist undertones at a particular 1980s football match, for example – "nostalgia" is too strong or too limiting (I'm not sure which). Instead, I should simply refer to memory or recollection, which, whilst more neutral terms, are equally powerful.

What is certain is that such memories or recollections – of which the nostalgic reminiscences are a sub-set – can easily be evoked by particular triggers in film or music or literature. In this particular case, there is a direct line of association in my thought process which runs from this month's Eurovision Song Contest to Bonnie Tyler to Wembley Stadium to Martin Offiah to Ayrton Senna to the telephone conversation with my father.

The UK last won the Eurovision Song Contest on the night of the 1997 Challenge Cup Final. The big winners that day were St Helens (who defeated the Bradford Bulls at Wembley) and Katrina and the Waves. Since then, whilst St Helens have continued to enjoy regular success, the combination of political point-scoring and bloc voting – and, it has to be said, a frequently uninspired choice of British entry – has conspired to keep the UK well away from the Eurovision winners' podium. More than once, this (increasingly) grumpy old man has wondered how much the UK taxpayer/BBC licence fee payer is contributing to the funding of this ritual national humiliation.

Maybe this year will be different. Bonnie Tyler will have the odds heavily stacked against her in a couple of weeks time. But I wish her well.

www.anordinaryspectator.com/news-blog May 2013

Rugby League/Clarkson

Scores and Values

> *Dad and I were watching the early evening television for news of the rugby scores… How could it happen? How could a Hunslet team, with the players I had now seen perform several times, be beaten by such a score? My father…sat in his armchair…and pursed his lips. 'Something funny's happened there.' After all these years, I can still remember him saying these words and shaking his head slowly. [OS, page 13]*

The best laid schemes…

In *An Ordinary Spectator*, I make several references to the first live sporting event I was taken to see: the Hunslet vs Whitehaven rugby league fixture at Parkside in August 1961. I also refer to the reverse encounter in that season's fixture list – played the following March – when Whitehaven defeated Hunslet by 61 points to nil.

A few weeks ago, it finally occurred to me that – after all these years – it would be appropriate to exorcise this particular demon by going to see yesterday's match between Whitehaven and the Hunslet Hawks. It would have been manageable as a day trip from Glasgow, leaving some time to look around the town as well as take in the match. Unfortunately, other events intervened and it turned out that the timing of the outing did not fit in with the recuperation programme that I am currently undertaking following some recent surgery. My trip to the Recreation Ground will have to wait for another day.

(For the record, Whitehaven won yesterday by 22-14. Another Hunslet defeat, but not quite by the same margin).

It was during my time in hospital that the actress Angelina Jolie announced that, as she carried a mutated gene which meant she stood a high probability of being afflicted with breast or ovarian cancer, she had had a double mastectomy. The general media response was one of sympathy and support.

In *The Sunday Times*, Jeremy Clarkson offered his take on things. I read his opening paragraph and I wept.

A couple of days later, after I had spent some time reflecting on my reaction, I wrote to the newspaper:

> *To the Editor of The Sunday Times*
> *J Clarkson and A Jolie*
>
> *The opening line of Jeremy Clarkson's column (19 May): "When I heard that Angelina Jolie's breasts had been removed, my first thought was, "Oh, can I have them?.".*
>
> *I declare an interest: my family is no stranger to breast cancer. Against this background, I draw three conclusions.*
>
> *1. Re Mr Clarkson – ignorant, cruel and obnoxious. But, hey, who cares when there is the opportunity for casual insult and resultant distress? The blokeish reputation is enhanced, the books fly off the shelf and the money flows in.*
>
> *2. Re the editor of The Sunday Times – apparently quite content for his publication to inhabit the same space as the crudest of lads' magazines ie in the gutter. A sad betrayal of the noble traditions of a once honourable newspaper.*
>
> *3. Re my continued weekly purchase of The Sunday Times – you must be kidding.*
>
> *Yours*

The gist of Mr Clarkson's article – in as much as it had a serious point – seemed to be that, if he were confronted by the type of choice faced by Ms Jolie, his response would be different.

> *If I were to be told I had an 87 per cent chance of catching testicular cancer, would I whizz round to the doctor and ask him to snip off my bits?... I [would] choose to do nothing at all.*

Fair enough. That's a brave decision – and a bold statement – for a hypothetical situation. I hope that Mr Clarkson is never faced with the actual reality. For my part, there is something of an irony in the nature of the surgery I mentioned earlier, though, for the present, all remains well.

What particularly interests me in all this are the respective values that are revealed. For Mr Clarkson, it is clearly acceptable to "joke" about an individual's risk of life-threatening illness, notwithstanding any physical and/or emotional turmoil that she might be suffering in dealing with that risk. Again, so be it: that's his privilege and he hasn't broken any laws.

At the end of *An Ordinary Spectator*, I reflect on the principles and standards of behaviour – honesty, compassion, hard work, a sense of humour – with which I was brought up and how they were reflective of the values that my parents had derived from their own families.

> *The original sources of those influences had a wide geographical distribution – North Yorkshire and Scotland, London and Germany – and so there has been an inevitable complexity in the way that my own values were shaped. My parents provided the filter for these influences, of course. And in my father's case...the principles that he passed on to me – and which I was happy to take – incorporated the values that had been absorbed in his own childhood in south Leeds, including on the terraces at Parkside. [OS, page 373]*

In short – and as for most people – the sources of the values that I hold dear will have been myriad and complex: parents, grandparents, teachers, *et al*. However, I am quite sure that, somewhere in the mix, will have been the behaviours and actions that I witnessed on the rugby pitch and cricket ground as a young and impressionable sports spectator. They would have provided insights about courage and effort and discipline and comradeship. And respect.

I should say that I do not claim the moral high ground here. My values are different from those of Mr Clarkson. I will leave it at that.

As for *The Sunday Times*, it did not publish my e-mail. However, my communication did prompt an immediate and apologetic personal response from an Associate Editor whose own regular columns I recognise as characterised by thoughtful analysis and sympathetic presentation. Perhaps all is not yet lost.

www.anordinaryspectator.com/news-blog June 2013

Cricket

The Western Terrace

[Note: I have been a (very) occasional contributor to a couple of online supporter/member forums covering the fortunes of Yorkshire CCC, initially on the Club's official website (until the forum was removed in 2013) – as here – and latterly on www.network54.com.Forum. This short piece responded to a contribution recollecting a Headingley test match some 30 years earlier].

I enjoyed Dave Hawksworth's reminiscences of the Headingley test match of 1984. My principal recollection – on the Monday after Malcolm Marshall had demolished England's second innings – was of the absolute contempt with which Gordon Greenidge and Desmond Haynes set about knocking off the 120 or so needed for victory. The former thrashed one long hop from the demon Derek Pringle to the square cover boundary with as much ferocity as I have ever seen anyone hit a cricket ball.

My father and I watched the (half) day's play from the same vantage point on the Western Terrace that I had favoured since my first visit to Headingley almost 20 years earlier. In those days, it remained an open and generous part of the ground, from which the cricket would be watched by interested and knowledgeable spectators.

Mr Hawksworth notes that he has deliberately refrained from commenting on the reputation of the crowd on the Terrace. However, it is surely relevant that his fond memories of the 1984 test match are from the period before the lager louts took over large sections with their rowdiness and drunken boorishness. Within a few years – certainly by the end of the decade – the area was ruled by the sizeable minority who were principally interested in sitting in the sun, drinking all day, insulting the opposition, littering the ground with torn-up newspapers, and leering at any female who had the misfortune to walk around the cycle track in front of them.

I have written elsewhere of how, by the time of the 1989 test series against Australia, we had graduated to the balcony of the Main Stand, from where we looked down – literally and figuratively – and thanked our lucky stars that we had not bought tickets for the Terrace. I offered this silent prayer for many years afterwards. As I did so, I reflected with complete sympathy on those fathers, who had not been familiar with tribal geography of Headingley, who had brought their sons (or, even worse, daughters) for a day out at the test match and who had found themselves in the middle of the crowd from hell.

I note Mr Hawksworth's comment that the Terrace's reputation has been done to death, and I have no desire to open old wounds. However, I do think the evolving nature of crowd behaviour on the Terrace is relevant to the fascinating discussion – in this Forum thread and elsewhere – on the "Headingley experience" and how this has changed over the years, whether for better or worse. For me, the "loss" of the Terrace for many years at test matches was a sad development and – notwithstanding the subsequent determined efforts of the Club to mitigate the lager lout factor – it permanently affected my sense of attachment to the ground. Perhaps it is just the power of the remembrance of times long past, but my level of affection for Headingley has never been restored to that of my youth and adolescence.

One final observation. The loutishness was not specifically a Headingley or Western Terrace phenomenon, although its effects might have been exacerbated here. A far more authoritative commentator than I – Mike Brearley in *The Art of Captaincy* – stated that, in general: "Cricket crowds are getting more unpleasant… Vocal violence is also worse. Jeering, exultation and abuse have all increased, while humour has decreased. Mindless chanting is commonplace. Crowds…demand instant satisfaction; their criticisms are crudely sexual. A cricket match is often, now, an outlet for a vicious streak." Brearley's book was first published in 1985.

http://forum.yorkshireccc.com/ June 2013

Cricket

Proper Cricket

> *I like applauding the good shots and the fine pieces of fielding and the tight maiden overs and the individual or team landmarks. I like being part of the ruddy-faced crowd with its tightly packed holdalls and its cushions and its newspapers and its sensible clothing for all weathers. [OS, page 350]*

Last Friday I had a day at the cricket at Headingley. Proper cricket too: the first day of the County Championship fixture against Surrey. It was my first visit to the ground since the 2010 fixture against Warwickshire reported towards the end of *An Ordinary Spectator: 50 Years of Watching Sport*.

I had identified this particular game when the fixtures came out as the one to attend in Leeds this summer as it was the only weekend in which a Yorkshire fixture at Headingley could be matched with a home fixture of the Hunslet Hawks rugby league club. After that, my appetite was whetted by Surrey's flagship signings of two test match captains: Graeme Smith of South Africa and Ricky Ponting of Australia. After that again, the game was earmarked as the one in which Kevin Pietersen would make his long-awaited (by some) return to first class cricket in anticipation of easing his way into the forthcoming Ashes series.

It didn't quite turn out like that, of course: Smith has been injured for several weeks and has returned home; Ponting dropped out on the morning of the match; and, after Yorkshire had been invited to bat first in cloudy swing-friendly conditions, Pietersen's contributions to the day consisted of some stiff-legged fielding and four overs of gentle off-spin.

But it was a splendid day. And – as noted – proper cricket. The morning's play was attritional stuff as the Yorkshire openers, Adam Lyth and Alex Lees, were tested by the aggressive bounce of Chris Tremlett and the nagging accuracy of Jonathan Lewis. 50 runs from 20 overs represented a fair return before bad light and an early lunch. Then, three quick wickets, including both openers. Then, a partnership of over 200 runs between the Yorkshire captain Andrew Gale – clearly a batsman in good form as he reached a third successive century – and Gary Ballance, the latter playing a cautious and mature innings that belied his burgeoning reputation for rampant stroke play. And then, finally, two wickets late in the day for the persevering Lewis. 292 for 5 at the close of play.

"Did you enjoy the day?" a middle-aged lady asked me as we waited for the pelican crossing to change at Shaw Lane whilst walking on to our next engagements: she and her husband to pick up the car for their drive back to Malton, me to find a booth in Bryan's fish and chip shop. I said that I had indeed. "Shame about his hundred," said the lady, referring to Ballance's late dismissal in the 90s. I suggested that he had looked a little uncomfortable against the second new ball and we agreed that the Surrey bowlers had bowled well at him when this had been taken. I wished them (the couple from Malton, not the Surrey bowlers) a safe journey home.

A little later, when I was tucking into my haddock and chips and mushy peas, I reflected on why I had answered the lady's question in the affirmative. Partly, it was due to Yorkshire's successful day, of course, as they strove to enhance their position at the top of the County Championship table. But there were a couple of other factors as well.

One was Headingley itself. I have recently commented elsewhere – http://forum.yorkshireccc.com/ – on why I no longer have the affection for the ground that I had in the 1960s and 1970s, notwithstanding those improvements that have been made to "the spectator experience" since the days of my youth and adolescence. But, whatever might be thought about the physical development of the ground in the last 10 years, it still does have a variety about it. During the day, I took up spectating positions in the Football Stand balcony, the Trueman Enclosure at the base of the Carnegie Pavilion, inside the Long Room and in the seating of the East Stand. The last of these was when Gale and Ballance were scoring heavily in the late afternoon sunshine and, it has to be said, the "experience" was entirely pleasant.

Second, as I had previously noted, I was pleased to be reminded of the rituals of County Championship cricket and of being part of the spectator engagement with those rituals.

On this occasion, there was again plenty to like in the detail of the day: the excellence of the Surrey wicketkeeper, Steven Davies, and his slip-fielders; the warmth with which the spectators greeted Gale's century;

the willingness of the boundary fielders to sign autographs; the clear and efficient presentation of the game's progress on the main scoreboard.

The final factor was the crowd, of course. As ever, the vast majority paid close attention to the evolving rhythm of the day's play. However, it is a well-known fact that, whilst doing so, there are many within a Yorkshire crowd who also like a bit of a natter. Many spectators do sit in silence. But a sizeable proportion natters. Sometimes it can get a bit much – there is a fine line between nattering and boring – but, as noted, at Headingley there is always the option of changing your seat and your viewing (and listening) perspective. Inevitably, therefore – and without consciously eavesdropping – you pick up those snippets of conversation (or monologue) that either make immediate sense or don't make sense at all or, most intriguingly, leave you wishing for more. Within one period of a few minutes, I heard, separately: "…I got all 5 days for twenty-five quid…" "…Lewis's run-up is too long…" "…she must have wondered what he was doing…" and "…it's not a brewery, it's a bloody beer factory…"

If Alan Bennett were ever to run short of raw material, I could recommend a very good source.

Postscript

Kevin Pietersen had to wait until the third morning to start his innings. A more alert Yorkshire fielder would have run him out first ball. He went on to make 177 not out. As Sir Alex Ferguson might have said under different circumstances: "Cricket, eh?" The match was drawn.

www.anordinaryspectator.com/news-blog June 2013

Rugby League/Football

A New Season

The beginning of a season was a period of unbridled anticipation. I can clearly remember receiving Hunslet's 1966-67 fixture card and devouring the names on it. The home fixtures were given in upper case and the away games in lower case and, at the top of the list, after the Lazenby Cup pre-season match against LEEDS, were listed HULL KR and BARROW. Great, I thought: two home fixtures with which to start the season, and an excellent opportunity to get some points in the bag for the league table. I poured over the rest of the list – CASTLEFORD, Keighley...WIDNES, York – and over the syllables within each of the names and then over the individual letters in each team. [OS, page 62]

The 2013-14 season for the top tier of English football – the Barclays Premier League – begins next Saturday, August 17th. By that time, the seasons in the Sky Bet Championship and the Scottish Premiership (without sponsorship as yet) will be two weeks old, their campaigns having begun on August 3rd and August 2nd, respectively. It is a new season and – for all supporters – a time of hope, aspiration, concern and/or fear (delete as appropriate).

In the early 1960s, when I pored over the new fixture list for the Hunslet rugby league football club, the professional season began in August, of course. It was known that, within that same season, the mellow days of early autumn would be followed by the darkness of winter, the re-arrangement of postponed matches to be played on light spring evenings and the conclusion of the campaign well into a new calendar year. There was light at the beginning of the season and light at its end.

By contrast, in the modern era, the rugby league season starts in

February. This year, the build-up to an early fixture of the Hunslet Hawks RLFC coincided with an appeal to supporters to assist in clearing a heavy fall of snow from the pitch at the South Leeds Stadium. For the Super League, the climax to the season will be the Grand Final at Old Trafford on October 5th. The season will end – as it began – in darkness.

And what of the autumnal start to this football season? There are two main reasons for suggesting that its general anticipation might be somewhat more muted than that with which I was familiar in my youth (and notwithstanding the overwhelming media hype that now accompanies the start of the Premier League/Championship/SPFL leagues as a whole).

First, there is the truncated nature of the "off"-season. Even this year – when there has not been a summer World Cup or Euro Championships to attract our attention – the football supporter has had a catalogue of other options, especially if a subscriber to a satellite sports channel. The Under 21s Euro Championship, the Under 20s World Cup, the Women's European Championship…there has been no shortage of opportunities to follow a series of embarrassing failures by a succession of England teams. These tournaments – plus the Confederations Cup – have been followed by the interminable speculation of the transfer window and the regular items of urgent "breaking news" of the latest score from one of the Premier League clubs' money-making pre-season friendly matches in the Far East or America.

Reflecting the spirit of the age, we are effectively in the era of the "rolling" football season. Of course, there is an arbitrary break to differentiate one year from the next, but the clarity of definition of that break – as characterised by an identifiable period of footballing truce – has been lost.

Second – and this reason will be relevant for those who, like me, are followers of more than one major sport – there is the encroachment of the football season into more of the summer. 50 years ago, in 1963, Leeds United played their first competitive match of the season (in the old Second Division) on August 24th. That also happened to be the Saturday of the fifth and final test match between England and the West Indies. This year, playing in the corresponding division, Leeds United opened their account (on August 3rd) during the third test in the five-match Ashes series.

Perhaps there is something in the wiring of my cerebral sporting calendar, but my preference would be for the main business of the summer to be at least nearing its conclusion before the winter's activities get under way. (In fairness, I should acknowledge that the increased overlap between the cricket and football seasons is also the result of the decision of the cricket authorities in England to stretch their own season into early autumn. The last of the series of one-day England/Australia internationals is scheduled for September 16th, whilst Yorkshire CCC's first class season is planned to end on September 27th).

No matter. I hope that today's 11 year-old football supporter enjoys the same sense of excitement, as the new season kicks off, that I experienced in my preferred sport at that age. In particular, I hope that he/she will have the same sense of *personal* excitement in the anticipation of the fortunes of his/her favoured club.

A word of caution, however. The pre-season anticipation can quickly turn into stark reality. Hunslet lost heavily to Hull KR in the first match of the 1966-67 campaign and only drew with Barrow in the next game. So much for getting "some points in the bag for the league table." After two home fixtures, I knew that it would be a long and difficult season.

www.anordinaryspectator.com/news-blog August 2013

Cricket

"He's a Player"

To the Clydesdale Cricket Club in Pollokshields on the south side of Glasgow last Thursday for the Yorkshire Bank 40 overs fixture between Scotland and Lancashire – or, to use the modern branding, the Scottish Saltires versus the Lancashire Lightning.

Lancashire needed to win the match to maintain their chances of qualifying for the knock-out stages of the YB40 competition. For Scotland, it was a different story, the side having lost 10 of their previous 11 group matches this year. With several of their more experienced or effective players under contract with English counties, it had been difficult to remain competitive in this league.

It was the Roses match at Headingley in the county championship of 1966 that was my first exposure to watching professional cricket. That was a Lancashire side including Geoff Pullar, Harry Pilling, Ken Higgs and Brian Statham. Yorkshire won by 10 wickets inside two days.

The current Lancashire side is captained by Glen Chapple, a Yorkshireman in his 40th year, who played his first match for the Red Rose in 1992 and has been one of the central figures of English county cricket during the last two decades. He leads from the front too. He inserted Scotland after winning the toss, opened the bowling with an aggressive and testing spell, and marshalled his team impressively in the field. When the match was won, he led his team down the pavilion steps and shook hands firmly with each of the incoming Scottish players.

The Scottish Cricket Union presented the game well. There was a cheerful welcome at the gate, the thoughtful distribution of seating around the ground and full access to the clubhouse.

The SCU could not control the weather, of course. The view across the open and spacious ground provided clear warnings of when each set of clouds was on its way, blown by a stiff breeze. When rain briefly stopped play for the second time just after Scotland had started their innings – and the covers were again quickly put on and then taken off again – I turned to my neighbour on the next wooden bench at the boundary edge. "It's going to be one of those afternoons," I said. He reached for his phone and tapped in some digits. "It says here that there will be a 40 per cent chance of rain later in the day," he replied helpfully. And then, after a pause. "They were hammered by Hampshire in their last match here."

After a brief early flurry of runs, the Scottish batsmen were kept in check by some accurate and disciplined Lancashire bowling. The middle order was also undermined by two direct hits for run outs by the athletic Steven Croft. Richie Berrington batted neatly to make 35 and the number 11 batsmen Calvin Burnett struck a few lusty boundaries at the end – his last wicket partnership of 36 with Preston Memmson was the highest of the innings – but the general view would have been that the total of 145 was below par. "We're 50 runs short," said a tall white-haired man – to no-one in particular – as the players left the field at tea.

When rain interrupted play again at the start of the Lancashire innings, I headed inside the clubhouse for shelter and a pint. By doing so, I missed the announcement of the number of overs by which the innings had been reduced. When played resumed, and I was walking around the boundary, I asked a middle-aged ginger-haired man wearing a flat cap if he knew. "No, I don't," muttered a Lancashire accent, his face immovably looking down on to the screen of his mobile phone. "Sod you, then," I thought but, probably wisely, did not say.

Scotland bowled with some skill and fielded with enthusiasm and vocal gusto, but Lancashire's main concern would have continued to be the variable weather coming from the south west. The Lancashire batsmen kept a close eye on the scoreboard, where the various intermediate targets set by the Duckworth-Lewis formula [to be used in the event of a rain-enforced early end to proceedings] were posted, as well as the overall (reduced) target of 124. Fortunately, there were no further interruptions.

Lancashire were always ahead of the required rate, although, at the end of one particular over, their score was only a few runs above the Duckworth-Lewis requirement. The matter was immediately resolved by Ashwell Prince – a scorer of 11 test match centuries for South Africa – who, with some crisp straight driving and the ruthless dispatch of a couple of short-pitched deliveries, played the best innings of the day. As I continued on my lap of the ground, I remarked on this to one of the assistant groundsmen. "He's shown his class," I said. The groundsman nodded his head in agreement: "He's a player."

I thought about the groundsman's reply when I was sitting at Maxwell Park station, waiting for a train for the short journey back into the centre of Glasgow. It had been spot on. Ashwell Prince is a player. I thought, also, how nice it was – after the unfortunate lapse – to have resumed the cricket spectating courtesy of meeting a stranger's unsolicited comment with a polite and respectful response.

www.anordinaryspectator.com/news-blog August 2013

Rugby League

Professional Sport: A Microcosm

One year ago – to the day – I reported (in "*No Trains to Featherstone,*" 5th September 2012) on my visit to watch Featherstone Rovers secure the League Leaders crown of the rugby league Championship (the second tier of the sport at the professional level) by beating the Keighley Cougars at Post Office Road.

On Sunday, I saw Featherstone repeat the feat, this time by defeating the Hunslet Hawks at the South Leeds Stadium. At the same time, other results on this final day of the league season not having gone their way, Hunslet were consigned to relegation to a lower division – Championship 1 – for next year (unless there is a twist in the tail and one of the promoted clubs from that league fails to meet the Championship's ground conditions).

Once Featherstone had broken through for their first try, it was clear that this was going to be a long afternoon for the home side. When they kicked off for the second half – down 0-24 and facing a stiff breeze – it was possible that the wheels could have come off completely. But they didn't. The Hunslet players stuck to their task, admirably led by Richard Moore – a dual-registered forward from the Leeds Rhinos – and scored a couple of neat tries themselves.

A final breakaway try by Featherstone straight from a Hunslet kick off produced a final score of 46-8. I could see why Featherstone were continuing to do well. Their big forwards ran strongly – notably the impressive Lamont Bryan – the tackling was precise and aggressive and, as last year, the skilful half back combination of Liam Finn and Andy Kain provided an incisive cutting edge to the attack.

The game was held up for 10 minutes during the second half when the Hunslet forward, Tommy Haughey, required attention for what appeared to be a serious injury following a Featherstone tackle. He remained motionless on his side as the medical staff ministered to him before (eventually) a stretcher was brought on to the pitch. His departure from the field was marked by sympathetic applause from both sets of players and supporters.

Later, just as full-time approached, an ambulance drew up on the running track in front of the main stand. Haughey was carried out to it from the changing room on a stretcher, his head supported in a neck brace. The final whistle blew and, after shaking hands, the players and officials moved off to the side of the pitch.

It was a somewhat bizarre scene: the Featherstone players and coaching staff jumping up and down and singing in front of their jubilant supporters in the stand; their Hunslet counterparts consoling themselves at the end of a difficult season; and the ambulance setting off down the running track to take the unfortunate Haughey to hospital.

I realised, of course, that the *tableau* in front of me was simply a microcosm of professional sport – the ecstasy of hard-won success, the despondency of honourable failure, and the danger and pain associated with striving to attain one and avoid the other.

Thankfully, the latest information on a Hunslet supporters website is that Tommy Haughey's injuries were not as serious as first appeared. I hope he makes a full recovery.

Later, I sat at the back of the bus taking me back into the centre of Leeds. Opposite me was an elderly man in a light jacket wearing the old-fashioned Hunslet scarf with which I was very familiar from my boyhood attendance at the old Parkside ground. He unwrapped a couple of slices of fruit cake from some silver foil. I didn't disturb him as he was listening through a pair of headphones to what I assumed was a local radio station's round up of the afternoon's match reports. The man looked wistful. Perhaps, like me, he was wondering what the future would hold for the Hunslet Hawks rugby league club.

www.anordinaryspectator.com/news-blog September 2013

Football

Killing Time(s)

To rolling Ayrshire on Saturday for the second round of the William Hill Scottish Cup: Auchinleck Talbot (top of the West Super League Premier Division) versus St Cuthbert Wanderers, based in Kirkcudbright and currently fourth in the South of Scotland Football League.

As with so many towns and villages in west and south-west Scotland, Auchinleck has been buffeted by economics. The local pits closed in 1983 and the Barony Power Station followed suit in 1989 with the result that, according to Wikipedia, "Auchinleck village subsided into post-industrial recession." The same entry retains some optimism, however, noting the signs of "green shoots" prompted by new building in the area.

The football team provides the main focal point for local identity. Auchinleck Talbot FC has a rich history – formed in 1909, ten times winners of the Scottish Junior Cup and the trophy's current holders – and appears to be thriving. I generally find that a good benchmark for judging a club's current state of health is the quality of its match programme and, on this occasion, Talbot's was first class, including a good introduction to the opposition's players, a nice article about Bob Shankly (brother of the famous Liverpool FC manager, Bill), who started his playing career with the club, and plenty of local advertising.

The Beechwood Park ground is well maintained, with sturdy terracing, some shelter from the elements (not needed on this occasion), a neat stand and an immaculate playing surface. (On the downside, the toilet facilities can best be described as rudimentary). I arrived early and watched the growing number of black and gold scarves form a queue at the burger bar (roll and sausage £1, Bovril 70p), from which a heady aroma wafted over that part of the ground. In the second half, as the players' shadows lengthened in the bright sunshine, I sat in the stand, occasionally glancing across to the tower of the parish church and, in the distance, the tranquil hills.

The home side was too strong for their opponents, 3-0 up at half time, by which time St Cuthbert had seen one of their central defenders dismissed for conceding a second penalty kick. Talbot were sharper in midfield and more aggressive down the touchlines, though the player who really caught the eye was Craig Pettigrew, playing in a *libero* role, who sprayed a series of long accurate passes to his eager forward line. That Talbot added only one more goal, late in the second half, was due to some fairly inept finishing and, more particularly, an outstandingly heroic display by the St Cuthbert goalkeeper, Jack Johnstone. Without him, I thought to myself at the end, it would have been 10-0.

After the match, having missed my connecting bus into Kilmarnock, I had some time to kill before the next one was due. I walked down to the parish church, next to which is Auchinleck Old Cemetery. Near the entrance to the church, under a spreading tree, is a stone obelisk commemorating the nine Covenanters who were killed by government troops at the Battle of Airds Moss in July 1680. The monument also commemorates Alexander Peden, a Covenanting priest, who died in 1686 and was initially buried in the churchyard, but whose remains were disinterred by the authorities a few weeks later and re-buried two miles away, beneath the gallows in Cumnock.

It was a reminder, of course, that the Ayrshire hills had not always been so peaceful. The Covenanters were Scots who signed the National Covenant, which, from 1638, demanded that there should be no interference by the Crown in the affairs of the Presbyterian Church of Scotland. For the next half century, the risk of transportation, imprisonment or death meant that the Covenanters' preaching usually took place on the fields and moors. The culmination of these bloody, religious wars – between 1680 and 1688 – became known as The Killing Times.

I took my seat on the next bus. At a later stop, three elderly women got on, travelling to Kilmarnock for their Saturday night out. One of them asked, to no-one in particular: "How did Talbot get on? I heard they were winning 2-0." A young man, wearing a black and gold scarf, turned around from the seat in front. "They won 4-0. Their goalkeeper played the game of his life. Without him, it would have been 12." I nodded silently to myself. 10 or 12: we were on the same wavelength.

www.anordinaryspectator.com/news-blog October 2013

Sport/General

"It Makes Me Realise What I Had Without Knowing It"

Some reflections on the personal responses to *An Ordinary Spectator: 50 Years of Watching Sport* that I have received since the book's publication. (In the cases of those comments that have come in private correspondence – by letter or e-mail – I have anonymised the sources unless specific permissions have been given).

Several people have commented on the specific events that I related; others have contacted me about their recollections of different occasions and different times. In all cases, I have appreciated the efforts made – by acquaintances and strangers like – to provide some feedback via their own reminiscences. Some of the responses have been quite poignant.

The responses have been of three broad types. First, there have been those from my contemporaries (known and unknown to me) who watched the same events that I described in *An Ordinary Spectator*. One of these – Andrew Carter – is mentioned in the book as a good friend and companion at Yorkshire CCC matches in the 1970s and early 1980s. In one example, I refer to the Gillette Cup semi final at the Oval in 1980, specifically recalling the late start, Geoff Boycott square driving an early boundary off Sylvester Clarke, the tight bowling of Robin Jackman and, at the end of the Yorkshire innings, the futile efforts of a visiting supporter in a Hull FC rugby shirt to kick the boundary rope a few more inches back towards the edge of the ground.

Andrew's principal recollections cover incidents that were different from the ones that I had identified: specifically, an early delivery going for four wides that gave us hope that Clarke would be too wayward to be a threat that day, and then the same bowler, bowling round the wicket, spearing a ball on to Boycott's toes to trap him lbw. Andrew summarises this as us having "…shared memories [of] similar paths [with] some points where the paths came together": a neat description, I think, and one which is thought-provoking on how we choose to store or reject particular items in our memory.

Some correspondents contacted me to say that we must have attended the same fixtures of Hunslet RLFC at Parkside and/or the Elland Road Greyhound Stadium in South Leeds (the club's temporary home after Parkside had been sold for warehousing). One of them – a Leeds supporter – remembered Hunslet's win over his team at the latter venue (reported in the book) in 1980, when the floodlights failed at half time and the stadium announcer asked if there was an electrician in the ground (not reported in the book, though I wish it had been). Another fondly remembered "the Parkside of Billy Langton, Geoff Gunney and Co" as well as the Headingley/Cardiff rugby union fixture at Kirkstall (in 1969) when Barry John and Gareth Edwards were scheduled to play for the visitors, but didn't (also reported). I found his conclusion that the book "makes me realise what I had without knowing it" to be both moving and rewarding.

Harry Edgar's comments on some of the events described in *An Ordinary Spectator* have already been published, as he kindly reviewed the book in his capacity of editor of the *Rugby League Journal*. Harry refers to the "remarkable symmetry" with his own lifetime of watching sport, beginning with the Hunslet/Whitehaven rugby league fixtures in the 1961-62 season. The review refers to my "feeling of angst" (in reality, a flood of tears in the living room) when Hunslet were on the wrong end of a hard-to-believe scoreline of 61-0 (at Whitehaven in 1962), Harry stating that "the symmetry was already complete because I was at that game and, like all the other spectators present, could not believe what I was seeing." In our subsequent spectating careers, we have both graduated from the rugby league fields of northern England to more distant pastures such as Sydney Cricket Ground (to watch the St George rugby league team) and Soldier Field in Chicago.

The second group of respondents have been those who can relate the content of *An Ordinary Spectator* to their own (different) experiences of watching sport at a younger age. For many of these, the roles of their respective fathers were particularly significant. A distinguished professor at a Scottish university, reflecting on visits to Cardiff Arms Park and Edgbaston, referred wistfully to "fond memories of less busy times." A respected sports journalist at two national newspapers reported in an e-mail that "it sounds like you received a similar sporting education from your dad as I did from mine." A senior sports administrator in Scotland informed me that the book had got him thinking about the influence of his own father in watching sport; in his case, it had been at the age of about

10 or 11 that he had been allowed to stay up late with his dad and brother and watch the Masters golf tournament on television. A friend stated that he had had cause to reflect on times with his own children. My relationship with my father is a central theme of the book, of course, and it is no surprise to learn of this theme having been important elsewhere.

For Peter Todd, General Manager of the Hunslet Hawks RLFC, the earliest memories of watching sport in the 1960s were, like mine, through cricket (Vic Wilson captaining Yorkshire at Headingley) and rugby league (the international scrum half Tommy Smales playing for Huddersfield against Leeds). He recalled, as a young Leeds supporter with his brother and friends, being allowed "to get on to a Wallace Arnold coach to go to exotic-sounding places such as The Boulevard, Central Park and Watersheddings." In a detailed and fascinating note, Peter described the different guises in which he has watched rugby games over the years: fan, disinterested (though not uninterested) spectator, coach, scout, non-participating referee and parent. I was struck by – and could relate to – his acknowledgement of occasionally taking his eye off the main action in order to follow a particular individual, be it player, referee, water carrier or physio; there are similar such references in *An Ordinary Spectator.*

The third group of respondents – smaller in number – are those from previous generations. These are exemplified by Harry Jepson OBE, the 93 year-old President of the Leeds Rhinos rugby league club. Mr Jepson was born in Hunslet – a near-contemporary of my father – and had a distinguished career in rugby league administration, combining this with his duties as a schoolteacher in Leeds.

Mr Jepson has been kind enough to write to me with his appreciative thoughts on the book, supplementing these with reminiscences of his own spectating career. In many respects, this has run in parallel with mine, albeit with a time lapse of between 30-40 years: a first rugby league match at Parkside in 1926, being immediately "hooked" (ditto 1961); his father taking him to watch Yorkshire play at Headingley in the 1920s, sitting on the Western Terrace (ditto 1966); the Leeds and Hunslet Schools trip to Wembley for the Rugby League Challenge Cup Final in 1934 (ditto 1966). I was honoured to receive Mr Jepson's (hand-written) letters and they take a treasured place in my files.

Finally, I should report on a couple of responses to this occasional series of blogs, which I have also received with gratitude. In May ("*Martin Offiah, Ayrton Senna and the Eurovision Song Contest*"), on the 19th anniversary of his death, I recalled the shocking moment when I learned that Senna had been killed at the San Marino Grand Prix at Imola in 1994. A friend here in Milngavie e-mailed me to say that it was also the 27th anniversary of the death of Henri Toivonen, one of the most gifted rally drivers ever. These things are remembered, I'm pleased to say.

Earlier, in March, ("*The elderly, frail-looking figure on the Blackpool right wing*"), I noted that Brian Bevan, the great Australian winger, had probably had the earliest year of birth (1924) of any sportsman that I had seen playing in the flesh. (I saw him play for Blackpool Borough against Hunslet at Parkside in 1963). This was duly trumped by a rugby-playing college friend who e-mailed to say that he had seen Stanley Matthews (born in 1915) play in 1964 or 1965 for Stoke City against Tottenham Hotspur. However, even this was put in context, my friend also mentioning that he had once known an old Russian lady who had met someone who had defended Moscow against Napoleon in 1812 (!)

The responses to the book/blogs have confirmed (and amplified) several of the themes previously explored: the resilience (and selectiveness) of memory; the shared pleasure of individual and collective nostalgia; the role of sport in building (or strengthening) family relationships; the bonding of spectators across the generations.

Sport as a shared experience: humbling and inspiring.[2]

www.anordinaryspectator.com/news-blog October 2013

Cricket

The End of an Era

After a thousand articles and a million words – and that's probably only in the last week – it is difficult to know what else to add about the retirement of Sachin Tendulkar. This being cricket, we can start with the statistics – 200 Test matches over 24 years, 15,921 runs at an average of 53.79 with 51 centuries, plus 463 One Day Internationals with 18,426 runs at 44.83 and another 49 scores of a hundred or more. The numbers are too large to really take in, however: we can look at them and seek to remember some of them (in the way of Don Bradman's final Test match average of 99.94), but we might never succeed in comprehending them, such has been the magnitude of Tendulkar's achievements.

Second in the test match run stakes is Ricky Ponting, the former Australian captain, who also retired this year: 168 matches, 13,378 runs at an average of 51.85 and 41 centuries. As noted in an earlier blog ("*Proper Cricket*," 27 June 2013), I had hoped to see Ponting play for Surrey against Yorkshire at Headingley this year but, unfortunately, he dropped out on the morning of the match. He has a special place in my sporting memory bank, however, as *An Ordinary Spectator* book records that my father and I saw him score his first test hundred – against England at Headingley in 1997.

I wonder if anyone will match these totals in the future: Alastair Cook, perhaps, or, a little further down the line, Joe Root. Much obviously depends on whether test match cricket itself survives to anything like its current extent – for my tuppence worth and some responses to it, see the earlier blogs "*The Future of Test Match Cricket*" (5th January 2013) and "*The Future of Test Match Cricket: Feedback*" (16th February 2013). It may well be that, after Cook, there will be no-one with the frequency of opportunity and the longevity of test match career to be in a position to re-write the records.

Writing in 2010, the Australian journalist Gideon Haigh perceptively noted that (as with Bradman) one of Tendulkar's key attributes over the years had been his ability not to disappoint – on or off the pitch – notwithstanding the enormously high levels of expectation that accompanied his every appearance. He certainly did not disappoint in the Headingley test match of 2002, when he was approaching the peak of his powers.

India produced a batting masterclass. After the dismissal of Rahul Dravid, whose innings commenced when the pitch was at its liveliest, but whose unflappable temperament and immaculate technique took him to 148. Sachin Tendulkar batted with equal skill and panache to make 193, accelerating rapidly towards the end of his innings.

On the Friday evening, during Tendulkar's near-250 run partnership with his captain, Sourav Ganguly, the lights on the scoreboard came on – one, then two…then eventually all five – to signify that the light was deteriorating. In the meantime, the ball kept disappearing across or over the boundary, Tendulkar depositing a delivery from Andrew Caddick several rows back into the members' seating in front of the old bowling green and Ganguly striking some massive blows off Ashley Giles's bowling over and around the old pavilion. It was thrilling and exhilarating and, as the darkness gathered, somewhat surreal.

I recall that my father and I would naturally have wanted England to be winning the match, rather than watching the side toil as we did. However, throughout our spectating careers together, we were also keen to see the best exponents in their particular sports performing at the top of their games. The Indian batsmen certainly fell into that category.

That particular test match was the last sporting event that I attended with my father. Two months later, he was diagnosed with a malignant mesothelioma – the growth in the lining between the lung and the chest brought about by exposure to asbestos dust. (The West Yorkshire Coroner later recorded that this had occurred because of the nature of many of the jobs at which he had been present in his routine work as a joiner and foreman).

My dad had taken me to my first live sporting encounter – a rugby league match – in August 1961. The Headingley test match of August 2002 – an occasion enriched by Sachin Tendulkar and his colleagues – marked the end of an era.

www.anordinaryspectator.com/news-blog November 2013

Rugby League

50th Anniversary of a Torrid Ashes Battle: "Rough Play On Both Sides"

We have been reminded throughout this year that 2013 marks the 50th anniversary of a number of politically or culturally significant events: the first Beatles' LP, the Beeching Report, the Profumo affair, the Great Train Robbery... November of that year saw the assassination of President Kennedy and the first appearance of Doctor Who.

My contribution to this journey back into the past is to record that it was exactly 50 years ago – on November 30th 1963 – I attended my first international match: Great Britain versus Australia in the third test at Headingley. I was 9 years old and filled with excitement and trepidation. I had already been a two-year veteran of Hunslet's matches at Parkside, attending with my father, and I had even been to the Leeds stadium before (for the Yorkshire Cup Final of 1962), but this was something different. This was the latest instalment of an intense international rivalry that dated back to the early years of the century.

The occasion was memorable, therefore, for personal reasons. However, with the huge benefit of hindsight, it is also evident that the 1963 Ashes series had a profound historical significance for the sport as a whole.

In the jargon of today, there was a "context" to the Headingley test. For one thing, Great Britain had enjoyed a highly successful tour of Australia in the summer of 1962 when, if not for a touchline conversion in the last minute of the third test, they would have won the series 3-0. I had read about this tour so often in my *Windsors Rugby League Annual 1962-63* (in which I had invested the princely sum of two shillings and sixpence) that the pages had all come away from their binding.

More relevantly, however, the Australians had already extracted revenge in the first two tests of the current tour, winning both games (at Wembley and Swinton) comfortably and scoring no fewer than 50 points in the second test. This time, it was to be Great Britain's turn to attempt to avoid the whitewash.

From the perspective of the modern era – when we tend to pay homage to all things Australian – it is useful to remind ourselves that, for a long period, the scales of rugby-playing power were not so much more evenly balanced, but skewed the other way. Indeed, prior to 1963, Great Britain had won 9 of the 10 home series that had been played against Australia since the first tour in 1908. (Moreover, Australia's sole success, in 1911-12, had been assisted by 4 New Zealanders). Of the 32 test matches played on British soil (including the 1960 World Cup encounter at Odsal), Australia had won only 8 with 3 drawn.

Of course, these historical records counted for nothing to the 1963 Australian tourists. Captained on the field by Ian Walsh (whose obituary appeared in the Summer 2013 edition of *Rugby League Journal*) in the injury-enforced absence of tour captain Arthur Summons, they had come to win the test series and to take back the Ashes that had been in Great Britain's possession since their third test win in Swinton in 1956.

The Australians were not invincible – they had lost 4 of the 21 matches played on tour before the third test (to Yorkshire, Lancashire, Featherstone Rovers and Castleford) and also drawn with Swinton – but, as ever, it was the international matches that really mattered.

The results of the first two tests – Australian victories by 28-2 and 50-12 – sent shock waves through the British game. We could point to some mitigating circumstances – the loss of Wigan's Dave Bolton through injury after 20 minutes at Wembley, for example, or the injuries to Eric Ashton and Frank Myler at Swinton, resulting in Britain playing with 11 men in the second half – but there was no hiding from the underlying truth.

In *The Guardian*, Harold Mather reported after the second test that "Britain were hopelessly beaten for speed…it was like watching a carthorse trying to catch a thoroughbred." *The Times* drew the same conclusion: "where Britain were ponderous and often slow-witted, the Australians were alert to every chance and went through the gaps like greyhounds." It was "a staggering indictment of Britain's team and possibly, up to a point, their selectors."

The selectors took the hint. Their response was to make nine changes to the team for the third test. The 10th change – imposed when Vince Karalius of Widnes dropped out through injury – meant that this equalled the biggest shake-up in selection between tests that a British team had ever seen. Seven home players (Geoff Smith, Keith Holden, Alan Buckley, Frank Collier, Johnny Ward, Ken Roberts and Don Fox) were awarded their first test caps. Tommy Smales, the Huddersfield scrum half, was recalled to captain the side.

This astonishing turnover of personnel meant that Great Britain were to use a total of 29 players in the series. Only Ken Gowers, the Swinton full-back, played in all three games.

Meanwhile, the 9 year-old rugby league historian researching earlier Ashes encounters was cheered by one fact. Great Britain had never lost to Australia at Headingley, all 7 of the previous matches having gone the way of the home side. Admittedly, it had been a somewhat precarious achievement – three of the wins had been by one point and two others by only two – but, surely, this was a good omen.

I still have our tickets for the game (twelve shillings and six pence each) and the match programme (one shilling). My father, uncle Vic and I had seats in the main stand, on the left side, just inside the 25-yard line. We were close to the concrete ramp down which the players made their entrance on to the corner of the pitch. The coaching staffs walked down the touchline in front of us to reach their respective benches on the half way line.

The game was one of unremitting ferocity, notwithstanding the stern discipline imposed by the referee, Eric Clay from Leeds, who sent off two Australians, Brian Hambly and Barry Muir, and the British prop, Cliff Watson. In my memoir of half a century of sports spectating, published last year, I recall "sitting in the stand and being awed – and, it has to be said, somewhat frightened – by the violence of grown men."

More experienced commentators than I drew similar conclusions. In his match report in the sports edition of the *Yorkshire Evening Post*, John Bapty stated that, even before Hambly's dismissal mid-way through the first half: "It was distinctly unpleasant… There was a snarl about it all."

In *The Guardian* on the following Monday, Harold Mather commented that "when a game is played with such ill feeling and bad temper…it leaves a very bitter taste in one's mouth." He identified an early foul on Don Fox as being the catalyst for the repeated bouts of fisticuffs. *The Times* reported on "a match marred by incidents" quaintly noting that "there was some rough play on both sides."

There was some decent rugby played as well, however, mainly by Britain. To confirm this, I would recommend the excellent *1962 & 1963 Ashes Tests* DVD available from Open Rugby. Look, for example, for the two high kicks to the corners by Dave Bolton that led to tries for the British wingers, Geoff Smith and John Stopford: superb skill under pressure, of which Kevin Sinfield or Lee Briers would justifiably be proud.

Notwithstanding the heightened drama of the various "incidents," my father and uncle were keen to reveal the finer points of the game to me. It was part of my rugby education. I have a clear recollection of Vic pointing out that, in broken play, when the Australian backs threw the ball across the line, their forwards stood behind them, out of the way. He was implying that this allocation of responsibilities had been carefully predetermined and that any forward slowing the action down by being part of the movement would incur his coach's wrath.

The Australian backs had some talent, of course, one of the centres being Reg Gasnier, who had scored 5 tries in the first two tests and who, according to *The Times*, "for years now has probably been the finest player in the world." I thought back to the match – and Vic's tactical tutoring – many years later, when I read the first volume of Clive James's autobiography, *Unreliable Memoirs*. James recounts, as a boy at Sydney Technical High School, being commandeered to provide practice opposition to Gasnier's first grade schoolboy rugby side. Gasnier was "the brightest schoolboy rugby prospect in years... He was all knees and elbows. His feet scythed outwards as he ran, like Boadicea's hub-caps... The way he shifted his weight in one direction while swerving in the other, was a kind of poetry." James's account of his two brave attempts to tackle Gasnier provide a painful warning of the likely fate meted out to mere mortals by the rugby gods.

But, on that day at Headingley, Gasnier and his team did not prevail. The home side's tackling was more effective than Clive James's had been. Great Britain scored 4 tries – by debutants Smith, Ward and Fox and the Swinton winger Stopford – with 2 goals from Fox completing a 16-5 win to avert the whitewash.

I'm not sure that the Australians took the defeat particularly well. Their frustration was demonstrated by one of their coaching staff who, walking back along the touchline to the exit from the field by the corner flag, threw the contents of a bucket of water over the celebrating spectators located in the section of the stand below us.[3]

On the short journey home to our house in Moortown, the obvious thought occurred to me. The unblemished Headingley record had been maintained. It was clearly the case – or so I thought at the time – that Great Britain would always be destined to defeat Australia on that particular ground. In fact, the record lasted for another two fixtures – the first test of 1967 and the pool match of the 1970 World Cup – before Australia finally came out on top in the latter year's World Cup play-off final. Since then: a complete role reversal. Great Britain has lost all 7 internationals played against Australia in Leeds, either at Headingley or Elland Road.

The British win in the third test of 1963 persuaded the selectors to look for some continuity in their next selection. The side to play France just over three months later contained 8 of the victorious team – supplemented by a couple of my Parkside favourites, Geoff Shelton and Dennis Hartley. But the Headingley test marked the final appearances of two of Britain's greatest players – Dave Bolton and Dick Huddart. It was also the last game for two of the debutants. The test careers of Keith Holden and Don Fox might have been brief, but they also consisted of a 100 per cent success rate against Australia.

It is the long passage of time that reveals the real significance of the 1963 Ashes series. Notwithstanding the result in the final game, the pendulum had swung to a new (and apparently fixed) position. Having come out on top in that year, Australia has (to date) won all of the last 10 official test series held in Britain. The British tourists were gloriously successful Down Under in 1970, of course – and we have also had some notable one-off victories on domestic soil – but our last home series win was in 1959.

It is to be fervently hoped that, before too much longer, the relevant authorities find a way of resurrecting what was once an iconic competition – the three-match Great Britain versus Australia rugby league test series – and restoring it to its proper place in the international sporting calendar.

In the meantime, I shall treasure my memories of my first exposure to that competition, and, that same evening in November 1963, of hiding behind the sofa as the newly arrived time-travelling Doctor confronted his own scary foes.

The Rugby League Journal Winter 2013

Football

Into The Valley

The first professional football match that I attended was at Elland Road in September 1968: Leeds United (second in the First Division, for those with long memories) versus Charlton Athletic (top of the Second Division) in the second round of the Football League Cup. The match programme stated that the Charlton manager was "Mr Eddie Firmani, a former strong and clever forward of theirs who did a stint as a player in Italy before returning." It was to be over a year later before I saw my first league game, when Leeds played the newly promoted and high flying Derby County in October 1969. On that occasion, the programme noted that Derby "are led by Mr Brian Clough, one of the most dynamic of the younger school of managers," who had done "right well" at the Baseball Ground.

Last Saturday, during a long weekend in London, I caught up with some old acquaintances. I went to watch Charlton Athletic play Derby County at The Valley.

Forty-plus years on from those Elland Road dates, the sides began the day in 21st and 4th positions, respectively, in the Sky Bet Championship (or Second Division in old-speak). By the end of the afternoon, a 2-0 win for the visitors had consolidated those places, Derby's sixth successive victory leaving them handily placed in the play off positions, whilst Charlton were left to look over their shoulders at the three sides just below them in the division's relegation places.

Charlton began the game brightly with a number of dangerous crosses coming in from the right wing. Derby weathered the storm, however, and, after taking the lead at the half hour mark through a deflected free kick by Jamie Ward, generally exerted control through a combative midfield and a well-organised defence. Charlton rallied in the second half, after Ward had missed a chance by striking the bar, but failed to take a couple of half chances of their own. A neatly taken late goal by Craig Bryson sealed the Derby win to the delight of the sizeable travelling support in the Jimmy Seed stand.

Whenever I parachute into an unfamiliar sporting location, I am always interested in both the history and tradition of the club or institution I am visiting and the current circumstances which that club faces.

Charlton Athletic was obviously no exception: founded in 1905; First Division runners-up in 1937; FA Cup runners-up in 1946 and winners in 1947. Many years ago, I recall being captivated by photographs of the huge sweep of The Valley's east terrace. Indeed, the Leeds-Charlton match programme of 1968 had described the ground as being "spacious, rather Odsal-like" – a good reference for a rugby league follower – the record attendance having been over 75,000 for a cup game against Aston Villa in 1938. (Saturday's attendance was 16,870 – the 3rd largest of the afternoon's 11 Championship fixtures – in a ground that now holds 27,100).

The club's sense of history is evident. The Jimmy Seed stand is named after the club's most successful manager (from 1933 to 1956). In front of the West Stand, the impressive bronze statue of Sam Bartram recognises the goalkeeper whose period at the club almost exactly matched Seed's: Bartram made 623 appearances for Charlton between 1934 and 1956. (Lest Derby were to feel left out, I should also record that the large banner unfurled by their supporters included its own historical reference: to the year of the club's foundation, 1884).

When history matters, present-day ritual is also important. We took our seats to the sounds of the The Skids' "Into The Valley" – surely containing one of the most evocative guitar riffs of the late 1970s – before the teams walked on to the field to the accompaniment of "When the Red Red Robin Goes Bob Bob Bobbing Along." As they did so, it occurred to me that the last time I had heard that particular refrain was probably whilst watching Hull Kingston Rovers play sometime in the 1980s. Another rugby league reference, I'm afraid.

To the casual observer, it appears that much is happening off the field at Charlton. The previous day's *Evening Standard* had stated that the club had been the subject of a number of takeover bids this season, including from American interests, and that this was affecting the offers of new contracts to the manager, Chris Powell, and several players. The excellent independent fanzine *Voice of the Valley* reported in a series of articles on how a potential change of ownership might be linked to a move away from The Valley and on the pros and cons (mainly the latter, it argued) associated with this. It is difficult to avoid the conclusion that a marked sense of uncertainty is hanging over the club's fortunes, both in the short term and beyond.

I enjoyed my visit to The Valley. I had been impressed by the helpfulness of the lady in the sales office when I had first enquired about tickets; I was struck by the courtesy of a middle-aged supporter when we sought his advice on the correct entrance to our places in the stand; later, as we were leaving the ground, the security guard smiled and wished us a friendly goodnight. During the second half, I found myself joining with the home support in willing an equaliser and was out of my seat in anticipation when a far-post header just missed the target.

I would not pretend to know what the long term future holds for Charlton Athletic. Clearly, various scenarios are possible. More immediately, however, a dispassionate football sense suggests that, in a highly competitive division, Charlton will do well to retain their current league status at the end of the season. On and off the pitch, I wish them well.[4]

www.anordinaryspectator.com/news-blog December 2013

Rugby Union

A Weekend in Bristol

Towards the end of Billy Wilder's affectionate *The Private Life of Sherlock Holmes*, when the great detective is asked by Queen Victoria about the progress of his current case, Holmes replies ruefully that: "It has not been one of my more successful endeavours." I had a similar feeling last Sunday afternoon in Bristol.

The previous day had been much more rewarding. I participated at an Open Day arranged at the Foyles Bookshop in Cabot Circus by SilverWood Books, the publishers of *An Ordinary Spectator: 50 Years of Watching Sport*. The event was arranged for the benefit of budding authors considering the self-publishing route and had contributions from expert speakers and short readings from SilverWood authors. A splendid initiative from an impressive publishing company and a supportive retail outlet.

I took my reading from the introductory chapter, which refers to the bookends of my spectating journey over half a century: the rugby league matches between Hunslet and Whitehaven in August 1961 and the Hunslet Hawks and Barrow Raiders in August 2011. After I had finished, I was approached by Jenny Martin, who has published an anthology of poetry about the Whitehaven area and then by a gentleman who had played his youth rugby in Barrow. Unexpected and touching connections.

On Sunday, I had been looking forward to going to watch Bristol play Plymouth Albion in England's rugby union Championship. Two famous teams, particularly the home side (Bristol Rugby in its modern guise) – the club of Tom Richards, John Pullin, Alan Morley and Alastair Hignell – which had celebrated its 125th anniversary in 2013.

In doing my research (via Wikipedia) on the Bristol club, I had noted two things in particular. First, the Memorial Ground stadium had been built in 1921 to commemorate those members of the club who had died in the Great War; second, the City Council had approved plans in 2013 for the ground to be demolished for a new supermarket, though the Memorial Gates are to be retained and enhanced.

I was struck by the similarity with the history of the Headingley rugby union club in Kirkstall, Leeds. Over 200 Headingley men enlisted in the Great War, of whom 50 were killed and 21 gained military honours. After the war, club members raised £2,500 to buy the first team pitch as a memorial to those who had lost their lives.

In 1992, Headingley merged with the Roundhay rugby union club to form Leeds RUFC: an attempt to create a strong rugby union side in Yorkshire to match the likes of Leicester and Wasps. However, it is a clichéd truism that, when one medium-sized rugby club merges with another medium-sized rugby club, the end result is a medium-sized rugby club. Not a bad description in this case. The former Headingley ground now constitutes the training pitches for the Leeds rugby league and rugby union sides; the old Roundhay ground is now a housing estate.

The other part of my research was to Google the route from the centre of the city to the Bristol Rugby club. This was a five mile (and 40 minute) journey to Henbury on the number 76 bus – or so I thought. It turned out that my detour took me to the adjacent grounds of the Clifton and Bristol Saracens rugby clubs. Once I had realised my mistake, there was the small matter of a near-suicidal crossing of the dual carriageway at Cribbs Causeway, as the rain clouds gathered, in order to catch the bus back into the city. It was only on the return journey that I realised I had actually passed the Memorial Ground (in Horfield) when travelling down the Gloucester Road. Moreover, I discovered, the match had been postponed at 10.00am due to a waterlogged pitch.

(Memo to the Bristol Rugby ticket office: When postponements occur, it's useful to update the message on the answerphone. At 1.15pm, the message was still reporting that tickets were available for the match).

So that was my Sunday afternoon. A round trip of an hour and half to the wrong location to watch a rugby game that had been called off several hours earlier. Plus a near-death experience crossing the road. As Sherlock Holmes remarked, it was not one of my more successful endeavours.

Perhaps I'll get to the Memorial Ground on another occasion before it is demolished. I hope so. In the meantime, I am delighted to report that there are three copies of *An Ordinary Spectator* on the shelves of Foyles Bookshop in Cabot Circus available for purchase by the discerning Bristol book-buying public.

www.anordinaryspectator.com/news-blog January 2014

Rugby Union

Bragging Rights

In the last blog, four weeks ago, I reported that I had been in Bristol to give a reading at an Open Day in the Foyles bookshop organised by SilverWood Books (and that I had also been unsuccessful in locating the ground of the Bristol Rugby club for a postponed match with Plymouth Albion). The same weekend there had been a fixture scheduled between West of Scotland and Dumfries Saints in Division A of the Scottish Rugby Union Championship. As it happened, that game was also called off because of the weather.

At the time, both West of Scotland and Dumfries had a mathematical chance of finishing in the top seven of their 10-team division and thus qualifying for the National Division 2 of the re-structured Scottish club league for the 2014-15 season. However, results over the last month have meant that both teams will now be in the National Division 3, effectively the fourth tier of the Scottish club hierarchy. For the West of Scotland FC – founder members of the Scottish Rugby Union and the club of Gordon Brown and Sandy Carmichael and Gordon Bulloch – it is a sad decline.

West of Scotland and Dumfries fulfilled their fixture last Saturday at Burnbrae. It was a cold, dull afternoon with the continual threat of rain to worsen an already heavy pitch. There were about 50 spectators present. In the words of West's club president in the match programme, the teams were playing for the bragging rights that go with 8th place in Championship A. It did not auger well. When West kicked off, the foregone alternative of an afternoon in a warm living room watching back-to-back Six Nations matches looked very attractive.

How often, when watching the live sporting contest in the flesh are our expectations – optimistic or downbeat – undermined by the events on the pitch. This was an excellent match.

The Six Nations could wait for its later viewing on Sky Plus. I knew, in any case, that I had already witnessed my international rugby highlight of the season. In the first game of the championship, when Scotland were desperately defending their line against a ferocious Irish second-half attack in Dublin, Jim Hamilton, the Scottish second row forward, was penalised for an infringement – not for the first time – by the referee, Craig Joubert. The latter's microphone picked up the detail:

Jourbert: "*Come here, please, Jim. The fact of the matter is that every time there's something…you're involved.*"
Hamilton: "*I'm sticking up for myself, sir.*"
Jourbert (suppressing a laugh): "*Not again. Do you understand, Jim?*"
Hamilton: "*I understand, sir.*"

All of rugby is in that short exchange: the referee's respectful admonition; the player's dignified response (a combination of schoolboy and defence counsel); the referee's assertion of his authority; the player's courteous acknowledgement, with the use of "sir" both natural and genuine. And, all around, the howling Irish crowd sensing that their team was going for the kill.

The players at Burnbrae on Saturday did not have the speed or the skill of their Six Nations counterparts. But I could not but admire their commitment and enthusiasm and ambition. (I also noted the accurate and sympathetic refereeing of John Shaw from the West of Scotland Referees Society). A steady line-out and some effective driving mauls took West to a 17-0 lead, before Dumfries gained some ascendancy in the set scrum and were rewarded with a converted try of their own. The half-time score of 22-7 was maintained throughout most of the second half before a further try apiece – that of the visitors involving some impressive handling in a long-range attack – took West to victory by 27 points to 14.

Towards the end of the match, I left my place in the stand and walked round to the banking on the lower touchline, where there were no more than half a dozen spectators. A West supporter remarked to me what a good game it had been, the players on both sides fully committed to their cause and, as shown by Dumfries's final try, keeping going impressively in the heavy conditions.

I agreed. The players had been a credit to their clubs and their coaches. Clearly, the bragging rights for 8th place in the Scottish Rugby Union Championship Division A had indeed meant something.

www.anordinaryspectator.com/news-blog February 2014

Rugby League

Match Programmes: Windows Into the Past

It is a reasonable assumption that, for those readers of *Rugby League Journal* who attended the league and cup games of half century or so ago, the purchase of a match programme was an essential task. It is probably also the case that, for at least some of those readers, the programme collections remain safely stored away, gathering dust at the bottom of a cupboard or in the corner of the attic.

In my case, the attempt to broaden the collection of programmes began in the late 1960s when, in my early teens, I placed an advertisement in the section of the *Rugby Leaguer* that dealt with programme swaps and purchases. As I recall, I offered to swap Hunslet home match programmes, the stock of which I had built up over five or six seasons, for those of clubs in the Lancashire League.

Needless to say, I was swamped with responses from the supporters of clubs that I had not only not visited, but was also unlikely to visit, given that Hunslet's fixture list comprised predominantly Yorkshire opposition, with only a couple of Lancashire clubs featuring in any one season. Now I was inundated with programmes from Salford and St Helens, Leigh and Warrington, Whitehaven and Widnes. Someone in Sydney sent four editions of the Australian *Rugby League News*.

My difficulty, of course, was that I did not have enough collateral. My stock of Hunslet programmes did not contain many swaps and I quickly realised that, if were to meet my end of the range of bargains that I had implicitly struck, I would either have to draw down my existing Hunslet programme collection or buy multiple copies at the forthcoming home games.

In the event, both these routes were taken, in the case of the former not without some remorse, as I was reluctant to part with too many of the home collection. On balance, however, I was happy with the trade, given the wide spectrum of other clubs that was now represented in my collection.

At the time, there were probably three main reasons for my interest in the programmes of other clubs. First, there were the differences in style and quality: the full range from the paper-based editions (Barrow, Dewsbury, Liverpool City, Workington Town) through to the ones with glossy covers (Blackpool Borough, Hull Kingston Rovers, Rochdale Hornets, Swinton) and those with, in my view (though I would not have expressed it quite this way at the time), the highest production values (Leigh and Salford).

Second, there were the programmes for those matches in which Hunslet were the visitors. There were several of these, reflecting the generosity of thought of respondents to my *Rugby Leaguer* advert, who had assumed that these were the editions which I would really wish to possess. I was naturally interested in what the programme writers said about my club in terms of its history, its results against the host team and its players.

The standard varied. A couple of programmes made no mention of Hunslet being the visitors and, in retrospect, probably had their content drafted without knowing who the opponents would be. Others were much better: Blackpool Borough 1967 (with a nice tribute to Geoff Gunney), Leeds 1967 (reviewing the full record of the fixtures between the clubs) and Wakefield Trinity 1964 (summarising the clubs' post-war matches).

Third, I was intrigued to see that, for several clubs, the basic template of the programme was almost identical. They shared the type of front cover with which I was already familiar from my visits to Leeds: the name of the club at the top of the page; an aerial photograph of the home ground; the name of the opponents and the date and time of the fixture in the bottom right hand corner; and a glossy surface with a broad stripe down the left half in one or more of the team's colours (Leeds yellow, Oldham red, Warrington yellow, York yellow and black).

A quick check revealed that they all shared the same printer – Frisby, Sons and Whipple Ltd of Leeds – a company which, if it had not exactly cornered the market, was clearly exploiting various economies of scale in its production processes. (I later discovered that the same template was also used by Norwich City FC).

Elsewhere, clubs used a variety of means of stamping their identity on the front cover. These included a couple of beautiful reproductions of the clubs' crests (Castleford 1967, Leigh 1966) as well as pen and ink action sketches (Batley 1964, Hull Kingston Rovers 1966, Liverpool City 1966). When photographs were used on the cover, they were often of the main stand (Bramley 1966, Doncaster 1967, Keighley 1965) or of teams with silverware (Hunslet 1963, Halifax 1966). A more dynamic use of photographs was through close-up shots of action on the pitch (Widnes 1963, Wigan 1965, Wakefield Trinity, 1964.)

Viewed from today's perspective, the 1960s match programme have other fascinations. They varied in size and scope. Those in my collection range from a single sheet of A3 paper folded over twice to make a neat 8-page A5 document (Whitehaven vs Swinton, 1966) through to The [Wakefield] Trinity Programme's 28 pages in the same year. However, even the latter was small in size and could easily fit into a coat pocket. The key point here is that the programmes of this era were invariably relevant, functional and affordable – not the padded, bulky "match day magazines" seen today.

Not at all surprisingly, the content of most clubs' programmes was very parochial. There was a focus on the immediate – the review of the home side's recent matches, injury news, transfer speculation, the welcome to the day's visitors, the re-arrangement of fixtures, the winning bingo or prize draw results, the appeal for more pools and lottery agents – all of which would have been keenly devoured by home supporters seeking up-to-date information on the club and its prospects.

At the centre of each programme (almost without exception) was to be found its main purpose: the listing of the teams. In many cases, this simply comprised two basic columns with the respective numbers and surnames; in others (Hunslet 1962, Rochdale Hornets 1966, York 1964), the names were set out in battle formation. In several of the programmes I received from my *Rugby Leaguer* exchange, it is clear that these centre pages also constituted a rudimentary scorecard, with the tries and goals registered against individual players.

Sometimes the programmes would contain articles of more general interest to the rugby league follower. Changes to the laws of the game would usually be reported and commented upon; there were interesting references to the new "four tackle rule," for example, from the point of view of Hull KR (vs Hunslet, 1966) and St Helens (vs Barrow, 1966).

Other issues for discussion included the uncertainty surrounding international competition involving France (Dewsbury vs Keighley, 1964), the financing of floodlights (Barrow vs Wigan, 1966; Widnes vs Brookhouse, 1966) and, in particular, the decline in attendances. The last of these was a consistent topic in several well-written articles in Wakefield Trinity programmes, amongst others, in the middle of the decade.

It was relatively rare for the contents of match programmes to stray into broader areas, though occasionally they would do so. It is touching to see the reference to the Supporters Club of Hull KR (vs Hunslet, 1966) raising £41 11s 3d in a raffle for the Aberfan Disaster Fund. It is also interesting to read (Warrington vs Halifax, 1965) that "it is expected that BBC2 will open in the North in time to cover the Swinton vs Oldham [Floodlit Trophy] game on 19th October." Elsewhere, there were a surprising number of warnings about the threat of hooliganism, including at Castleford (vs Dewsbury, 1965) and in a Rugby League Council notice (Wakefield Trinity vs Hunslet, 1966).

Of course, modern readers of the 1960s club match programmes have one particular advantage. We know what happened next. We can look at the content of the programme notes – a cup draw, a serious injury, a transfer request – and move the story on.

We can also identify whether or not the optimism or pessimism regarding a club's playing prospects, as set out in the programmes, were borne out by subsequent events. A fascinating example of the latter is given in the Featherstone Rovers programme (vs Dewsbury) on the last day of 1966. There was clearly genuine despair at the "problems and troubles" facing a club that had been nilled in the previous two games (against Bradford Northern and Wakefield Trinity) and was languishing in 21st place in the league: "what we are sadly lacking are the basic requirements… we are at rock-bottom." Within five months, Featherstone were lifting the Challenge Cup at Wembley, having beaten both Bradford and Wakefield – as well as league leaders Leeds – on their way to the final.

A consistent feature of all the match programmes concerned the clubs' links with their own communities. This is revealed in the huge range of local companies that took out advertising space: it really was the butchers, bakers and candlestick makers. To give one notable example, the impressive Rochdale Hornets programme (vs Oldham, 1966) – whilst also providing informative club news and up-to-date statistics – carried no fewer than 46 advertisements, of which 36 were for businesses in the town.

Advertising space was also widely taken by the game's early sponsors (Mackeson through most of the decade for team points scoring and Player's No 6 from 1967 for "Player of the Match" and "Player of the Year" awards) and, occasionally, by large employers looking to recruit to their workforce – for example the National Coal Board (Wakefield Trinity, 1964) and Rowntree & Co Ltd (York, 1967) – but the vast majority of advertisers were small-scale businesses.

Across the whole of the Northern Rugby Football League, the volume and range of advertising provided clear evidence both of the support that the local communities gave to the local clubs and of the central role of the clubs within those communities.

Some of the advertising was from other parts of the leisure industry. It seemed that virtually every club had the support of a regional or local brewery. In addition, several clubs' programmes advertised the local night-time attractions. I wonder what became of the Regency Club (Widnes, 1966), the Cigar Club (York, 1967) and, especially, the Silver Blades Ice Rink (Bradford Northern, 1969) – "If you think girls and excitement go together – go ice skating, it's got both!"

Needless to say, in this regard, it was the Blackpool Borough programme that held all the trump cards. Its full-page adverts for the Blackpool Tower Company's attractions (vs Huddersfield, 1966) included the shows involving Ken Dodd and Arthur Askey and the following year (vs Hunslet, 1967) Kathy Kirby and a certain Bruce Forsyth.

There is no doubt that, from a modern perspective, some of the programmes' content makes uneasy reading. My eyebrows were raised, for example, when I saw that the Bradford Northern Supporters Club Notes (vs Hunslet, 1966) had stated (without any apparent irony): "We are appealing once again for young ladies to put forward their names for Miss Bradford Northern. Last season the entries were very disappointing to say the least."

Present day sensitivities would also be alert on the subject of ethnicity. The Warrington programme (vs Hull, 1965) reported that "wingers Barry (sic) and Clive Sullivan are coloured boys from Cardiff's Tiger Bay" and, similarly, later in the year (vs Halifax 1965), that "there are two coloured players in the [Halifax] side – Johnny Freeman and Colin Dixon." (For reference, I might also add that, some considerable time later – in the match programme for the Leeds vs Bradford Northern Yorkshire Cup tie in August 1981 – Ellery Hanley was noted as being "an exciting, coloured centre").

Of course, from the perspective of 2014, we might easily scoff at the naivety or crassness of some of the advertising lines and programme notes of half a century ago. That is not my intention here. Rather, it is to make the serious point that the match programmes of the 1960s were products of their times. They reflected – and were influenced by – the cultural norms of the era.

I would argue that my collection – and those other collections hidden away in the attic corners of *Rugby League Journal* readers – not only provides a source of personal reminiscence and enjoyment, but also constitutes a set of significant social documents in its own right. As such, the match programmes of the 1960s should be of interest both as memorabilia for rugby league enthusiasts and as important references for cultural and social historians. They are windows into the past.

The Rugby League Journal Spring 2014

Football

Hoardings and Plaques

> *I am attracted to the sports event and all that is attached to it...as a reflection of the much deeper currents that are all around us. [OS, page 364]*

It takes about 20 minutes to walk from the railway station in Stirling to the Forthbank Stadium, the home ground of Stirling Albion FC. The journey begins by crossing the Forthbank Bridge, a modern structure partly funded by the European Union's Regional Development Fund. I know about the funding because I was a senior official with responsibility for European Structural Funds in the Scottish Executive/Government between 2006 and 2011. I also recall the strict conditions that are imposed by the EU on its financial support, with the risk of at least partial clawback by its auditors if the conditions are not met. These include the requirement for some sort of plaque stating the source of the funds and showing the EU flag.

On Saturday, I continued my slow – and irregular – progress through the teams of the Scottish Professional Football League. My choice of match came down to two games: either Stirling Albion versus Montrose in the SPFL League 2 (the fourth division of the club hierarchy) or Airdrieonians versus Forfar Athletic in the SPFL League 1. I decided on the former. By half-time, the score stood at 0-0 and there had been one shot on target. Meanwhile, according to the lad sitting behind me in the West Stand, who insisted in giving a running update to his mate of the latest scores flashing up on his mobile phone, there had been four goals and a sending off in the other match. Ah well, I thought: you win some and lose some.

*

In the second half, I definitely won some. Four goals – two of them absolute crackers – including a last minute penalty for the visitors that produced a 2-2 scoreline.

The result has some significance. In the 10-team league, there is one place open for automatic promotion and, as things currently stand, this will probably go to Peterhead. The next 3 teams will play off for the second promotion place with the side that finishes second bottom of the SPFL League 1. Stirling Albion began the day in 4th place. However, such was the competitive nature of the division that Montrose (in 6th place at the start of play) and even Albion Rovers (in 8th) could still harbour hopes of promotion, given that about one-quarter of the fixtures were still be to played.

"All those missed chances," I consoled a middle-aged man in a red and white bobble hat after the referee had blown the final whistle. The man looked crestfallen. Accompanied by his young son, he had seen Stirling miss 4 or 5 opportunities to extend the lead that the neat midfield player, Craig Comrie, had given them early in the second half. The inevitable had then happened. The battling Montrose centre forward, Garry Wood, won a free kick about 20 yards out and Paul Watson curled a left-footed shot just inside the post that Lionel Messi would have been proud of. The quirks of football: a couple of minutes earlier, Watson had been booked for a clumsy foul that the home supporters around me were adamant had warranted a card in one of the colours of my neighbour's headgear.

The Binos took the lead again when a sweeping move down the pitch culminated in David McClune striking a powerful drive that was a fitting way to win any match. And so it seemed until a final Montrose attack led to a scramble near the home goal, the award of the penalty, and Wood putting the seal on a hard afternoon's work with a confident spot-kick. The goal was ecstatically celebrated by the small knot of Montrose supporters in the left hand section of the stand.

It was an enjoyable and interesting afternoon. I liked the enthusiasm of the supporters – 529 in total on this occasion – and the competitiveness of the (part-time) players. *The Albion* official magazine was comprehensive and informative and a good addition to the collection of match programmes. For their part, Montrose – notwithstanding that they "have spent the vast majority of their recent history in the relative obscurity of the Third Division" (Wikipedia) – contributed fully to the occasion and, as shown by their late score, confirmed that they are also competing resolutely for a place at a higher level.

The Forthbank Stadium was neatly presented with the hoardings around the ground showing a healthy display of advertising from the main sponsors (Prudential), an array of local businesses (whisky distillery, cafe, taxi firm, garage *et al*) and the Scottish National Party. I was intrigued by the last of these, as I'm not sure that I have seen a political party advertising at a sporting event before. (I suspect that this might be more common in Europe). It was a simple display in the party's colours of its initials and logo – and a reminder of the serious political events that are unfolding in Scotland this year.

After the match, I walked back into the centre of town in the early evening sunshine. Stirling Castle dominated the skyline in front of me. To my right, across the valley, the Wallace Monument projected itself above the trees and, to its right, some light clouds skirted across the top of the hills in Clackmannanshire. When I reached the Forthbank Bridge, I noted the plaque on the wall. The bridge had been opened by the Provost of Stirling in May 2009. There was a small EU flag and the usual homily: "Project part-funded by the European Union. Europe and Scotland: Making it Work Together."

Sporting contests reflect the societies in which they take place. On Saturday, whilst my primary objectives had been sport-related – travelling to and attending a football match – it was inevitable, therefore, that my attention would also be drawn to characteristics of the broader environment. As I sat on the train for the short journey back from Stirling to Glasgow, I reflected on the political messages I had been receiving that afternoon and the media through which those messages had been transmitted.

In their own small ways, the SNP's hoarding at Forthbank Stadium and the EU's plaque on Forthbank Bridge are components of two significant political debates currently taking place: the future of Scotland within/ outwith the UK, and the role of the European Union in the UK/Scotland. These are important issues and there is a continual pitch – from all sides, not just the interests noted here – for hearts and minds. Often that pitch is loud and hectoring; in these examples, it was subtle, almost subliminal.

I was reminded that, even when casually attending a local sporting event, it is very difficult to distance oneself completely from the broader societal context. In this case, going to watch two SPFL League 2 teams play in front of a few hundred people on a sunny afternoon did not give me full immunity from the reach of the political pitch.

And that is no bad thing, I think. Sports spectating does not take place in a vacuum.

www.anordinaryspectator.com/news-blog March 2014

Sport on Television

Television Lines

The focus of my writing about sports spectating – book, blogs, articles – has been on watching events live and in the flesh. Here, exceptionally, I turn my attention to sport on television.

In doing so, I am aware of two things: that this is a big subject; and that I should not retreat into "grumpy old man" mode. Hence, I shall resist the temptation to generalise about the overall standard of modern day commentary and analysis. Or to state the obvious fact that, as television is a visual medium, viewers really do not need to be told what we can see on the screen for ourselves. Or to suggest that having been a top-rated sports participant does not automatically mean that that excellence is transferred to commentary. Or even to venture that a more appropriate understanding of English grammar – "he's one of them players…" would not sometimes go amiss. In addition, regrettably, space constraints mean that I shall also refrain from outlining the virtues of those commentators and analysts who are first class: Tony Cozier, Michael Holding, John McEnroe, Brian Moore…

Instead, I shall identify half a dozen pieces of sports commentary that stick in my mind. Why these items in particular, it is difficult to say. A couple of them relate to very famous pieces of sporting action, but that is not the main reason for their inclusion. Rather, I suspect, it is to do with each commentator's ability to think in an instant and to say something that was absolutely appropriate for that moment.

- Football. Kenneth Wolstenholme. World Cup Final, Wembley, July 1966

"Some people are on the pitch. They think it's all over… It is now." Probably the most famous line in all television coverage of English sport.

I include it here, not only because it is a reminder of a great English sporting triumph, but because, when Wolstenholme began speaking the line, he would not have known what its third part would be. As he began, England were leading 3-2 in the last minute of extra time and Geoff Hurst was running with the ball towards the West German goal. By the time the commentator had concluded his quick-witted coda, Hurst had completed his hat-trick by thumping the ball into the net. English football has been waiting for a comparable moment ever since.

- Rugby league. Eddie Waring. Challenge Cup Final, Wembley, May 1968

In an extraordinary conclusion to an extraordinary match – the "Watersplash Final" played on a surface covered with huge pools of water following torrential rain – Don Fox of Wakefield Trinity missed a straightforward conversion that would have given his side victory over Leeds with the last kick of the game. Fox had been judged the game's best player – winning the coveted Lance Todd Trophy – but that was no consolation as he sank to his knees in anguish and, as the final whistle blew, the victorious Leeds players ran triumphantly past his slumped figure. *"He's in tears is the poor lad,"* said Waring.

Over the years, Eddie Waring divided opinion amongst rugby league followers. For some, he was an enthusiastic evangelist for the sport, spreading awareness across the national airwaves; for others, he was guilty of portraying rugby league with a wilful mockery of its northern working-class roots. On this occasion, however, he revealed a genuine and personal compassion for a player's clear distress.

- Golf. Henry Longhurst. The Open Championship, St Andrews, July 1970

A similar compassion was shown by Longhurst two years later, when Doug Sanders missed the three foot putt that would have won him the Open Championship: *"And there it is. And there but for the grace of God."* The difference between this and the previous example was that Longhurst had seen it coming. A poor approach shot had left Sanders with two putts for the Championship from a long way across the green. The build-up was slow – Sanders was partnered by Jack Nicklaus and Lee Trevino, who completed their own rounds first – and, when Sanders reached the green, Longhurst speculated on "the man who had two putts to win the Open, took three, and lost in a play-off," which is precisely what happened.

(Nicklaus won the play-off). As Sanders started to address the fateful putt, Longhurst remarked that "that's not one I would like to have." This was not sensationalist speculation by a commentator seeking to ramp up the tension; it was genuine concern about a possible outturn that he did not wish to see. When he did, he addressed it perfectly.

- American Football. Merlin Olsen. Super Bowl XX, New Orleans, February 1986

In the 1980s, the NBC Sports coverage of American Football – fronted by Dick Enberg and Merlin Olsen – was skilfully packaged into hour-long weekly highlights programmes on Channel 4. For this audience, the full-length coverage of the Super Bowl would have been something different, not only for its hype and excess, but also because of the length of time it actually took to play the game with its frequent breaks for advertisements and time-outs.

In the 1985-86 season, the Chicago Bears were the dominant team in the National Football League and they confirmed this clear superiority in the final game, when they overwhelmed the New England Patriots by 46-10. By that time, the Bears' star players had become well-known faces on our television screens – the quarterback Jim McMahon, the running back Walter Payton and the defensive tackle William Perry. The last of these – "The Fridge" – was 23 years old and weighed 308 pounds.

Perry took an active part in a total of two offensive plays during Super Bowl XX. In the third quarter, he trundled (unstoppably) into the end-zone from one yard to register a touchdown and take the Bears' score over the 40 point mark. However, in the first quarter, he was halted when attempting another run. In the action replay, Olsen explained how the Patriots defensive line had managed this particular feat: *"They weren't taking any chances. They said 'we'll go get him with six of us.'"*

- Rugby union. Cliff Morgan. Barbarians vs New Zealand, Cardiff, January 1973

My friend Llyr James once pointed out to me that, the week after this famous rugby match, the television critic of the *New Statesman* had offered the view that Cliff Morgan had turned rugby commentary almost into an art form. In the book, I stated that the skills on the pitch were complemented by those behind the microphone. It was good to know that I was on the same wavelength as Russell Davies.

For this match, Morgan was a last minute replacement to do the commentary after the scheduled broadcaster dropped out through illness. How fortunate we were. He combined the experience of his own excellence as a player with Wales and the British Lions with, crucially, the articulate musicality of his Welsh roots. When the game started sensationally with a sweeping length-of-the-field move by the Barbarians that brought a try for Gareth Edwards – incidentally, in my opinion, the best rugby union player that I have seen in half a century of sports spectating – Morgan's sheer delight could not be disguised: *"Oh, that fellow Edwards… What can touch a man like that?"*

- Horse racing. Peter O'Sullevan, King George VI and Queen Elizabeth Stakes, Ascot, July 1970

"And here comes Nijinsky and Lester Piggott on the stand side." At first sight, it is difficult to explain why this line is included in this short compilation. It seems a fairly ordinary description of the horse and jockey making their move at a crucial part of the race. And the race itself, whilst prestigious, was not one of the English "Triple Crown" – the 2000 Guineas, Derby and St Leger – all three parts of which Piggott and Nijinsky also won in 1970 (the last occasion on which this feat has been accomplished).

It is, I think, that very simplicity that I like so much. This was Nijinsky's first outing against older horses, the field including the previous year's Derby winner, Blakeney. Notwithstanding the high quality of the opposition, it was as if, when O'Sullevan said the line, he knew that the race was effectively over, even with two furlongs to run. And he was right. As Nijinsky approached the winning post, Piggott having been able to ease his mount with half a furlong still to run, O'Sullevan's voice was a combination of admiration and incredulity: *"Lester's just letting him canter. What a horse this is."*

The above list is a personal choice, of course – readers will have their own selections – and, no doubt, with further thought or gentle prompting, I could be persuaded to amend or add to it. It is probably no coincidence that the most recent item is from nearly 30 years ago and that most are from my teenage years. Perhaps that was when I was at my most impressionable as a viewer of television sport. Or perhaps the commentaries of that era were just more memorable than the efforts of today. Perhaps – indeed – I have been in grumpy old man mode after all.[5]

www.anordinaryspectator.com/news-blog April 2014

Football

A Polish Masterclass and "Our Club"

To Berlin for last weekend's encounter between Hertha BSC and Borussia Dortmund in the Bundesliga and the game between FC Union Berlin and TSV 1860 München in the Bundesliga 2.

The matches – on Saturday and Sunday, respectively – were in the final rounds of games in this season's leagues. Three of the teams had mid-table respectability in their divisions; the fourth – Dortmund – were guaranteed second place in the top league, well behind the champions Bayern Munich, but clear of FC Schalke 04 and Bayer Leverkusen, vying for third place. Not much to play for, one might think.

However, no-one seemed to have mentioned this to the players or the spectators. Two fast, skilful, hard-fought games. Two noisy, colourful – and capacity – crowds: 21,000 plus for the Bundesliga 2 fixture and, for Hertha BSC/Borussia Dortmund, over 76,000 in the Olympiastadion.

Where to start? In preparing this blog, I thought that might be a difficult decision. As it happens, it is straightforward: Robert Lewandowski. I have referred before to the pleasures derived from watching the top performers at the peak of their abilities: Sachin Tendulkar, Ellery Hanley, Gareth Edwards *et al*. To this list I can now add Dortmund's Polish centre-forward. He gave a masterclass with his speed, his footwork, his ability to read the game and, whilst closely marked, his passing and link play with the dangerous Marco Reus. And, for good measure, his goals: Lewandowski opened the scoring just before half-time and then, in the closing minutes, curled in an exquisite 25 yard free kick to register Dortmund's third goal in their 4-0 winning margin. He finished the season as the leading scorer in the Bundesliga.

Although Hertha had their moments in attack – they actually forced 9 corners to none by the visitors – Dortmund were convincing winners. In addition to Lewandowski, they fielded 5 of their 6 members of the German World Cup squad announced earlier in the week and – through their pace, movement and cohesion, allied to a strong defence – they were hugely impressive.

But the Hertha supporters did not desert their team. In the *Ostkurve* section, where about 15,000 of them stood for the whole match (in the all-seater stadium), the noise from the blue and white sea of waving scarves was just as loud in the 90th minute as it had been at the kick-off. When the game was over, the fans paid full tribute to the season-long efforts of their team, which had been promoted at the end of the previous campaign, with particular recognition for the departing captain, Levan Kobiashvili.

I had to pinch myself occasionally – the fingernails-in-the-palm trick – to remind myself where I was. My college friend Llyr James had managed to persuade a security man to escort us through the barriers to the Hertha club shop before the game to pick up a couple of the last remaining tickets. Once inside, we tried to take in the history and the "bombastic gigantism" (as described in the *Berlitz* pocket guide) of the Olympic complex. Whilst the stadium has been redeveloped twice since the 1936 Summer Olympics – for the World Cups of 1974 and 2006 – much of that history is still evident: the Olympic rings straddling two tall towers; the swimming and hockey stadiums; the bell tower; and the Maifeld (Mayfield), a vast area used by Hitler for May Day and other celebrations. We smiled when we saw how the Maifeld was being used on this occasion: a home fixture for the Berlin Cricket Club.

Llyr and I were in Berlin to meet up with another contemporary from college, Stephen Evans, who has been a distinguished correspondent in the city for the BBC for the last 4 years. As a native of Bridgend, Steve's overwhelming preference is for the oval ball game, rather than its round ball counterpart, but he did mention that he was interested in taking in a fixture at FC Union Berlin, which plays in the delightfully named Stadion an der Alten Försterei (Stadium Near the Old Forester's House).

It was an inspired choice. The FC Union Berlin ground is in east Berlin and, to reach it from the Kopenick S-Bahn station, there is a 10 minute walk along a path through a forest; I expected Hansel and Gretel to appear at any moment laying a trail of breadcrumbs. The stadium itself, rectangular in shape, has covering on all four sides, but seating in only a new stand – completed in 2010 – down one side of the pitch. The rest of the spectators stand on the terraces; it felt like old times.

TSV 1860 München led 1-0 at half-time, the reward for a well-timed header by Grzegorz Wojtkowiak from a superbly delivered corner and reflective of a general superiority in the midfield exchanges. However, FC

Union Berlin were much more purposeful in the second half and equalised when Patrick Kohlmann curled a right-footed shot into the top corner of the net. Thereafter, chances fell at both ends, but 1-1 was a fair result.

Steve's interest in FC Union Berlin was partly stimulated by the progress in recent years of a relatively small and under-resourced club, but also by its complex and politically charged history. The origins of the club date back to 1906, but it went through a number of name changes until becoming 1. FC Union Berlin in 1966. Wikipedia notes pointedly that, in this period, the East German government favoured "elite" clubs such as the Stasi-sponsored Dynamo Berlin (winners of 10 DDR *Oberliga* titles in a row "in highly dubious circumstances") at the expense of "civilian" clubs such as FC Union Berlin.

We stood behind the goal that the home side were attacking in the second half. A sturdy meshed barrier separated us from the TSV 1860 München supporters to our left. The slogan prominently displayed at the top of the opposite stand – "*Unsere Liebe, Unsere Mannschaft, Unsere Stolz, Unsere Verein*" ("Our Love, Our Team, Our Pride, Our Club") – reflects FC Union Berlin's close identification with the east Berlin community. (Indeed – I note again from Wikipedia – it was the fans themselves who rebuilt the stadium after 2008 when the club's finances were tight and modernisation was required).

This was my first visit to Berlin since the mid 1980s. The sights and sounds of the city will stay with me for some time. As will the memories of two fascinating – and contrasting – expeditions to the football: the vociferous, chanting crowds; the widespread consumption of beer, including inside the grounds; the helpfulness of the Hertha steward; the supporters' flags; the commanding excellence of Borussia Dortmund; the Polish masterclass; "Our Club."

And so the season draws to a close and the planning begins for the next campaign. For Dortmund, that planning must cater for the absence of Robert Lewandowski, who will be a Bayern Munich player in 2014-15. In the meantime, however, there is one final match in the current season: next Saturday's German cup final – Borussia Dortmund versus Bayern Munich in the Olympiastadion.[6]

www.anordinaryspectator.com/news-blog May 2014

Cricket on the Radio

"Hit For Four"

In April's blog, I listed half a dozen examples of television sports commentary that have stuck in my mind over many years. Most were from the 1960s and 1970s and the most recent was from 1986. I am following these up today with two of my favourite clips from radio, both by the same commentator.

John Arlott commentated on his first cricket matches for the BBC during India's tour of England in 1946. Two years later, he reported on Don Bradman's all-conquering Australian tourists, who beat England 4-0 in the Ashes series. The BBC Radio Collection's *John Arlott: The Voice of Cricket* includes a wonderful excerpt from the fourth test at Headingley, which the home side actually began well, the opening partnership between the local Yorkshire hero, Len Hutton, and Cyril Washbrook of Lancashire putting on over 150 runs before Australia took the second new ball.

Arlott provides a mental picture of Australia's champion fast bowler, Ray Lindwall, preparing for action by going through his "physical jerks" with "the shirt now comfortably loose." He then describes the first delivery of the new spell:

> *...and he [Lindwall] comes up now from the Grandstand end and bowls the first ball to Hutton...*
> *[raises voice, urgently]*
> *...a magnificent out-swinger...*
> *[sound of spectators' applause]*
> *[pause]*
> *...hit for four...*

John Arlott had many skills as a commentator. First, there was his use of language, reflecting someone who wrote poetry and had been the BBC's

Overseas Literary Producer; hence, in sending the ball to the boundary, Hutton had "hit it firmly past the somnolent Toshack at point." In addition, of course, Arlott had a deep understanding of – and love for – the game of cricket: its history and values and personalities and, in particular, its rhythm. In one interview on the BBC's tapes, he refers to cricket being "a contemplative game" that produces art and writing and poetry with commentary being "just a step down from that." Another asset – again obvious – was his voice, the Hampshire burr that mellowed over time with age and the connoisseur's appreciation of red wine.

Perhaps most important, however, was his sense of timing. In the excerpt given above, after he has described Lindwall's preparation and delivery, Arlott lets the sound of the Yorkshire crowd's polite applause speak for itself before he himself talks again. For the listener during this period of background noise – his/her imagination working overtime about the devilish ball bowled by Lindwall – the only conclusion to be drawn was surely that Hutton had been beaten, perhaps even dismissed. And then, after this pause, the punchline delivered as a matter-of-fact statement: "…hit for four…" Hutton had won that particular battle after all; the local hero's wicket was intact and his score had moved on to 81. The first time I heard that piece of commentary, I found it absolutely thrilling – and I still do.

Sport being sport, there was more to follow. Immediately. Lindwall dismissed Hutton with his very next delivery, bowling him off his pads with a sharp in-swinger.

The second of my favourite pieces of John Arlott commentary is probably much better known. It was another England vs Australia test match, in 1975, when a streaker sprinted across the sacred Lord's turf.

> *We've got a freaker down the wicket now. Not very shapely. And it's masculine. And I would think it's seen the last of its cricket for the day.*

Arlott was on BBC *Test Match Special* duty at the time, giving – if you'll pardon the expression – ball-by-ball commentary. I think what I like about this description is its very Englishness: not quite getting the correct name for this odd cultural import from America; pursuing accuracy in the factual content; and, not least through the final phrase, revealing a typically understated humour.

It was at yet another England/Australia test match – the Centenary Test at Lord's in 1980 – that John Arlott gave his final commentary. I was out of the country at the time – in the USSR of all places, where the reporting of English cricket (even Centenary Tests) was not seen as a priority. Wikipedia notes that the public address announcement that Arlott had completed his final commentary session prompted the crowd to give an ovation. The entire Australian team in the field and the two England batsmen joined in, with Geoff Boycott removing his batting gloves to applaud. Arlott retired to his home in Alderney, where he died at the age of 77 in December 1991.

I shall return in a future blog to the subject of *Test Match Special*, which played a central role in my cricket education. In the meantime, I note that John Arlott has his own centenary this year – he was born in Basingstoke in February 1914 – and I raise a glass of Rioja in recognition.

www.anordinaryspectator.com/news-blog June 2014

Gaelic Football

"Hard but Fair From Gun to Tape"

For many football supporters in the west Ireland province of Connacht, a hugely important match will be played on Sunday: a game that will bring glory or despair to the respective battalions of players and spectators for some time to come.

Meanwhile, the World Cup Final between Germany and Argentina will also be played on the same day.

At MacHale Park in Castlebar, Mayo will take on Galway in the Connacht Senior (Gaelic) Football Championship Final. The winners will not only gain bragging rights as the province's leading county side – a position held by Mayo for the last three years in succession and 45 times in total since 1901 – but a direct route to the quarter-finals of the All-Ireland Senior Championship at the beginning of next month; the losers, whilst not eliminated from this year's All-Ireland scene, would be required to win another play-off match before reaching the quarter-final stage.

I will not witness the Mayo/Galway encounter as it will take place after my return home from a short break in County Mayo assisting my wife in her family history researches into the McManamons of Newport and the surrounding townlands. However, more than adequate compensation was obtained in viewing last Saturday's match between Westport St Patrick's and Hollymount/Carramore. This was a club (rather than county) fixture, but it was sufficiently revealing for me to sample the full flavour of this fast and demanding sport.

It was with a wry amusement that I always acknowledged my late father's capacity – which I have inherited, of course – for being an expert on any new sport he happened to watch on television within about 10 minutes of switching on the set. In the age of the internet, we can reveal our newly acquired expertise (or ignorance) at an even quicker pace.

Accordingly, as my wife and I stood behind the low stone wall next to the touchline at the Westport GAA ground waiting for the game to start, I explained for her benefit (and perhaps for readers of this blog who are more familiar with my occasional musings on soccer or rugby) that the goalposts are a combination of those from the other two sports, with three points for scoring a goal into the net and one point for kicking it over the bar. (That the pitch is considerably larger than in soccer or rugby – 130-145 metres in length and 80-90 metres wide – presents a significant challenge to fitness and stamina for a 15-man team). These methods of scoring are separately identified: thus, Hollymount/Carramore quickly went into a 1-3 (ie 6 point) to nil lead and it looked as if a heavy defeat for Westport might be on the cards.

Westport and Hollymount/Carramore play in Division 1B of the 12-team Mayo Senior Football League. Prior to Saturday's match, Hollymount/Carramore had won 3 of their 4 league games to date, whilst Westport had managed 1 win out of 3. As both teams had lost a couple of players to the Mayo county squad, so their respective strengths in depth were also being tested. By half-time, Hollymount/Carramore had pulled away to a 1-10 to 1-4 lead, the reward for some swift movement of the ball and energetic support running in midfield and a steady aim in front of goal.

Westport closed the gap in the second half, but could not quite overturn the half-time deficit. As the players on both sides tired, the pace slowed, mistakes crept in and chances were missed. The key moment (in the view of this instant expert) occurred in the closing minutes when the Hollymount/Carramore goalkeeper made a brave point-blank save when a three-point score for Westport looked inevitable. "Good save," I said to myself, though rather louder than I had intended. "Twas a great save," agreed the middle-aged Westport supporter to my right. I felt satisfyingly vindicated. A last minute scramble in the Hollymount/Carramore goalmouth came to nothing and, as it turned out, it was the save that had proved decisive in the visitors' margin of victory of 1-11 (14 points) to 1-8 (11 points).

We enjoyed the match and the occasion. After a torrential pregame downpour, the match was played in the bright sunshine of a fresh early evening against the backdrop of a row of green and rugged hills. On the pitch, I liked the way that, just before the start, the players shook hands with their immediate opponents. There was an impressive skill in the challenges for the high kicks sent out by the goalkeepers – the Hollymount/Carramore number 9 was noticeably effective in this regard (it was a shame that there was no match programme) – and a fierce determination in securing the subsequent breaks of the loose ball. It was clear also that, to play in the forward positions, one needs a range of skills, not only speed and adroitness to shake off the tight defensive marking, but also a keen sense of spatial awareness either to take advantage of the positioning of team-mates or to size up the opportunity for a points attempt.

Both 30-minute halves of the match flew by. The following Tuesday's report in the excellent weekly *Mayo News* summarised the encounter well: "The game itself was played in good spirit with both teams going at each other hard but fair from gun to tape."

There is – obviously – a basic similarity between all these team sports that involve moving a ball down a pitch and depositing it over a line or bar or into a net. Soccer, rugby union, rugby league, Gaelic Football, Australian Rules, American Football…are they all not codified descendants of much earlier traditions of rival sets of villagers fighting to convey some sort of rudimentary ball down a lane or across a field towards a marker post or wall. They are all – as I once heard an American television commentator describe his own sport – "a battle over real estate."

Of course, these sports now have different rules, reflecting their evolution over time and the impact of local or national customs and preferences. In the case of rural Ireland, the particular characteristics of Gaelic Football and hurling have an obvious and powerful place within the fabric and traditions of the local community. But I do find the subtle similarities to be intriguing. As I watched Westport play Hollymount/Carramore, my mind went back to Chandos Park in Leeds, where the Roundhay rugby union club used to play its home fixtures. In particular, I thought back to those sunny days in the 1970s, when Roundhay might have been playing – say – Fylde or Durham City or Vale of Lune: amateur players, keen commitment, flagging energy levels, a few dozen supporters, mutual respect, an afternoon well spent.

Indeed, it occurred to me afterwards that the Gaelic Football scoring system also has parallels with rugby, albeit from a much earlier age. Before rugby adopted a points system, the scores were registered as so many goals and tries per side and, until the late 1880s, matches were simply decided by the number of goals scored, with tries as a tie-breaker. The records show, for example, that, at the Cardigan Fields, Leeds, in 1884, England defeated Wales by 1 goal and 2 tries to 1 goal.

The Roundhay rugby union club no longer exists, having merged with the Headingley club in 1992 to form the Leeds RUFC; the Chandos Park ground is now a housing estate. I sincerely trust that Westport will avoid any similar fate in the years to come and, indeed, the full touchline length of local and other advertising hoardings offers a positive marker. From my (very) detached perspective, I suspect that – as has happened in rugby union following the introduction of overt professionalism in 1995 – the future of small clubs will be critically dependent on how the lead administrators in the governing body (in this case the Gaelic Athletic Association, of course) deal with the various pressures exerted by global forces in commerce and the media.

More immediately, however, having won only one of its opening four league games – and thus standing "one and three" as the American commentator would say – the Westport club is now looking up the Division 1B league table from the second-bottom position, albeit with a game in hand. The *Mayo News* set out the local fears: "Westport now find themselves in a real dogfight to avoid relegation to the third tier."[7]

www.anordinaryspectator.com/news-blog July 2014

Football

Outcomes and Hopes

I am not exactly sure when the dividing line between one football season and the next actually falls, but it's probably reasonable to regard last Sunday's World Cup Final as the last match of the 2013-14 season, at least for those followers of the sport in the winter seasons of Europe. Meanwhile, of course, the 2014-15 season has already begun: the first qualifying round matches for the Europe League were played a fortnight ago.

I reported on a select – and eclectic – number of football matches in these news blogs in 2013-14: Auchinleck Talbot vs St Cuthbert Wanderers in the Scottish Cup second round in October ("*Killing Time(s)*"); Charlton Athletic vs Derby County in the Championship in December ("*Into The Valley*"); Stirling Albion vs Montrose in the SPFL 2 in March ("*Hoardings and Plaques*"); and, in May, Hertha Berlin SC vs Borussia Dortmund in the Bundesliga and FC Union Berlin vs TSV 1860 München in the Bundesliga 2 ("*A Polish Masterclass and 'Our Club'*").

For completeness, I should report on the fates of these sides in 2013-14:

- Auchinleck Talbot were beaten by Stranraer in the following round of the Scottish Cup, but retained their West Super League Premier Division title;

- St Cuthbert Wanderers finished as runners-up in the South of Scotland Football League;

- After flirting with relegation for much of the season (and sacking their manager in March), Charlton Athletic reached the quarter-final of the FA Cup and ended the Championship season in the safety of 18th position;

- Derby County finished third in the Championship and, having reached the Wembley play-off for a place in this year's Premier League, contrived to outplay Queen's Park Rangers for virtually the whole match before losing to a last-minute goal;

- Stirling Albion also reached the play-offs in their division, but with more success, defeating Annan Athletic and then East Fife for a place in the 2014-15 SPFL 1;

- Montrose ended up with mid-table respectability by finishing sixth in the 10-team SPFL 2;

- Borussia Dortmund qualified for the group stage of the 2014-15 Champions League by finishing runner-up to Bayern Munich in the Bundesliga, albeit by the distant margin of 19 points; the club was also runner-up (to Bayern) in the German Cup Final (the *DFB-Pokal*). Dortmund provided four members of Germany's World Cup-winning squad;

- Hertha Berlin finished 11th in the 18-team Bundesliga, a satisfactory consolidation of their place in the top league, having been promoted the previous season;

- TSV 1860 München and FC Union Berlin were both placed safely in Bundesliga 2, in 7th and 9th places, respectively.

And so to a new season. New hopes. New expectations. New fears. The merry-go-round starts again.

www.anordinaryspectator.com/news-blog July 2014

Cricket/Rugby League

Casual Conversations of a Sport Tourist

Geoff Gunney had been sent off. This was not consistent with my known view, firmly established at ten years of age, of how the world operated. [OS, page 60]

A long weekend in Yorkshire for some rugby league and cricket: the First Utility Super League clash between the Leeds Rhinos and Castleford Tigers at Headingley; Halifax versus Whitehaven in the Kingstone Press Championship at the Shay; a NatWest T20 Blast fixture between the Yorkshire Vikings and Warwickshire Bears (who seem to have become the Birmingham Bears in this competition) at Headingley; and the first day of the Yorkshire versus Middlesex LV County Championship fixture at Scarborough. Not a bad haul.

I shall report on the visit to the Shay separately. Perhaps inevitably, the other three match-ups represented repeats of earlier (sometimes much earlier) encounters, some incidents in which are clearly crystallising even more firmly in the memory as the years pass.

In 1969, before the Boxing Day Leeds/Castleford encounter at Headingley, the sheer weight of numbers outside the Kirkstall Lane turn-styles flattened one of the large wooden gates and I was swept through by the surging crowd (thereby getting in for free, of course); in 1972, Mike Brearley, the captain of Middlesex (though not yet of England), was out twice leg-before-wicket in the county championship match at Headingley for a total of three runs; in 2010, at my first (and hitherto, only) attendance at a T20 match, a Yorkshire side including overseas players Herschelle Gibbs and Tino Best was well beaten by Warwickshire.

Events over the weekend stirred other memories. In the T20 match, the Bears' off-spin bowler, Jeetan Patel, took a hat-trick, dismissing Kane

Williamson lbw and then bowling Andrew Gale and Adam Lyth with successive deliveries. Three high quality victims. I thought back to the previous occasion on which I had witnessed a hat-trick on the Headingley ground: by Ken Higgs for Lancashire in the Roses match of 1968. Higgs's feat had straddled two separate overs, however, and, as I recall, had gone largely unnoticed at the time.

Earlier, Yorkshire's star T20 player – the Australian, Aaron Finch – had opened the batting under some pressure, as he had only registered one sizeable score in his eight innings in this year's competition. He circumspectly left the first two balls of the innings, which were wide of the off stump. "Get 'em hit," suggested a supporter somewhere to my left. A couple of overs later, Finch duly hit one straight up into the air and was caught at mid-off. In a tight finish in the early evening sunshine, the Birmingham Bears won by five wickets with two balls to spare, thanks to a mature and skilful innings of 69 not out by Laurie Evans, who won the obligatory "man-of-the-match" award. Personally, I would have given it to Patel.

On the previous evening, towards the end of a pulsating – and, at times, frenetic – Rhinos-Tigers clash, which ended in a 24-24 draw, the Leeds captain Kevin Sinfield was dismissed from the field for head-butting an opponent following an exchange of words and skirmish at a play-the-ball. The incident occurred at a point level with my seat in the North Stand and I had a clear view, though, if I had been in any doubt, there were also – in the modern way – several replays on the big screen.

Sinfield is one of the most respected players in rugby league, if not in British professional sport more widely. He has played for Leeds since 1997 and this was his first dismissal. I looked across to the late middle-aged man sitting a couple of seats to my left – the intervening seat was empty- and, in silent harmony, we both gave an uncomprehending shake of the head.

Again, however, my thoughts were soon delving into the memory vault. Was I the only person in the ground thinking back to a Hunslet versus Wakefield Trinity match in February 1965, when Geoff Gunney, the great Hunslet forward, was sent from the field for striking an opponent? Up to that point, Gunney had had a similarly unblemished disciplinary record, in his case of over 13 years in the professional game. (My uncomprehending reaction at the time is noted above).

As Sinfield left the pitch, the crowd in the North Stand rose – virtually as one – to applaud him tumultuously. For any detached observer of sport – as I am these days – or, indeed, any observer of social behaviour more generally, this was a fascinating coda to Sinfield's evening's work. Surely no-one could condone his act of serious foul play (and the Rhinos' coach,

Brian McDermott, stated later that he had agreed with the referee's decision) nor not be concerned that his absence would present difficulties for Leeds in maintaining their 24-18 lead (which it certainly did, as Castleford scored the equalising try and conversion soon afterwards, though this was an argument not conceded by McDermott)?

This would be grist to the mill of any behavioural psychologist examining the actions and reactions of large crowds. I know, of course, that the Leeds supporters fervently identify with Sinfield, who has led the club with distinction for several seasons. Were they somehow simply recognising the longevity of his commitment to the cause? Or was it something more tribal: the crowd identifying with the fallen leader in the Leeds shirt at this particular moment, notwithstanding the severity of his offence and the possible consequences for his side? Perhaps, when considering these interesting and difficult questions, attention should also be paid to the case of Zak Hardaker, the Leeds full-back, for whom the Castleford Tigers match was his first game back after serving a 5-match ban for venting homophobic abuse at a match referee. The announcement of his name, as the team line-ups were announced before the kick-off, brought one of the biggest cheers of the evening.

The tribalism is all. The match is all. Nothing else matters. Before the game, I stood for a while under the end of the Western Terrace of the Headingley Cricket Ground and watched supporters of both Leeds and Castleford go down the short tarmacadamed path that leads to the seating of the North Stand and North Paddock and the terracing of the West Stand. A young black nun, smartly attired in a full habit, was holding a collection bucket labelled "Sisters of the Poor: Collection for the Elderly." In the three or four minutes that I watched, every single supporter ignored her.

I went over and put a modest donation into her bucket. "God bless you," she said. "How are you getting on?" I asked. "It's very hard…" she smiled, "…a hundred people pass by…" "God bless you," she said again, touching my arm gently.

I walked away feeling both blessed and sad, if that's possible. Of course, no-one is obliged to contribute to every collection bucket that is placed in their vicinity. However, I did wonder about these supporters, the vast majority of whom were attired in their expensive replica shirts and many of whom were carrying their pricey pints of beer into the arena. Their concentration was elsewhere. The match is all.

I spent the following morning in the Leeds Central Library researching an article to be published in due course in a well-known rugby league magazine. After four hours trawling through the microfilm records of 1960s newspaper reports, I adjourned to the adjacent cafe of the Leeds Art

Gallery for some lunch. I had been seated for a few minutes when the next table was taken by a late middle aged man and his wife. "Did you enjoy the game?," I asked my neighbour from Headingley's North Stand.

We talked for a few minutes. About Kevin Sinfield. About how Castleford had deserved to win the game, rather than draw. About our respective careers: mine as a retired civil servant in Glasgow; his as an about-to-be retired civil servant in Leeds. About our respective daughters: his studying at the University of St Andrew's; mine having graduated from the same university last month. The man's wife asked what had brought me down to Leeds and I explained that I was here to watch some rugby and cricket. "You're a sport tourist," she said. I could not disagree.

On Saturday, I arrived at the Scarborough cricket ground about half an hour before play was due to start. It was announced that Middlesex had won the toss and had put Yorkshire in to bat. As I passed the sight-screen on my way round to the raised stand on the far side of the ground, I met the President of the Yorkshire CCC. "Who do you fancy this morning?" I asked. "Oh, it'll go all over" replied Dickie Bird, drawing on the experience of 23 years as a Test Match umpire and waving his arm to indicate a viciously deviating cricket ball. "Just look at it," he said, gesturing towards the green tinge on the pitch and the humid conditions. "We'd have put 'em in if we'd won the toss. But what can you do?" "We can hope that the sun comes out," I ventured.

We bade our farewells and went our separate ways. I had never met Dickie Bird before and he didn't know me from Adam, but I suspect that this friendly and idiosyncratic man would happily discuss anything about cricket with anyone at any time.

In the light of the President's concerns, I wondered if Yorkshire might do well to get to three figures. In the event, following a mid-afternoon break for a heavy downpour, they had reached 207 for 4 wickets by the time that I left the ground just after 7 o'clock to catch the train back to Leeds. The opener, Adam Lyth, had played an excellent innings of 116 not out (he was out shortly afterwards for 117), combining some elegant driving through the covers with resolute defence in testing conditions against a probing Middlesex seam attack led by Steven Finn.

During the course of his innings, Lyth became the first batsman in the First Division of the LV County Championship to reach 1,000 first class runs in the season, (thereby curiously repeating a feat that I had also seem him achieve in an innings against Warwickshire at Headingley in 2010). If he does not win an England cap before too long, I should be very surprised.[8]

Finally – perhaps to offer a counterweight to my observation of the nun's experience – I should report what happened when I was waiting for the number 56 bus to take me to Headingley from Leeds city centre. I was towards the back of an informal queue of about a dozen people. A couple of places in front of me was a sullen-looking youth wearing a faded T-shirt and baseball cap. He had a thin, pale face and a few straggly whiskers of beard. To the side of the queue were two elderly ladies, smartly (and identically) dressed; they could have 80-year old twins. The queue edged forward, but the youth waited and bent his head forward slightly. "Are you waiting for the bus," he enquired gently, repeating the question when the ladies did not hear the first time. He gestured with his hand that they should proceed in front of him.

On the train journey back to Glasgow, I reflected on the casual conversations and other encounters that had accompanied my weekend as a sports tourist – those mentioned here and a dozen more – and which I would not have experienced otherwise. Some were conversational, others observational. They add up to something, I think.

www.anordinaryspectator.com/news-blog July 2014

Rugby League

The Shay and Mrs Simpson

Last Sunday afternoon in Yorkshire presented me with an opportunity to go to one of the rugby league grounds in the region that I had not previously visited. The choice boiled down to the John Smith Stadium in Huddersfield, where the local Giants were playing the Bradford Bulls in the First Utility Super League, or the Shay in Halifax for the home side's clash with Whitehaven in the Kingstone Press Championship.

Given that the Bulls were on the verge of relegation, having won only 4 of their 20 league fixtures, I thought that the Super League game might be a bit of a mismatch. By contrast, the lower league's sides were placed 3rd and 7th in their division, respectively, with both having something to play for before the end-of-season shake-up of league reconstruction.

The Halifax rugby league club has shared the Shay with the town's football team since 1998, when the former moved from Thrum Hall, its home since 1886. From my childhood in the 1960s, I recalled that the ground had doubled – rather exotically I thought at the time – as a venue for both football and speedway, hosting the Halifax Dukes, though the bike riders moved on to Bradford in 1986. It was high time for a visit.

And a very pleasant afternoon it was too. I had a friendly welcome at reception when I enquired about buying a ticket and an excellent view from the East Stand. The vast majority – though not quite all – of the 1370 spectators were home supporters, of course, and they encouraged their side throughout the game, not least in the opening exchanges, when the determined efforts made by the Halifax prop forwards to gain the extra couple of yards before being tackled were duly recognised.

The first few minutes were evenly fought, but after Ben Johnston had side-stepped his way through the defence to set up the first try for Tommy Saxton it was one-way traffic. The opening 6-0 margin had widened to

34-0 by half-time with Halifax gaining a noticeably productive return on the left hand side of their attack. "A fantastic first half performance from the lads there" said the public address announcer as the players left the field.

When Halifax scored again shortly after the re-start, I did wonder if the floodgates would really open. But Whitehaven did not give up, being denied only when their right winger was stripped of the ball when over the line and attempting to touch down. "Come on 'Haven," shouted a lone voice to my right, supplementing the small knot of visiting supporters on the terraces of the South Stand. Two late tries gave them some consolation before a final score of 52-12.

(For reference, the margin of victory in the competing attraction was not quite as wide, but still emphatic. Huddersfield Giants defeated Bradford Bulls 52-26 in what the following morning's *Yorkshire Post* described as a "low quality contest," thereby confirming the Bulls' relegation).

The Shay has changed a great deal since its speedway days, but there is still an old-fashioned feel to the ground with its four discrete and covered stands, two of which were in use for this match. Most noticeably, the stadium is framed by a ring of tall, dense trees, which contribute to the sense of an enclosed dedicated space. It is not quite the "Stadion an der Alten Försterei" (Stadium Near the Old Forester's House) in Berlin – on which I reported in this occasional series of blogs in May, having watched FC Union play TSV 1860 München in the Bundesliga 2 – but the end result is not dissimilar. The public address was clear and informative – and good value for the players' sponsors, who were name-checked every time a try or conversion was scored or a substitution made. The match programme was also good value, with a nice article summarising key moments in the visitors' history.

After the game I walked over to Piece Hall – "Britain's oldest remaining Cloth Hall, opened January 1st 1779" as stated by the entrance – wondering if it might be open on a late Sunday afternoon. Not quite was the answer, as the Grade 1 listed building is closed for renovation until Spring 2016. I shall make a note to return to the Shay sometime in the following rugby season.

Instead, I had a rather good cup of coffee in the Wallis Simpson Cafe of the Imperial Crown Hotel near to the railway station. I asked the young man behind the bar what the link with Wallis Simpson had been. He explained – helpfully, but somewhat anti-climatically – that a considerable amount of research had been done on the subject, but no firm connection had been established. However, he said by way of mitigation, Edward VIII had opened the local borough market when he was (briefly) king. That would have been in 1936; Halifax RLFC, playing at Thrum Hall, finished 13th (out of 30) in the league that year.

www.anordinaryspectator.com/news-blog July 2014

Swimming

We "Gie It Laldy" at Tollcross

Glasgow is hosting the 20th Commonwealth Games with pride and friendliness and humour. And imagination and efficiency. And a certain amount of luck: today is the third day of competition and – so far at least – the weather has been unseasonably hot and sunny, even for a Glasgow summer. Having lived in a Glasgow postcode for over 20 years, my family is – with tens of thousands of others – basking in the reflected glory of a successful event.

Yesterday evening, we took the train to Carntyne – the travel provided free as part of the ticket purchase – and walked through the park to the Tollcross International Swimming Centre. It felt as if we were part of something: the volunteers cheerily guided us on our way; a young soldier politely carried out the security check outside the arena; an Australian t-shirt or South African accent reminded us of the multinational presence.

This being a highly significant year in Scotland as a country and a nation, I was – inevitably – looking for clues about the broader political picture. How would the royal visitors – the Earl and Countess of Wessex – be received? What reaction would be induced by the senior Scottish politician at the medal ceremony? Above all, how would the competitors of England be received by an arena full of excited and passionate spectators?

I need not have worried. The evening's first event – the Men's 50 Metres Butterfly Final – was won by Ben Proud of England. His achievement was rapturously received by the whole crowd – not just the sizeable English-supporting contingent – both at the point of victory and as the winner and his fellow medallists took their lap of honour after the medal ceremony.

The majority of the spectators were Scots and, of course, they were rooting for their own swimmers throughout the evening. But they were generous to all the competitors, not only those – from Australia, Canada and England – whose winning anthems were heard during the course of the evening, but also to those of other nations – Singapore, Sri Lanka, India – appearing in the semi-finals and finals.

"Flower of Scotland" was heard once. A devastating final length on the freestyle leg of the 400 Metres Individual Medley brought a gold medal for Daniel Wallace. He took the lead more or less as he was swimming past our seats half-way down the pool for the final time and the tumultuous noise of the crowd roared him home. Commentators often speak about it seeming as if the noise created by a crowd was about to take the roof off a sports arena. The deafening crescendo as the single light on the starting block registered that Wallace was the first man home was one of those occasions.

"Make Some Noise," implored the message on the big screen, followed in the local vernacular by "Gie It Laldy." We needed no such encouragement.

The evening went without a hitch. The arena was bright and warm and intimate, though with plenty of leg and arm-room in the seating areas. The announcers were informative and enthusiastic. The starters were brisk and efficient: there were no false starts at all. The races were keenly competitive with the modern technology allowing the results and times to be shown almost instantaneously on the big screen. And, in the tight finishes, the drama was enhanced by the lighting system at the end of the lanes – one, two, three – showing the order of the finishers. On two occasions, two sets of lights were illuminated for one place: the swimmers could not be separated to one hundredth of a second.

There was one Para-Sport event during the evening: the Women's 100 Metre Freestyle S8 Final. Maddison Elliott, a 15 year-old Australian, was an emotional winner, hugging her kangaroo mascot tightly throughout her lap of honour. In the sixth and final place was a Kenyan girl, Ann Wacuba, who is a double amputee above the knee. She finished almost a full minute behind the winner to a roar of the crowd that pretty well matched that given to Daniel Wallace. I just about held it together, but it was a close-run thing.

After we returned home to Milngavie, we sat in the living room for an hour and chatted about the evening. The windows were open and a warm post-midnight breeze aired the room. We supplemented the discussion with Pimms and lemonade and bacon sandwiches. A perfect coda to the evening.

We had engaged fully with the swimming at Tollcross and with the Glasgow Commonwealth Games as a whole. I had even high-fived a couple of the latex gloves worn by the volunteers on my way to and from the arena. For me, this was an act of exhibitionism comparable with shaking hands with Mickey Mouse in Disneyland in 1999.

And so on to next Thursday and the gymnastics at the SSE Hydro. To quote the slogan of the Glasgow Commonwealth Games: "Bring It On."

www.anordinaryspectator.com/news-blog July 2014

Gymnastics

The Pommel Horse and Darth Vader

I suspect that, for many spectators, the 20th Commonwealth Games currently being held in Glasgow are providing an opportunity to watch some sports live and in the flesh for the first time. I am no exception. The swimming and gymnastics gaps in my spectating CV have now been filled.

The gymnastics programme is being held at the SSE Hydro. Yesterday afternoon's schedule consisted of the Men's Finals of the Floor, Pommel Horse and Rings disciplines and the Women's Finals in the Vault and Uneven Bars.

A competitor's score is comprised of two components – the tariff for the degree of difficulty of the routine and the judges' mark on the quality of its execution – minus any fixed penalties for stepping outside the border line or falling off the apparatus. I was aware, therefore, that gymnastics is a sport that is fundamentally different from most of those that I have previously watched. Unlike sports that are quantitatively measured to determine the outcome – goals scored, runs accumulated, shots taken, time spent, and so on – here the judges' assessment is crucial. There is a dominant qualitative perspective, as there is in ice-dancing or diving.

However, I did not spend too long fretting about this philosophical point, for two reasons. First, a moment's thought confirms that the official's judgement often plays a critical role in determining the outcome in my "quantitative" sports, whether it be a referee's penalty decision or an umpire's leg-before-wicket verdict. It was only two weeks ago that I attended the Leeds/Castleford Super League match at Headingley that finished in a 24-24 draw. In my view, the video referee disallowed a perfectly good Castleford try that, had it been allowed to stand, would almost certainly have contributed to an away victory.

Second, the action at the Hydro was compelling: the speed of the gymnasts across the diagonal of the floor and the precision of the timing of their routines within the allotted time span; the agility and bravery of the vaulters; the athletes' grace and strength as they moved along the pommel horse; the rising tension as the dismount approached from the uneven bars; the straining of muscles on the rings where, at the critical points, the ultimate aim is not to progress but to remain still.

There was a nice sense of ritual. Some of this reflected the overall themes of the Games as a whole – the name and country of each individual competitor being announced to the spectators, the lone piper introducing a medal ceremony, the military representatives preparing for the hoisting of the medal winners' flags during the playing of the anthems – but other aspects were probably specific to the gymnastics itself. At the end of each routine, I liked the respectful nod of the head by each competitor towards the judges and the way that he/she then shook hands with the next entrant. Before this, the judges had formally marched into the arena to the Darth Vader theme from *Star Wars*. At the medal ceremony, the silver and gold medal winners did a mini lap of the podium in order to congratulate the bronze and bronze/silver winners before their own award was given.

In the usual way, being present at the live event allowed one to observe some of the detail that is unavailable to the television viewer: the assiduous cleaning of the uneven bars by the coaches or assistants of each competitor to remove the perspiration left by the previous entrant; the large red box needed (by some) in order to reach up and clean the higher bar; the hook on the end of the long pole used to bring the rings to a standstill after the previous dismount; the Canadian coach's assistance in removing the springboard for the South African bars competitor after she had begun her routine. Above all, perhaps, the sense of space within the overall arena with its different sections for each event and the successive concentrations of action in the various parts of the auditorium.

And, of course, there was the drama. The two competitors from Wales both lost their grip on the uneven bars; when one of them did so for the second time and left the stage after ending her routine, she was immediately consoled by her rivals from England and Australia. In the vault, Dipa Karmakar of India bravely took on an exercise that had a far higher tariff of difficulty than any of the others – a handspring double front, I learned later – and was rewarded with the bronze medal. And on the pommel horse, the score of 15.966 announced to the final competitor – Max Whitlock of England – meant that the gold medal had been won by Daniel Keatings of Scotland by the margin of 0.092 points. The Hydro spectators worked out the maths – almost instantly – with predictable effects on the decibel level.

Whitlock had earlier won the Men's Floor exercise and – as he was followed by Claudia Fragapane in the Women's Vault – "Jerusalem" received the first two airings of the afternoon as the winner's anthem. The man sitting two rows in front of me resolutely refused to stand up, notwithstanding that he had clearly been fit enough to take his seat in the first place. A minor political statement, I thought: it's a free country. However, he was, at least, consistent, remaining steadfastly on his backside for the later renditions of "Flower of Scotland," "Jerusalem" again and "O Canada." Each to his own, I suppose.

Within the overall context of the Commonwealth Games, this was something of a private contest. Of the 71 nations represented at the Games, just 9 had competitors amongst the 40 finalists whom we saw yesterday. The 15 medals on offer were shared between 6 nations, several of whose entrants doubled (or, in Whitlock's case, tripled) up across events. This is not carping; it's just an observation. For whatever reason, the concentrations of talents within many sports are like this – including at the Olympic Games – whether considered as a whole (rowing, show jumping, sailing) or within specific sub-sets (Jamaican sprinters, Kenyan middle distance runners).

But I digress. Let me reflect, instead, on an enjoyable afternoon at the Commonwealth Games Gymnastics – especially on the skill, fitness and courage of the competitors – and note that one of the missing pieces of my sports spectating mosaic is now in place.

www.anordinaryspectator.com/news-blog August 2014

Cricket on the Radio

Test Match Special

The June blog recognising the centenary of the birth of John Arlott has prompted me to reflect on *Test Match Special* (*TMS*), the BBC radio programme that, since 1957, has provided ball-by-ball commentary on test match and other cricket involving the England cricket team.

I can date my introduction to *TMS* to 1963 or 1964. This is not so much due to the cricket played by of either of the sides touring England in those years (the West Indies and Australia, respectively), but through the commentators and analysts of that time, whose names registered fully with the eight/nine year old boy: Robert Hudson, Rex Alston (whose last test match was in 1964), Alan Gibson, John Arlott, Freddie Brown, Norman Yardley, EW Swanton, Alan McGilvray.

For this eager listener, the immediate attraction of *TMS* was, of course, the access that it provided to live commentary on England's test matches. (This was several years before the first one-day cricket international). There were alternative sources of information and opinion – my father's *Daily Express* or the intermittent coverage on the single channel of BBC television – but, via an unfamiliar (to me) radio channel called the Third Programme, I could listen for hours to the cricketing action being described as it happened. This was even more exciting when one of my own Yorkshire side was involved: Phil Sharpe, Ken Taylor, Fred Trueman and Geoff Boycott all featured in the 1964 Ashes series.

It wasn't just the cricket though. It was the broadcasts themselves. Naturally, I realised that they were being delivered to the whole nation, but I also sensed that the commentators were speaking to me – alone – listening to my parents' old wireless set whilst sitting in the "comfy" chair in the dining room. I was transported to Lord's and the Oval and even to nearby Headingley, which I did not actually visit for a cricket match until the Roses fixture in 1966.

Most of all, it was the commentators and their voices: I was captivated by Arlott, Hudson and Gibson in particular. With the exceptions of McGilvray – how exotic I thought it was to be listening to an Australian commentator – and Yardley, they were the voices of southern Britain: Arlott's Hampshire, Gibson's mild west country (though he had been born in Sheffield), Swanton's stockbroker belt. No-one had spoken to me, directly, in these accents before. Each commentator was distinctive – and, after a while, immediately recognisable – but they were all articulate, knowledgeable and authoritative. Many years later, it occurred to me that this had been the first "grown up" radio broadcasting I had listened to.

The full coverage of test matches on *TMS* gave me the opportunity to record each delivery of the games in my "Compactum" scorebook. It was my teenage equivalent of train-spotting or stamp-collecting. In hindsight, these exercises undoubtedly helped me to develop some of the skills and disciplines – concentration, attention to detail, time management – which I was subsequently able to put to good use in broader fields. At the time, however, it was just good fun, especially recording some of the major test match innings of the era: Hanif Mohammed for Pakistan in 1967, Basil D'Oliveira for England in 1968, Graeme Pollock for the Rest of the World in 1970.

One match I did not record was the England/India test match at Headingley in 1967. This took place during the school term time and so a couple of lunch breaks were spent listening on our transistors to the progress of the innings by Geoff Boycott in which he made 246 not out in just over a day and a half and was then dropped by England for slow scoring. At the same time, my Jewish friends in the school were glued to their own radios listening raptly for the latest news bulletin on the Six Day War. As I reflect back on this particular time, I make the immediate mental connection between a specific test match and an Arab/Israeli war: an important sporting contest set against a conflict that really mattered.

(An aside. I wonder if, in 50 years time, my counterpart – currently 12 years of age – will similarly refer back to 2014 and the juxtaposition between an England/India test match series and the contemporary catalogue of terrors and horrors in the Middle East: in Gaza, Iraq and Syria. Some things don't change).

The Wikipedia entry on *TMS* states that it "has always had a distinctively irreverent style." This is not my recollection of my early exposure to the broadcasts. That is not to say that the commentators of those days took things too seriously. They were generally from the wartime generation, who knew that cricket – even test match cricket – had its proper place within the grander scheme of things and who, as individuals, had their own respective hinterlands. Arlott had been a policeman for 12 years in Hampshire, rising to sergeant; Brown had been decorated for gallantry in Crete; Hudson had seen service in Malaya as a lieutenant-colonel; Swanton had been a prisoner-of-war for three years, including in camps along the Burma-Siam railway.

TMS's light-heartedness became more noticeable later, following the introduction of Brian Johnston as a full-time member of the commentary team in 1970. Perhaps my "grumpy old man" qualities set in at an early stage, but I never really bought in to the school tuck-shop mentality of chocolate cakes, champagne moments and commentators' nicknames ("Aggers," "Blowers," "Johnners"). By the time John Arlott retired in 1980, my original batting line-up had long since left the crease: Hudson in 1968, Yardley in 1973 (replaced by Fred Trueman), Gibson and Swanton in 1975.

The recurrent (though not original) theme that sport reflects the society in which it takes place also applies to its presentation, of course, including the commentary on it. Accordingly, *TMS*'s light-heartedness subsequently evolved into laddishness. Wikipedia reports that, after pointing this out in 2008, Mike Selvey – an excellent cricket writer and analyst, in my view – was "asked to leave" the programme (after contributing for 20 years) for expressing a "sentiment [which] has been echoed by many of his contemporaries and the wider cricket community in general."

Listening to the commentary on an afternoon of the Headingley test match between England and Sri Lanka earlier this summer seemed to me to confirm the slightly uneasy combination of enforced jollity and informed analysis that *TMS* presents. At one point, some rather tedious badinage about Graeme Swann's dress sense in the commentary box was juxtaposed with a fascinating description by the former England cricketer of the dos and don'ts of shining the ball in order to facilitate reverse swing. Less of one, more of the other, I thought.

I suppose that much depends on the commentary team that is selected for any particular match. Last Saturday's commentators on the second afternoon of the England/India test match at the Oval – Jonathan Agnew, Simon Mann and Ed Smith – were almost low-key in their detailed description of a fascinating session in which four leading England batsmen were dismissed for 98 runs. It was left to Geoff Boycott to draw on his long experience to offer the view of the Indian team that "…they're hopeless, aren't they, absolutely hopeless…" The timing of this comment was slightly unfortunate in that it was just before the flurry of English wickets, but, judged by the tourists' performances in every other session of last three test matches of the series, it is hard to dispute.

At the same time, it is clear that there is still room for the nice descriptive asides on which *TMS*'s reputation partly rests. I liked Agnew's admiration of an A380 aircraft flying through the blue sky on its way to Heathrow and, especially, the perceptive Sunil Gavaskar's description of the Indian spin bowler Ravichandran Ashwin holding the ball just before his delivery stride as if it were a cocktail shaker.

And so, these days, I am something of a lapsed *Test Match Special* listener. But I remain a spiritual member of the church, even though my regular attendance at the services is lacking. My affection for the programme remains, seeded by that early exposure in the 1960s. Half a century ago.

www.anordinaryspectator.com/news-blog August 2014

Rugby League

Gateshead Thunder and the Passage of Time

It is a characteristic of my sporting memory that the recollections of certain matches – in rugby, cricket or other sports – are often associated with particular events in my personal or professional life. Hence, I can recall that a rugby league game that my sister and I attended at the South Leeds Stadium in June 2004 – Hunslet Hawks versus Gateshead Thunder – took place a few days after we had laid our father to rest in Lawnswood Cemetery in Leeds. Rosemary wore the Hawks scarf that Dad had brought for her as a Christmas present some years earlier; I wore the same myrtle, white and flame scarf that I had had on my earliest visits to Hunslet's Parkside ground in the early 1960s.

Later in 2004 – on the day of my 50th birthday, as it happened – we attended the inquest into our father's death. The West Yorkshire Coroner concluded that the cause of Dad's malignant mesothelioma was his exposure to asbestos dust during the course of his working life as a joiner and builders' foreman.

Ten years on, 2014 is – of course – the year of my 60th birthday.

Last Sunday, I made what has evolved, over the last four years, into my annual visit to watch the Hunslet Hawks at the South Leeds Stadium. The fixture was an Elimination Play-Off in the round of matches to determine the promoted team from the Kingstone Press Championship 1 division.

Hunslet Hawks's opponents were Gateshead Thunder.

For many people, the occurrence of "big" birthdays tends to concentrate the mind. I am no exception. What has happened over the last 10 years? To me? To my family? To the world? We think back and we project forward. Will I still be here in 10 years time? If so, where? Doing what?

I count myself fortunate that, in my personal circumstances, there has been a marked sense of continuity over the last decade. We live in the same house in Milngavie. We remain comfortably well-off with foreign holidays – this year, Ireland, France and Germany – as our main luxuries. The small group of local friends who will celebrate my birthday in November are mainly the same individuals who attended the 50th birthday dinner. We are indeed blessed.

In other respects, the passage of time has had its usual effects. With one exception – a 95 year-old aunt living in Australia – the generation of our parents and their spouses and siblings has all passed on. Our own bodies creak a little more; we have had our share of illness and surgery. I have now retired from full-time work. Our children – now in their 20s – are making their own way in an uncertain world.

I was tempted to consult the archives to remind myself of the main news items in 2004, but I did not spend long on this task. The abuse of Iraqi detainees at the Abu Ghraib prison, the expansion of the European Union from 15 to 25 countries, the re-election of George W Bush as US President... Is it really 10 years since this happened? In the sporting arena, some things have remained the same (the Leeds Rhinos and St Helens won rugby league's main silverware); others, not surprisingly, now look somewhat dated (Tiger Woods was ranked as the world's top golfer until September, when he was usurped by Vijay Singh; Arsenal went through the Premier League season unbeaten).

If – in 2024 – I make it to three score years and ten and I am able to look back to current times, what will I focus on? The dreadful path of IS through Iraq and Syria, the war in Ukraine, the spread of the Ebola virus in western Africa...? Is it any wonder, when the main contemporary global issues are catalogued like this, that we might be pessimistic about the future? For the optimistic perspective, we need resolution, confidence, respectfulness, ingenuity, courage... A formidable list of requirements, perhaps, but all is not lost.

As noted, the big birthdays tend to be occasions for reflection – and for soul-searching and speculation. For the most part, I think that I am in denial about my 60th. It is not happening: I am really still only 25. Or it is happening to somebody else, whom I am observing, from outside. Then, of course, the reality hits. The clock is not only ticking, it is ticking at a faster rate.

In the 2004 encounter, the Hunslet Hawks and Gateshead Thunder teams were evenly matched in the early stages of their contest before the Hawks took control and rattled up a half-century of points. Last Sunday, the story was exactly – and uncannily – the same. The final kick of the match – the successful conversion of the home side's ninth try – took the final score to 50 points to 6.

Some things change and some things stay the same. But the passage of time continues – inexorably and relentlessly.

www.anordinaryspectator.com/news-blog September 2014

Rugby Union

Return to Scotstoun

The first round of group matches in the newly established European Rugby Champions Cup was played this weekend. On Saturday, on a sunny and breezy afternoon, I went to see the Glasgow Warriors play Bath Rugby at the Scotstoun Stadium. I'm not sure about the validity of the "champions" tag: Glasgow were runners-up in the (then) RaboDirect PRO12 championship final last season, whilst Bath finished in fifth place in the Aviva Premiership in England and didn't qualify for the play-offs. But I suppose that anything goes in the hyped presentation of modern elite sport.

I had high expectations of Bath. The club has shown its ambition by investing heavily in the former member of the England coaching staff, Mike Ford, as head coach, and in the recruitment of the South Sydney Rabbitohs and England rugby league star, Sam Burgess, though the latter's first appearance has been delayed by the fractured cheekbone and eye-socket he incurred earlier this month in the Australian NRL Grand Final. More immediately, Bath had won four of their opening six league fixtures this season, including against the Leicester Tigers (by 45 points to nil) and Saracens.

Glasgow had also started the season well, the defeat last week in Ulster being their first setback in the PRO12 league. Both sides had an impressive array of internationals at their disposal with the visitors including at least half a dozen players who would hope to feature in this autumn's England games.

It was good to visit Scotstoun again: a neat ground with an excellent view from the Main Stand across the running track to the pitch and, if the action flags, beyond the opposite stand to the suburban trains running to and from Yoker and Dalmuir. It was my first visit since Glasgow played their home matches there in 1997: my match programme collection for the autumn of that year includes those for the fixtures with Wasps, Swansea, Ulster and the ACT Brumbies. (On the subject of sporting echoes, I should also report that I saw Michael Ford – as he was listed in the programme – play at scrum half for Castleford against Wigan in the Rugby League Challenge Cup Final at Wembley in 1992. He had previously played in the final as a teenager for Wigan against Hull in 1985).

Unfortunately, Bath were a great disappointment. Their only try followed a speculative high kick which was inadequately dealt with by the Glasgow defence; with the conversion, this gave them an early 10-7 lead. After that, Glasgow scored 30 unanswered points to go in at half-time leading 23-10 and to run out final winners by 37 points to 10.

Glasgow were not flattered by the scoreline. They were consistently quicker in thought and deed and 4 of their 5 tries were scored by members of a dangerous back division, including two by the impressive Mark Bennett in the centre. In the second row, Leone Nakarawa complemented his work in the tight phases with some exciting running and skilful offloading of the ball in the tackle, illustrative of his pedigree as a Fijian Sevens international. The Glasgow defence in midfield and around the fringes of the rucks was robustly accurate and, apart from a couple of miscued kicks into touch on the full (both of which anti-climatically followed long mauling drives by the forwards), their tactical kicking was generally effective.

By contrast, whilst the Bath forwards provided a good supply of set-piece possession, there was a general lack of zip about the visitors' play. Their own high-profile backs had a fruitless afternoon: Gavin Henson was replaced early in the second half without having broken sweat; Kyle Eastmond, a successful recruit from St Helens rugby league, went off injured in the first half; the dangerous Anthony Watson had one impressive swerving run down the wing, but was otherwise little seen. Only for a brief period in the second half, when the introduction of an international front row from the replacements bench seemed to galvanise the whole team, did Bath place the Glasgow try-line under any serious pressure. At that stage, the half-time deficit could have been overturned by two converted tries, but a dropped ball over the line signalled the end of that particular threat.

An underlying theme of my sports spectating has been how often my expectations of success or failure by particular teams in individual matches or over the course of a season were undermined by the subsequent courses of events. From Saturday's showing, it would appear that the European Rugby Champions Cup prospects of the Glasgow Warriors are somewhat brighter than those of Bath Rugby. But it is a tough group – which also includes Montpellier and Toulouse – to be played out over the draining months of autumn and winter. Things might look a little different in the spring.[9]

www.anordinaryspectator.com/news-blog October 2014

Rugby League

The Garden Gate

Last Friday lunchtime, the "Hunslet Rugby League Remembered" Heritage Room was officially opened at the Garden Gate public house in south Leeds. I had received an invitation from Peter Todd, the General Manager of the Hunslet Hawks RLFC.

The room is dedicated to the history of the Hunslet Rugby League Club and contains some neatly presented display boards containing descriptions and photographs of the key events in the club's history from its formation in 1883 largely through to the disbanding of the original club – and the sale of its Parkside ground – in 1973. There are special features on Alan Snowden, the club's record holder for the number of tries in a season (34 in 1956-57), and Billy Langton, the club's record points scorer (2,204 between 1954-65).

The Garden Gate is an appropriate venue for the Heritage Room. It was built in 1903 and, since the 1970s, its status as a Grade II listed building has thankfully preserved it from the urban planners and developers. Moreover, I was told, it was the hostelry in which the Hunslet team gathered with their supporters to celebrate the completion of their "All Four Cups" feat in 1907-08. There is a main bar and three other small rooms – one of which is the Heritage Room, another containing the piano, the third on this occasion used to dispense the lunchtime pies and peas – connected by a narrow corridor. I sensed that, according to circumstances, it could be a place for both communal festivity and private discourse.

I was aware that, previously, I had had only brief acquaintance with a couple of people at the event and would therefore be faced with the tricky task of striking up conversations with folk who were already well-connected within the group. I need not have worried. The first person I met was Keith Rowson, who played for the Hunslet first and reserve teams in the 1960s. He greeted me by the entrance and we immediately struck up a friendly conversation.

As we waited in the sunshine, Harry Jepson arrived. This remarkable man, now aged 94, is the distinguished President of the Leeds Rhinos RLFC and a former Secretary/Manager of Hunslet. I introduced myself by saying that I had sent him a copy of *An Ordinary Spectator* and that I had been very touched by the warm letter that he had sent in reply. He placed me instantly and we had a nice chat. In his letter, he mentioned that he had first watched Hunslet at Parkside as a young boy in 1926 and had been instantly "hooked" on the club and the sport. He smiled when someone asked if he had been present for the Hunslet's team triumphant homecoming in 1908.

There was a consistent warmth of greeting from everyone I met. I kept my introduction short: "Hello. My name is John Rigg. My father brought me to watch Hunslet play at Parkside when I was a small boy." "Hello, John" responded Ray Abbey, a reserve member of the Challenge Cup Final squad of 1965, with a firm handshake and a friendly nod of the head. Next year is the fiftieth anniversary of that match, of course, and I wondered if any special commemoration was being planned. Ray Abbey counted through the squad on the fingers of his hands: 8 members are still alive, though sadly not all are in the best of health.

Earlier, after my nervous approach and introduction, a similarly friendly response. "Hello, John" said Geoff Gunney, with another handshake and warm smile. Geoff Gunney: a Great Britain tourist to Australasia in 1954, the winner of 11 international caps, a Wembley finalist in 1965, a driving force behind the establishment of the New Hunslet club in 1973. And also – with apologies to the advocates of Albert Goldthorpe and Jack Walkington – arguably Hunslet's greatest-ever player.

The short official opening speech was given by Peter Jarvis, another former player at Parkside and chairman of the Hunslet Rugby Foundation heritage group. He concluded by leading a rendition of the traditional Hunslet club song: "We've Swept The Seas Before Boys." This was a poignant moment. As I joined in from my position in the crowded corridor, the sounds of the verse coming from each of the rooms and from those placed back towards the entrance to the pub, I thought of my late father. He had been born in Hunslet and, like Harry Jepson, had formed an emotional attachment to the club in his childhood that stayed with him throughout his life. Peter Todd might have addressed his kind invitation to me, but I was there representing my dad as well.

I reflected on the concept of the Heritage Room on my journey down to London on Friday afternoon (prior to returning to Glasgow on Saturday).

For the individual Hunslet players and officials – past and present – I would imagine that it contributes towards their individual senses of personal identity: of who they were and are. Linked to that is clearly an already well-established sense of comradeship and bonding that many of those players have with their former colleagues: those who, at one time, were with them in the mud and rain at Batley or Hull or Whitehaven.

Perhaps most important, however, is the Heritage Room's role in the Hunslet community, hopefully not only as a locale to celebrate the past achievements of the area and its inhabitants but also, crucially, as a venue from which current and future generations can take inspiration to make good, if not in sport than in some other field. The best – and most interesting – heritage centres are those that not only describe and interpret the past, but also provide insights on the present and suggest pathways for the future. It does not take a genius to realise that the future of the Hunslet Hawks RLFC is critically dependent on the maintenance and development of strong links with the local community. The club is already devoting significant efforts towards this. At the same time, the firm link with the past also remains: the last line of the club song – "So We Shall Again" – appears on the Hawks's crest.

At present, the Heritage Room occupies a relatively small space. My personal view – without wishing to push the religious analogy too far – is that it would benefit from having a few more "relics." The presentation of physical objects – in this case, a shirt, a match programme, a pair of boots – can greatly assist in the presentation of historical narrative. I realise, of course, that this creates a separate set of issues to address, not least those concerning security, insurance and storage.

Peter Jarvis is ahead of me on this, however, and already thinking along the same lines. The *Yorkshire Evening Post*'s report on the Heritage Room's opening included a request from him to the public to donate memorabilia to add to the collection. I do hope that his appeal is taken up, that the collection expands into a second room at the Garden Gate, and that the efforts of the Hunslet Rugby Foundation heritage group in establishing the Heritage Room are fully rewarded.

www.anordinaryspectator.com/news-blog October 2014

Cricket

Suspended Animation

The Headingley test match of 1981 has entered cricket folklore for the performances of Ian Botham (with the bat) and Bob Willis (with the ball), respectively, in the England and Australian second innings. Having followed on 227 runs behind, England set Australia a target of 130 to win and bowled them out for 111. Botham scored 149 not out and Willis took eight wickets for 43 runs.

I was not at the ground for any part of those two feats.

But I have a startling and clear memory of one particular incident from earlier in the match.

Over the first two days, Australia compiled 401 for 9 declared in the first innings on a difficult pitch. The opening batsman, John Dyson, showed a sound technique and made an impressive century. England spilled some straightforward catches, including two by Botham. The weather was cold and blustery, and the breaks for rain did not cheer the home support.

The incident that is seared upon my memory came at the start of play on the Saturday morning. It occurred at the resumption of the England first innings, which had only just begun on the previous day – Geoff Boycott was nought not out overnight – and, more than 30 years on, its recollection instantly raises the hairs on the back of my neck.

When Boycott received the first ball from Australia's champion bowler, Dennis Lillee, the ground was nearly full, which meant that there would have been about 18,000 present. I sat next to my father on the Western Terrace. As the delivery passed by the outside of the off stump, left alone by Boycott, and travelled through to the Australian wicketkeeper, Rodney Marsh, we could have heard the proverbial pin drop. All activity had stopped. There was not a single sound: not a murmur or a whisper or any movement at all. It was as if, apart from the players, every single inhabitant of the ground had been placed in a state of suspended animation. And then, after the ball had thumped into Marsh's gloves and he had passed it on to one of the slip fielders, there was the collective realisation that Boycott had survived his first ball. 18,000 people – minus a few Australians – breathed out a communal sigh of relief.

That incident – which lasted for that part of a second that it took for the ball to travel from Lillee's hand to wicketkeeper Marsh – is one of the most astonishing I have witnessed on the sports field. My father and I looked at each other immediately afterwards and made a mental connection of what we had seen. We only discussed the moment later in the evening, when we were reflecting on the day's events. We were absolutely of the opinion that there had not been a breath of sound across the whole of Headingley until the ball smacked into Marsh's secure grasp. And we also agreed that that eerie feeling of complete suspense – and then relief – was only felt, in its purest form, for the first delivery that Boycott received from Lillee. A tension remained for the rest of the over – and, indeed, for the remainder of Boycott's innings over the next hour and a half (he was out for 12) – as the crowd watched the evolving proceedings with respectful attention, but the feeling was not quite the same as it had been for that unique delivery.

During the rest of Saturday's play, England made a poor attempt at responding to the Australian total, being dismissed for 174. Just before the close, after England had followed on, Graham Gooch was dismissed for the second time in the day without scoring.

The rest is history, of course, courtesy of Botham and Willis's heroics on the Monday and Tuesday. However, by the time that play resumed after the weekend, I was heading back south via Cambridge to London, where I was living.

In my recent memoir of sports spectating, I sought to identify the factors that have continually drawn me to the live event over the course of half a century. I decided that at the top of the list – above even the skill or leadership or courage of the participants – is the quest for drama.

I was the person who attended the 1981 Headingley test and failed to see the most famous instances of Botham's batting and Willis's bowling. But I did experience a split second of action – as Geoff Boycott survived the first delivery of the Saturday's play from Dennis Lillee – the memory of which remains crystal clear as one of the most exciting pieces of sporting drama that I have ever witnessed.

Backspin Winter 2014-15

First World War

Ruhleben

The centenary of Britain's entry into the First World War was widely commemorated on 4th August. Over the next four years, there will be many occasions on which the 100th anniversary of other defining events of that conflict will be recognised: the first landings at Gallipoli on 25th April 2015, the first day of the Battle of the Somme on 1st July 2016, the signing of the Armistice on 11th November 2018…

For individual households, there are other – more specific – reference points. In my case, I will note that Sergeant Robert Rigg of the Royal Horse Artillery and Royal Field Artillery was killed in action near Amiens in northern France on 7th August 1918. Just over a fortnight later, on 24th August 1918, also in France, the gun battery manned by his brother – John Rigg – was blown up. His casualty report of 26th August stated that he was "seriously ill" and that his next of kin were to be informed. John Rigg was my grandfather.

In *An Ordinary Spectator*, I refer to the Oxford versus Cambridge University Boxing Matches of 1977 and 1979, which I went to see at the Kelsey Kerridge Sports Centre in Cambridge. In the first of these, the Oxford bantamweight – weighing in at 8½ stone or under – was Colin Moynihan, later an Olympic medal-winning rowing cox, still later the Minister for Sport, and now a member of the House of Lords. It was the 1st Baron Moynihan – the distinguished surgeon, Sir Berkeley Moynihan (1865-1936) – who had operated on my grandfather on his return to Britain. This was some three years before my father was born.

My mother's father is also mentioned in the book. Alfred Edgar Niblett was born in Osnabruck, Germany, in 1888, one of the ten children of an Englishman from Cheltenham, Charles James Niblett – variously described in the official records as a merchant or business schoolteacher

– and his German wife (from Hannover). Alfred was a graduate of the University of Birmingham and, at the start of the First World War, was completing his doctorate at the University of Munich.

On 6th November 1914 – exactly one hundred years ago today – the German military authorities ordered the arrest of around 4,000 British men of military age then living in Germany and their internment at the Ruhleben racecourse, near Spandau just outside Berlin. Alfred Niblett was one of them. He was interned for the war's duration.

There is some excellent material available on the Ruhleben camp. I would recommend, in particular, the website created by the researcher and genealogist Chris Paton (http://ruhleben.tripod.com) – to which I have contributed a couple of paragraphs on Alfred Niblett – and the authoritative *British civilian internees in Germany: the Ruhleben camp, 1914-18* (Manchester University Press, 2008) by Matthew Stibbe of Sheffield Hallam University.

Professor Stibbe points out that the conditions in Ruhleben, whilst not as tough as in other First World War camps for "enemy aliens" in Germany, were especially poor (notably in terms of the quality of food and the crampedness of living space) during the first months, although the internees were perhaps fortunate that the camp's siting near to Berlin meant that it was easily accessible by neutral observers, including (until 1917) diplomats from the US Embassy. It is also clear that the internees' difficulties could be psychological as well as physical and, moreover, that this continued after the war through their reaction to the perception by some in Britain that they had been lucky to avoid the carnage of the Western Front and other theatres of war.

Sport featured prominently at Ruhleben, as the internees looked for ways to pass the time and to let off steam. Professor Stibbe reports that "football stood out in particular as a collective obsession, reflecting its dominance in pre (and post) war British popular culture," whilst boxing bouts "attracted big crowds, including German guards and officers who came to watch as spectators." (One of the internees was the famous footballer, Steve Bloomer, who had scored 28 goals for England between 1895 and 1907, a record that was not beaten until 1956).

Both my grandfathers lived into old age. John Rigg resumed his career in the police force in Leeds and died in 1959 at the age of 72. Alfred Niblett, who enjoyed careers as a businessman, schoolteacher and tutor, lived to the age of 84 and died in 1973. My mother, who was born four years after the end of the First World War, said that he did not speak at all about his experience in Ruhleben. What he did do, however, was retain two editions of the *Ruhleben Camp Magazine* – dated Christmas 1916 and

June 1917 – which respectively run to 64 and 72 pages of neatly printed articles and sketches. They have been passed down to me and are amongst my most prized possessions.

Today, Ruhleben is the name of a small railway station at the end of the U2 line in the orth west suburbs of Berlin. It could be a commuter halt in one of a thousand towns or cities. Outside the entrance, on the other side of the main road, is the local branch of Lidl, which includes (as I can attest) a rather good bakery section. The internment camp was situated a couple of miles down the road, bound by the main Hannover-Berlin railway line and the River Spree. The site later became a sewage processing centre and, as far as I know, there is nothing to mark its former use.

From today's perspective, the First World War – of which the Ruhleben narrative is a tiny part – took place in another time. All the participants, military and civilian – Robert Rigg, John Rigg, Alfred Niblett, Steve Bloomer, Berkeley Moynihan *et al* – are long deceased, of course. But – thankfully – there will be many occasions on which to remember them. And today – the centenary of 6th November 1914 – is one of those.[10]

www.anordinaryspectator.com/news-blog November 2014

Football

A Stramash in Paisley

On Saturday, I resumed my occasional tour of the football grounds of the west of Scotland. This time, I ventured to St Mirren Park in Paisley for the home side's fourth round William Hill Scottish Cup tie against Inverness Caledonian Thistle. The day had begun at the annual Christmas tree festival at St Paul's Church in Milngavie, where the musical accompaniment included a recital by Rachel Rutherford on the clarsach.

In my childhood, St Mirren was one of those names on my mother's football pools coupon that I could not locate in the *Philips' Modern School Atlas*. There were several of them across Scotland, of course – where exactly were Raith, St Johnstone, Hibernian, Third Lanark *et al?* – and the subsequent discovery of their respective locations always gave me a feeling of achievement.

The St Mirren club was located in Love Street in Paisley for the 115 years from 1894. On selling the ground to Tesco in 2009, they moved to a new 8,000 seat stadium in Ferguslie Park. The ground is neat and compact and the spectators are close to the action. For Saturday's cup-tie, it was barely one-quarter full, however, and, during those periods when the crowd was relatively quiet, the players' voices echoed around the stadium. In the opening minutes, the stentorian – and quite colourful – instructions to his defence from the Inverness goalkeeper were clearly heard by those of us in Row J of the Main Stand.

The course of the game reflected the two sides' respective positions in the Scottish Premier Football League. St Mirren are second bottom and separated from Ross County only on goal difference, having won only 2 of 14 league games so far; by contrast, Inverness are joint top of the league, behind Celtic again only on goal difference. However, although the visitors had the better of the early exchanges, it was St Mirren who took the lead just after the quarter-hour thanks to a crisp finish from Marc McAusland after Inverness had failed to deal with a corner kick.

In the second half, Inverness attacked for long periods, prompted from the midfield by the effective combination of the energetic James Vincent and the skilful Ryan Christie. I thought the latter was particularly impressive with his excellent close control and the vision for a penetrating pass with his cultured left foot. At 19 years of age, he is a player of rich promise: rather like Rachel Rutherford, perhaps, albeit in a different field.[11] The visitors managed an equaliser with half an hour to go, but they were profligate with their other chances. The replay is in Inverness tomorrow.

My neighbour in the stand was a burly middle-aged man who was attending with his young son. After Inverness scored their goal – following another corner, when there were two headed challenges, two shots cleared off the line and another shot hitting the post before Josh Meekings fired the ball into the net – he spoke to me in an accent that originated somewhere in the Western Isles: "What a stramash! As Arthur Montford would have said: 'What a stramash!'" It was a comment that was absolutely fitting. It described the goal perfectly and, knowingly, it was a nice acknowledgement of the great Scottish broadcaster, who died last week at the age of 85.

I enjoyed my visit to St Mirren Park. The club remains rooted in its community and recognises the circumstances faced by many in the locality. The advertisements on the big screen included an awareness campaign for lung cancer fronted by Sir Alex Ferguson (though I don't know if this campaign is also being rolled out across all clubs) and an appeal on behalf of one of local charities helping people "at this difficult time of the year." The MC's half-time pitch interview was with the four members of a local rock band – Lemonhaze – whose (quite impressive) new video was also played on the screen. "What's next?" the MC asked, perhaps expecting a music-related response to follow up the earlier references to the band's new single, the video and a couple of forthcoming gigs. The answer was probably more focused on the short-term than he had expected: "We'll go for a pint after the game."

After the match, I walked into the centre of Paisley. The evidence of post-industrial malaise is not hard to find, ranging from the derelict former home of the Paisley Provident Co-operative Society Limited, just down the road from the ground, through to the vacant areas of wasteland opposite the car-wash centre and the wholesale suppliers. But – I was reminded – this is also a town with a proud local history and architectural heritage; in the case of my walk, the latter started with St James' Church in Underwood Road and extended through to Paisley Town Hall, both buildings dating from the civic confidence of the 1880s.

The jewel in the crown is Paisley Abbey, of course. I entered through a side door and came across a rehearsal of that evening's performance of Mozart and Mendelssohn by the Orchestra of Scottish Opera with the City of Glasgow Chorus. I stood for a few minutes as the notes soared high into the abbey's upper reaches. Later, I reflected on my day's music sampling – a clarsach rendition, a Lemonhaze video and *Die Erste Walpurgisnacht*: a pleasantly eclectic collection.

Later still, in the evening, BBC Scotland's *Sportscene* showed the two goals from the St Mirren/Inverness match. The pundit Pat Nevin said that Arthur Montford would have described the Inverness equaliser as a stramash.

www.anordinaryspectator.com/news-blog December 2014

Rugby Union

Stade Toulousain

In October (in *"Return to Scotstoun"*) I noted that the game between the Glasgow Warriors and Bath Rugby in the European Rugby Champions Cup had been my first visit to Scotstoun since the home side had re-located there in 2012; it had therefore been 17 years since I had last seen Glasgow play at this ground, which they used for a couple of seasons in the 1990s. The gap to my subsequent visit has been much shorter, I'm pleased to say: a mere 8 weeks to last Saturday's match with Toulouse.

Toulouse had a ghost to lay with me, I think. The last time I had seen them was at Murrayfield in April 2012, when they had played Edinburgh in the quarter-final of the Heineken Cup. I recall that, whilst I had enjoyed Edinburgh's skilful and committed performance, which had resulted in a 19-14 win, I had been disappointed – if not slightly bewildered – by the approach taken by the visitors. In the period when Edinburgh had had two players in the sin bin, the main Toulouse tactic seemed to have been to hoof the ball as far down the pitch as possible, instead of keeping possession and attempting to run the depleted home defence off its feet.

Even worse, I could not understand why one of the best players in world rugby of the last 15 years (and unquestionably my favourite French player) – Yannick Jauzion – had started at full-back, rather than in his usual position of centre, especially when a class full-back, Clement, was on the replacement bench. Jauzion had been exposed by a couple of well-placed high kicks, leading to Edinburgh scores, and Toulouse had only really threatened as an attacking force late in the game when Poitrenaud came on to take up the full-back role and Jauzion reverted to his proper position.

I had realised, of course, that the coaches and players of Toulouse had a record of sustained success in European rugby over many seasons:

4 Heineken Cup wins and two other final appearances tell their own story. They are a highly professional side and know what they are doing. But, as the game had progressed and the Edinburgh supporters around me had begun to appreciate that a famous victory was on the cards, that had not stopped me scratching my head and wondering why their opposition was shooting itself in the foot.

That was 2½ years ago. What approach would Toulouse take this time?

The answer – and I appreciate that this is a cliché that inserts itself within a great deal of sports writing – is that they were "professional." They did just enough to win – by 12 points to 9 in this case – thereby maintaining their 100 per cent record after four matches in the Champions Cup group that includes Montpellier as well as Bath. In a sporting context, it reminded me of the great football teams of the 1960s and 1970s – Leeds United and Liverpool, in particular – who often also did "just enough" to win: usually 1-0, away from home, on their way to another championship.

Toulouse drew on their individual and collective experience – hardened over the years – to control the tempo of the game, take the few (penalty goal) chances that came their way and maintain an impregnable defensive alignment. Glasgow competed strongly, but missed a couple of kickable penalties of their own and these lapses were bound to have an crucial impact on a scoreline that always seemed that it would be a relatively low multiple of 3-point scores.

I watched the game again when I got home, courtesy of my television recording. The commentators were generally downbeat, bemoaning the Glasgow dropped passes and missed goal kicks and the lack of attacking adventure from Toulouse.

But there was more to the game than that. Beforehand, I had expected that, in the modern way, the most decisive players (apart from the goalkickers) were likely to be found in the respective back rows. When the teams were announced, I was standing next to a young man wearing a Toulouse scarf. "Ou est Harinordoquy?" I asked. "Est il blessé?" My source seemed to cotton on immediately that French was not my native language. "Not in the team," he replied, before adding that Thierry Dusautoir *was* in the team (having been listed as a replacement in the match programme). Dusautoir – the captain of France in the World Cup final of 2011 – was indeed in the Toulouse back row along with Yannick Nyanga and Louis Picamoles: a formidable combination.

Sure enough, at the game's conclusion, it was announced that Picamoles had been the man-of the-match. It could easily have been Dusautoir or Nyanga. Equally, it might justifiably have been any of their direct opponents: Robert Harley, Ryan Wilson or Josh Strauss, the Glasgow captain. Each had played himself to a standstill.

Ok: there were some handling errors by Glasgow and there was a huge reliance by Toulouse on the bulky power of their forwards. But you don't need to have 6 tries by each side to make for an enthralling rugby match. The game turned out to be what I had anticipated. It was physical, attritional and close – with try-scoring opportunities at a premium – as exemplified by the titanic contest between the respective back rows. I enjoyed every minute.

In addition, if you looked closely, there was also a superb display of full-back positional play by Poitrenaud (my second favourite French player of recent times), another impressive performance by the 20 year-old Jonny Gray in the Glasgow second row and, for good measure, an outrageous quarterback's offload by the Glasgow replacement, Leone Nakarawa. (Plus, it must be said, some accurate and sympathetic officiating – one touchline decision apart – by the referee, Wayne Barnes, and his assistants).

And, for the record, the afternoon was not without its imaginative spontaneity off the pitch. Before the game, the match-day announcer requested that the crowd respect both teams, particular the goal kickers. Half-way through the first half, when the home crowd judged that two or three contentious decisions had gone the visitors' way, Jean-Marc Doussain attempted a long range penalty kick to the loud accompaniment of booing and jeering, which was followed by a mocking cheer when the kick was fluffed. The announcer's repeated plea – "Ladies and gentlemen, the Glasgow Warriors would like to ask you please to respect the kicker" – was then itself met (predictably) by a further chorus of jeering. There was a short pause before he gave the perfect response: "Well, that's me told."[12]

www.anordinaryspectator.com/news-blog December 2014

Rugby League

Boxing Day Repeats

For the followers of many sports, within any season, there are certain days that take on a special meaning: the first day of the Lord's test match, Gold Cup Day at the Cheltenham Festival, the Varsity Match afternoon at Twickenham... The actual date might change from year to year, but the event is marked in the calendar. The day's significance is derived not only from the importance of the sporting contest itself, but from the social activity that is attached to its attendance.

Indeed, there is often more to it than that. For many, the day's particular relevance does not so much result from the immediate off-the-field intercourse in the bar or the pavilion, but from the opportunity it provides for *repeating* the connections enjoyed in previous years – for renewing the bonds with family or friends, for remembering past triumphs or disasters and, especially, for catching up on the successes or disappointments of life in general during the previous year.

In the world of rugby league, before the professional sport moved over to a summer season in the mid-1990s, such an occasion was generated by the Boxing Day fixture. Across the code, this was a time for the resumption of the battle for local bragging rights – Wigan/St Helens, Whitehaven/Workington, Hull/Hull KR – at its regular place in the annual cycle.

The busy Christmas schedule had always been a feature of rugby league. In the very first season of the Northern Rugby Union (1895-96), the Leeds club played no fewer than 6 fixtures between 21st December and 4th January, including Liversedge away on Christmas Day and Oldham at home on Boxing Day. (For some clubs, Christmas Day fixtures remained on the schedule until the mid 1960s, no doubt an annual source of some major family tensions).

Growing up where I did, I was particularly fortunate that Leeds's

Headingley ground – for a time bracketed with only the Arsenal FC ground at Highbury and the Murrayfield stadium in Edinburgh as comparable venues – had been one of the first in the country to install an "electric blanket." Whilst this did not guarantee that a match would take place in the depths of winter, it greatly reduced the chances of a postponement, of course. In the years that followed the blanket's installation in 1963, the financial return to the Leeds club from the annual combination of a healthy match-day attendance (healthy in terms of numbers, if not recent calorie count) and the television revenue – once the BBC had realised that it would be able to transmit live rugby in its Boxing Day sporting schedule – must have been substantial.

And so, from the late 1960s onwards, I would accompany my father and my uncles (usually two of them, though sometimes three plus cousins) for an 11.30 Boxing Day kick-off at Headingley. The visiting team was usually Wakefield Trinity, though Castleford, Featherstone Rovers and my dad's team, Hunslet, also featured. We would meet in the tea bar under the Main Stand and then take our places on the terraces in the South Stand or at the St Michael's Lane end, my father and I silently supportive of whoever Leeds's opponents might be. As I moved into my late teens, the routine was extended to include the post-match adjournment to one of the crowded pubs in Headingley, usually the Original Oak.

I have a series of memories from these matches: before the game with Castleford in 1969, the main wooden gate in Kirkstall Lane being flattened by the weight of the swelling masses outside the ground (thereby enabling me to gain a fortuitous free entry); the brilliant Wakefield stand-off David Topliss majestically shredding the Leeds defence in 1976; the propensity of Wakefield in the early 1970s to have a man dismissed during the match so that their numerical disadvantage began to take on the status of an annual ritual, at this time of year, to sit alongside the Christmas Day editions of *Top of the Pops* and *Morecambe and Wise*.

Looking back from today's perspective, it was not the outcomes of any of these matches that really mattered, of course. Of far more significance – as I think I also realised at the time – was the occasion itself. By the end of the 1970s, in particular, the Boxing Day game provided a fixed point of reference in our fluid world. At home and at work, there was change and uncertainty: I was away at university trying to make progress with a research degree; my uncle Vic, a die-hard Leeds supporter from his youth, had long been resident in Hampshire, though with an elderly mother still in the city; one of my other uncles and his son were launching a new business in Kent.

How precious, therefore, were those couple of hours in the pub when we would chew the fat, when we would bring each other up to date with our news and, on the rare occasions that Leeds had been beaten, when dad and I would good-naturedly seek to review the match in detail with Vic. Inevitably, the conversation would move on to dad and Vic casting themselves back to matches and players of the past. When my father raised the subject of Hunslet's Challenge Cup final victory over Widnes at Wembley in 1934 – as he always did – Vic would respond by referring to his long-standing friend, Cyril, with whom he had worked for many years. This was Cyril Morrell, who scored one of the Hunslet tries that day, breaking his collar bone in the process.

The post-Boxing Day match discussion in the Original Oak followed more or less the same script every year. But I did not mind: indeed, that was the point. It was a routine that was familiar and comforting and ours. We had anticipated the day, it had arrived, and it did not disappoint.

I am pleased that the tradition of the Boxing Day fixture continues. Last Friday, the Leeds Rhinos played the Wakefield Trinity Wildcats in their now-regular "Tetley's Festive Challenge" as part of the preparations for the new Super League season that will begin in February. It might not have been the same as a full-bloodied competitive match, with its high scoring (50-28 to Leeds) and the participation of several fringe players from the respective squads, but over 10,000 spectators turned out to watch and blow away the Christmas cobwebs.

I would guess that some old acquaintances might also have been renewed and some old stories revived.

www.anordinaryspectator.com/news-blog December 2014

Football

The Chances of Success

In December last year, I reported on the St Mirren versus Inverness Caledonian Thistle tie in the 4th round of the William Cup Scottish Cup ("*A Stramash in Paisley*"). Last weekend, ten weeks on, the 5th round matches were played: a curious and lengthy hiatus in the scheduling of this historic and prestigious competition.

After the first game, I checked the odds on Inverness winning the trophy with Ladbrokes (note: other bookmakers are available). They were 14 to 1. Following their success in the replay against St Mirren a couple of days later – the initial tie had ended 1-1 – and after the draw for the next round had been made, the odds fell to 12 to 1.

For Saturday's 5th round tie, Inverness were pitted against Partick Thistle on a sharp and clear afternoon at Firhill. It was a difficult match to predict. Inverness were standing at third place in the SPFL Premiership table – behind Celtic and Aberdeen, the latter only on goal difference – having accumulated almost twice as many league points as ninth-placed Partick. However, both the season's league fixtures had gone the way of Partick, with a total goal tally of 7-1. Moreover, Inverness sold their leading goalscorer, Billy McKay, to Wigan Athletic in last month's transfer window.

McKay's replacement in the Inverness forward line was the converted midfielder, Marley Watkins, who, within the first half hour, found himself on three separate occasions racing through the Partick defence to face the goalkeeper in one-on-one confrontations. He converted one of the chances. By the time that Greg Tansey scored the second goal, following a strong run and shot, Partick's early promise had fizzled out into a series of misplaced passes and attacking dead-ends. The home side left the field at half time to widespread boos and jeers from their own support.

At the risk of using a somewhat well-worn cliché, it was a game of two halves. After the break, Inverness seemed content to sit on their lead and move away from the crisp passing game that had characterised their first-half dominance. Then, midway through the second half, the Partick substitute Lyle Taylor, who had come in the reverse direction from English football in the transfer window (on loan from Scunthorpe United to be precise) – and who, when not waving his arms in chronic frustration at the referee, did enough to suggest that he might be a player of some talent – scored a rousing goal with a powerful volley from outside the penalty area. Partick pressed hard for the last 20 minutes of the match and there were a couple of narrow escapes for the Inverness defence, but the visitors held on to secure their passage into the last eight of the competition.

The draw for the quarter-finals was made yesterday. Inverness will play at home to Raith Rovers, who defeated Rangers on Sunday. This morning, their odds with Ladbrokes (note: obaa) to win the cup had been reduced to 7 to 2.

In statistical terms, the probability of an event occurring will range from 0.00 (definitely will not occur) to 1.00 (definitely will occur). In the case of Inverness winning the cup this season, the odds of 7 to 2 imply a 2 in 9 chance of success: ie a probability of 0.22. For the overwhelming favourites to lift the trophy, Celtic, the odds are 8 to 11, implying that there are 11 chances in 19: a probability of 0.58. Of the other clubs left in the competition, the odds range from 5 to 1 (Dundee United) to 2,000 to 1 (non-league Spartans).

Someone will win the Scottish Cup this year, of course. For the statistician, the probability of that occurring is 1.00. So, if we add up the implied probabilities of success of all 9 clubs remaining in the competition (there is one replay to resolve), does it give that figure? Answer: no, of course not. Based on the current odds for each of the clubs, the total probability is 1.20.

The difference represents the gross margin that goes to the bookmakers. This is needed to fund their costs – infrastructure, staffing, and so on – as well as their profit. For the consumer – ie the punter – it can reasonably be considered as the payment for having access to the betting market, whether in-store or on-line.

The other way to think of this is to scale up the odds on each team's success *pro rata* until the sum of their implied probabilities of success is reduced to 1.00. (Remember, this is an inverse relationship: the higher the team's odds, the lower the implied probability of its success). When this happens, the probability of Inverness lifting the cup falls from 0.22 to 0.19 and the implied odds are raised from 7 to 2 (or 3½ to 1) to 4.39 to 1.

In summary, therefore, the bookmakers' assessment – based solely on the relative strengths of the competitors left in the field, the current weight of bets and the known draw for the quarter-final – is that the odds on Inverness Caledonian Thistle winning this year's Scottish Cup are 4.39 to 1. However, because of their (very reasonable) requirements to meet costs and make a profit, the odds being quoted by the bookmakers to the punter are only 3½ to 1.

This does not necessarily mean that, at 7 to 2, a small wager on Inverness to win the cup represents a poor investment. The rational consumer simply asks whether he/she thinks there is a better chance than 2 in 9. However, if the bet is made – and if Inverness are to be successful – it might require the midfielder-cum-striker Marley Watkins to take more than one opportunity in three when one-on-one with the goalkeeper. Such are the chances of success.

www.anordinaryspectator/news-blog February 2015

Football

Internazionale

Last Thursday evening, benefiting from the two-thirds discount provided by my concessionary railcard for the over 60s, I paid £1-30 for the return journey from Milngavie to Bridgeton. "Are you going to the game," asked the clerk in the ticket office. "I hope we win. I fancy our chances tonight."

The game was the first leg of Glasgow Celtic versus FC Internazionale Milano – Inter Milan, of course – in the round of the last 32 of the UEFA Europa League. The ticket clerk and I agreed that a 0-0 scoreline would not be a bad result for the home side, as it would mean that Inter would not have an away goal to take back to the San Siro stadium for the second leg.

At the last football match on which I reported in this occasional series of blogs – the Partick Thistle versus Inverness Caledonian Thistle Scottish cup-tie a couple of weeks ago (*"The Chances of Success"*) – the official attendance was 2,915. For Celtic/Inter Milan, the corresponding figure was just over 60,500, the capacity of Celtic Park. It has been some time since I have been in a crowd of that magnitude – it would have been for the Scotland/New Zealand Rugby World Cup group match at Murrayfield in 2007 – but even these statistics do not tell the full story. Numbers alone do not convey the crowd's passion and involvement. And certainly not its noise.

On another of my previous visits to a Glasgow football ground – for the Rangers versus Leeds United European Cup tie at Ibrox Stadium in 1992 – the roar from the home support at the beginning of the match (the away supporters officially having been banned from entry) was one of the loudest that I have ever heard at a sports stadium. On that occasion, the bubble burst when Gary McAllister scored for Leeds in the first minute (though Rangers did go on to win the match).

On Thursday, the decibel level was probably higher. As the Celtic players broke up from their pre-kick off huddle, a deafening volume of sound blasted through the stadium. It was a roar of anticipation and hope and bloodlust. Unfortunately for Celtic, history repeated itself. The Kosovo-born Swiss international Xherdan Shaqiri was not quite as quick off the mark as McAllister had been all those years ago, but Inter were still 1-0 up after four minutes. After 13 minutes, it was 2-0, courtesy of a predatory goal from the Argentinian, Rodrigo Palacio. So much for the cunning plan concocted by the ticket clerk and me to keep a clean sheet.

For the first 20 minutes, it was men against boys. Inter Milan defended comfortably and passed the ball skilfully and quickly through the midfield. In attack, Shaqiri was a constant threat: short and stocky with a cultivated left foot – a faint echo of Ferenc Puskas, perhaps. By contrast, it seemed as if it were home side that had been overawed by the occasion with their misplaced passes and nervous positional play in defence. The crowd became anxious: collective groans were punctuated by individual verbal volleys of colourful disapproval.

Then Celtic scored twice within a minute.

Cue a further series of massive roars as Celtic took the initiative. For the rest of the half, they were in the ascendant, pressing the Inter goal. Then, perhaps inevitably, the pendulum swung again. A minute before half-time, a long, hopeful ball into the Celtic penalty area led to a mistake by the goalkeeper, Craig Gordon – yesterday's *Herald* referred to his "grotesque misjudgement" – and Palacio pounced for his second goal. The crowd's response was impressively supportive and, in its way, quite moving: "There's only one Craig Gordon" rang the chant.

The defences tightened up in the second half. Celtic had a couple of half-chances whilst, at the other end, Gordon made important diving saves from powerful shots by the excellent Shaqiri. But there had to be a climax, of course. In the third of the four minutes added on for stoppages at the end of the game, a volley by the Celtic substitute, John Guidetti, levelled the score at 3-3. By that time, some of the home support had decided to beat the rush leaving the stadium – an action I have always found somewhat bizarre – but that did not prevent the decibel level taking off again.

There was even time for one final twist. Inter were awarded a free kick in front of the Celtic goal just outside the penalty area. The defensive wall was formed; the referee marked its place with his can of foam; Shaqiri stood to the right of the ball and just behind it; the crowd combined holding its breath with baying for the final whistle; Shaqiri placed his curling shot into the precise angle between the upright and the crossbar. And Gordon dived across at full length to palm the ball to safety.

After the end of the game, I remained in my place for a few minutes to watch the stadium empty. I reflected that it was not often that the home side would draw the first leg of a European cup tie and be the ones doing the lap of honour. But the Celtic players had deserved the accolade. They had recovered from their dreadful start – and possible humiliation – to give themselves a chance in the second leg. They had paid their respects to their famous predecessors – the Lisbon Lions of 1967 – who had won by the European Cup by beating Inter Milan in the final. Most important – as I sensed from several snatches of conversation I heard before and during the game – they had not let the club down on this big occasion.

And I had seen the famous Inter Milan. Wikipedia informs me that the name of the club derives from the wish of its founding members (in 1908) to accept foreign players as well as Italians. In the global domain that is modern elite football, those members would have looked favourably on Thursday's line-up: there were just two Italians in the starting XI, which had representation from 6 other countries. (For reference, the corresponding numbers for Celtic were 5 Scots and 6 other nationalities).

It must be acknowledged that Inter Milan have fallen from the higher reaches of Italian (and therefore European) football in recent seasons: there have been 8 different managers since 2010, the side is only mid-table in this year's *Serie A* and the club is now owned by an Indonesian consortium. Alas, also, on this occasion, the team was not wearing the thick black and blue stripes that are synonymous with its past successes. But it is still the club with 3 European Cup/Champions League triumphs and 3 UEFA Cup wins and 18 *Scudetto* successes. The club of Javier Zanetti and Giacinto Facchetti and Sandro Mazzola. The club coached by Helenio Herrera and Roy Hodgson and Jose Mourinho. I'm not sure, however, how many of Herrera's sides of the 1960s would have let slip leads of 2-0 and 3-2.[13]

www.anordinaryspectator/news-blog February 2015

Top: The Alamodome, San Antonio, Texas, 2015.

Middle: Craven Park, Barrow, 2016.

Bottom: St James's Park, Newcastle, 2016.

Top: The Olympiastadion in Berlin prior to a Bundesliga match between Hertha Berlin and Borussia Dortmund, 2014.

Bottom: The Big Fellas Stadium, Featherstone, 2016.

Top: The pavilion of Yorkshire County Cricket Club.
Bottom: Leeds Rhinos rugby league ground.

Top: Nineteenth century cannons from the Royal Arsenal Munitions factory in Woolwich outside the Emirates Stadium of Arsenal FC.
Bottom Left: Statue of Sir Bobby Robson, St James's Park, Newcastle.
Bottom Right: The Memorial Board at Headingley Cricket Ground.

Top: Hunslet vs Castleford, 1946: "players serving in HM Forces."

Middle: Hull KR vs Widnes, Challenge Cup semi-final, 1977: "good jobs and long-term security."

Bottom: Wakefield Trinity vs Hunslet, 1964: television rental (black and white) for 8s 6d weekly "complete with matching legs and UHF tuner for BBC2."

Top Left: Backpass. Issue 51, August & September 2016.
Top Right: Backspin. Issue 11, Winter 2015-16.
Bottom: Rugby League Journal. Issue 50, Spring 2015.

Top: Artistic Gymnastics, Commonwealth Games. The SSE Hydro, Glasgow, 2014.
Middle: Ice hockey. Braehead Arena, Glasgow, 2015.
Bottom: Golf. The Open Championship, Royal Troon, 2016.

Der Rückenfigur in the Stadion an der Alten Försterei, Berlin, 2014.

Rugby League

A Close Rivalry of Half a Century Ago

When I first started watching rugby league – as a young boy supporting my father's team, Hunslet, in the early 1960s – I quickly formed the view that the league's most glamorous teams were Wakefield Trinity and Wigan.

The latter supplied the captain of Great Britain – Eric Ashton – who had been one of 6 members of his club side in the successful 1962 Lions tour party to Australasia. For their part, Wakefield had provided 5 tourists, all of whom – Gerry Round, Neil Fox, Harold Poynton, Jack Wilkinson and Derek Turner – had featured in at least one test match against Australia and/or New Zealand. Moreover, Wakefield had come within one match – the 1962 Championship Final defeat to Huddersfield – of repeating the "All Four Cups" feat that only three clubs had previously achieved. (The first of these, in 1907-08, had been Hunslet, of course, with its formidable pack of forwards: the "Terrible Six").

Hunslet were to play Wigan on nine occasions during the 1960s – the last of which was the famous Challenge Cup final of 1965 – winning just twice. By contrast, the Parksiders met Wakefield on a much more frequent basis, not only because of their joint membership of the Yorkshire League, but also due to the quirks of the draws for the Yorkshire Cup and the Challenge Cup. In the first half of the decade, especially, the Hunslet/Wakefield confrontations were amongst the most memorable in each season and, half a century on, they remain the source of fond reminiscence.

The teams met 24 times during the 1960s, with Wakefield winning 17, Hunslet 6 and one match drawn. This overall outcome reflected the respective league standings: Wakefield – coached throughout by the ex-Hunslet and Bradford Northern star Ken Traill – finished higher in the table every season after 1958-59. However, the Hunslet victories occurred in some of the key games of the period.

The unpredictable nature of the fixture was shown in the first round of the Yorkshire Cup at Parkside in September 1962. Hunslet were in the newly established Second Division, having finished 25th (out of 30) in the league the previous season. Wakefield were the cup holders, following their (near) all-conquering campaign. The result: a 34-9 victory for the home side in which the second-row forward Keith Whitehead scored two of Hunslet's six tries and Billy Langton kicked eight goals. Two months later, Hunslet were themselves the holders of the Yorkshire Cup, having defeated three other First Division sides, including Hull KR in the final at Headingley.

During the following two seasons – 1963-64 and 1964-65 – Hunslet and Wakefield met on no fewer than eight occasions. The league encounters were supplemented by another opening round tie in the Yorkshire Cup at Parkside in September 1963 – when, in a reversal of the previous year's outcome, the cup-holders (Hunslet) were again defeated (by 9 points to 4) by their first challengers – and three matches in the Challenge Cup.

In February 1964, Hunslet and Wakefield played a titanic first round Challenge Cup tie at Parkside, watched by a crowd officially recorded at 19,987. The game was tight and tryless – two Billy Langton penalties matching two from Neil Fox – the *Yorkshire Evening Post* (*YEP*) describing it as "as tense a cup-tie as Parkside has known."

In the replay at Belle Vue four days later, watched by an even bigger crowd of 20,822 – taking the aggregate attendance to over 40,000 for the two games – tries by Geoff Gunney and the powerful Welsh winger, John Griffiths, helped to secure a 14-7 win for Hunslet. The latter's try was created by Geoff Shelton's "supreme centre artistry and one of the greatest passes I have ever seen by a player as he went down to a two-man tackle," according to Leslie Temlett in the *YEP*. Fifty-plus years on, what a wonderfully evocative description this is of the skill of the classy centre three-quarter.

The next Parkside clash between the sides – a 16-2 league victory by Trinity in February 1965 – was memorable for entirely different reasons. In my memoir of sports spectating, published a couple of years ago, I recalled a particular incident from this game concerning arguably Hunslet's greatest-ever player.

> *I watched the match from my usual vantage point behind the fence at the front of the stand. A few yards away from me, and to my left, Geoff Gunney was tackled by a Wakefield player. Something must have happened in the tackle because, obviously severely provoked, Gunney stood up and, instead of playing the ball, flattened his opponent with one of the best punches that the ground could ever have seen.*

At this point, the detail gets slightly hazy. My recollection is that it was a classic right hook; however, the following Monday's Yorkshire Post stated that Gunney "felled Campbell, the Wakefield prop, with a straight left which Henry Cooper would have been proud to own."

The record shows that Gunney was duly dismissed by the referee – Mr DTH Davies, who, according to a nicely ironic line in the *Yorkshire Post* "…was probably as stunned as the crowd – not to mention Campbell…" – although this amounted to something of a technicality. He more or less condemned himself, walking straight in front of me towards the narrow exit from the pitch to the changing rooms and shaking his head ruefully to the referee as he did so.

(An aside. Last July, I paid a rare visit to Headingley for a Super League match: a pulsating encounter between the Leeds Rhinos and Castleford Tigers, which ended in a 24-24 draw. In the closing minutes, the Leeds captain, Kevin Sinfield – one of the most respected players in rugby league, with an unblemished disciplinary record after 17 years in the professional game – was sent off for an act of serious foul play. The crowd's initial reaction was one of utter amazement. As Sinfield left the field, I was struck by the powerful historical parallel with the events at Parkside all those years before).

And so to the Challenge Cup semi-final of 1965: a breezy April afternoon at Headingley, this time with over 21,000 in the ground. To reach that stage, Hunslet had won home ties against Oldham, Batley and Leeds, the last by 7 points to 5 in a tense quarter-final. Wakefield had beaten Dewsbury, Bradford Northern and Blackpool Borough.

Trinity were the favourites, having enjoyed a run of 17 games undefeated since December 1964 (when Hunslet had won by 20 points to 6 at Belle Vue) and standing fourth in the league. The formidable strike capability in their backs was exemplified by the contrasting skills of the wingers: the Welsh sprinter Berwyn Jones and the powerful South African Gert Coetzer.

But Hunslet would also have had some confidence, of course. By now, player-coach Fred Ward had moulded a formidable pack with international honours being won – either by that stage or later – by Dennis Hartley, Bernard Prior, Ken Eyre, Bill Ramsey and Geoff Gunney to complement the caps awarded to centre Geoff Shelton and stand-off Brian Gabbitas. Hunslet had had a good season in the league, solidly placed at 12th in the reconstituted single division at the time of the semi-final, but having been in fifth place at the turn of the year.

I attended the match with my father and two of my uncles, our seats (priced 12/6 each) on the 25-yard line in the left hand side of the Main Stand. It was another tense affair in which the close rivalry of the personal duals – Shelton/Fox, Gabbitas/Poynton, Ramsey/Haigh – was reflected in a match that remained scoreless with less than a quarter of an hour to go. The memoir picks up the story:

> *Hunslet had possession in the Wakefield 25. If my recollection is correct, they attempted a move in which Fred Ward received a pass, stood with his back to the opposition, and looked to offload to an oncoming player. However, the move did not work, and the ball was spilled to the ground, though it had not been knocked forward and was therefore still in play. Then, as the Wakefield defence momentarily hesitated, the ball was scooped up by Alan Preece, who promptly scuttled under the posts to score a try.*
>
> *It was a match-defining moment: if I close my eyes and think about that semi-final, the image that automatically comes to mind is that of Preece leaning forward and gathering the ball and thrusting himself over the line.*

I was to learn much later – when I had observed other similar incidents – that it is often when a pass inadvertently hits the ground that defences can be unlocked. The tackling line is thrown off guard or loses concentration, and the breach is made. Looking back to the Preece incident, it is highly likely that, had the move gone according to plan and Ward had found his intended recipient, the Wakefield defence would have dealt with this particular attacking threat.

> *I joined in the general celebration by the Hunslet supporters in the crowd. It was not the prettiest of tries. But it was a try. And it was under the posts, with a routine goal kick to come from the reliable Billy Langton. It wasn't until Wakefield had kicked off again, and the Headingley score board had resolutely remained at 3-0, rather than the 5-0 that we had casually anticipated, that we realised that Langton had somehow missed the conversion.*

But Hunslet were on a roll. John Griffiths scored a second try in the corner and, although Langton missed the difficult touchline conversion, he subsequently kicked a massive penalty goal from the half-way line. At this point, according to the match report in the sports edition of the *YEP*, "...the Hunslet war song was heard in something like its old style...with 'We've Swept The Seas Before Boys' ringing out." The final score was 8-0.

> *For my father, whose boyhood Hunslet team had won the Challenge Cup in 1934, when he was 13, there had been a wait of over 30 years before Wembley had been reached again. My perspective [at the age of 10] was different. My team had reached the Challenge Cup final. As with the Yorkshire Cup victory two seasons earlier, it seemed the most natural thing to have occurred.*

The pundits were quite clear about the basis of Hunslet's triumph. In the following Monday's *Guardian*, Harold Mather stated that "without doubt, all really was won and lost forward...[where] Wakefield were gradually worn down and outplayed." Hunslet had "played to a plan" which involved "getting on top in the forwards and then letting the ball out." On the face of it, this was a fairly basic approach – but it was also highly effective: in one period of play, Hunslet enjoyed 40 successive play-the-balls. Maintaining this theme, perhaps the ultimate accolade was provided in the headline of the Monday *YEP*'s review of the match: "'Terrible Six' would have been proud of Hunslet's pack."

Following the 1965 Challenge Cup semi-final, Hunslet defeated Wakefield on only one further occasion in the 1960s – by 10 points to 7 at Parkside in November 1969, when the 19-year old David Topliss played on the left wing for the visitors. Trinity won the other 9 encounters during the remainder of the decade, including yet another first round Challenge Cup match (by 28 points to 2) at Parkside in February 1967.

By then, Hunslet's star was in decline, of course – the match programme for the 1967 cup-tie listed only three of the Wembley side of two years earlier in the starting line-up – whilst Wakefield were going from strength to strength, winning the Championship in 1966-67 and 1967-68 and reaching Wembley for the "watersplash final" of 1968.

Most of these games remained tightly fought, however. Wakefield's margins of victory were only 6-0 and 8-3 in 1965-66 and 9-2 and 6-3 in 1967-68. In October 1966, it was even closer. I watched from the Belle Vue terraces – with some disbelief – as Trinity fought back to overhaul a highly improbable 0-17 half-time deficit and win 18-17 with a last minute drop goal by Don Fox from somewhere near the half-way line. I was devastated. Equally disappointed – it appeared – was the editor of the match programme for Hunslet's next home game later in the month, though he was suitably tactful in summing up the club's frustration: "...the injury time allowance seemed to most people to be very generous."

The Hunslet versus Wakefield Trinity fixtures of the early and mid 1960s. Can those matches really have been half a century ago? Can it have been 50 years since the dramatic interventions – still so clear in the mind – of Alan Preece and Geoff Gunney and Don Fox? It can indeed. In one of William Shakespeare's Sonnets, our greatest poet wrote that "nothing against Time's scythe can make defence." He was right, as ever.

The Rugby League Journal Spring 2015

Ice Hockey

The Clan and the Capitals

On Saturday I fulfilled a commitment that I made in the Spring of last year. The blog *"Television Lines"* (17th April 2014) on my favourite lines of television sports commentary generated a number of comments, two of which – from Denise Duvall and Anna Belfrage – referred to ice hockey commentaries. I promised in my response that, at some point during the current season, I would take in a match in Renfrew involving the Braehead Clan.

The Clan are having their best season in the Elite Ice Hockey League (EIHL) since the club's formation and entry into the league in the 2010-11 season. Prior to Saturday's fixture with the Edinburgh Capitals, they were second out of the 10 teams, one point behind the Sheffield Steelers and three points in front of the Cardiff Devils, though the latter had a game in hand. (The points awarded are two for a win and one for a drawn match that is subsequently lost in overtime or in a shoot out). It is a long and demanding season: before Saturday, the Clan had played 48 league games out of the scheduled 52.

The Edinburgh Capitals have been in the EIHL for longer than the Clan – since the 2005-06 season – but their highest finishing position has only been a couple of sixth places. This season is not going much better, as they were ninth prior to Saturday's match. However, there was still much to play for, as the Top 8 in the league go forward into a separate play-off competition which builds to a final in Nottingham next month.

My background research for the Clan-Capitals fixture – ie a Wikipedia consultation – suggested some differences between the two sides in addition to their respective league standings. The home squad began the 2014-15 season with 13 North Americans (9 from Canada and 4 from the USA) on its playing roster, supplemented by 3 Englishmen, 2 Welshmen and a Scot. By contrast, the Capitals have a tradition for "European-style" hockey, which is reflected in the presence on their roster of 5 Slovakians and a Swede in addition to 6 North Americans. The visitors' squad also has a far higher domestic component, with 8 Scots on the roster at the start of the season.

There were a few Capitals fans present on Saturday, but the overwhelming majority of supporters at the sold-out Braehead Arena were Clansmen (or women). Many – if not most – were bedecked in replicas of the home side's striking purple and black shirts. There is clearly a push to market the sport as family-friendly – the MC requested before the game that "when the temperature rises on the ice, please keep it cool in the stands" – and, in the west of Scotland in particular, it is not difficult to see its attraction to parents and children looking to identify with a local sports team whilst also avoiding the bitter tribal rivalries that dominate the region's soccer.

As with many sporting occasions, there was a significant element of ritual. The crowd would have been familiar with – indeed, demanded – much of the evening's script: the dramatic dimming of the arena's lighting prior to the entry of the teams on to the ice; the rhythmic drumming from the back of the stand to provide a driving beat to the rounds of coordinated spectator clapping; even the reassuring routine of the mechanical smoothing of the surface of the rink during the intervals between periods.

There was also, inevitably, the identification of the opposition team's villain: in this case, the Capital's goalminder, Tomas Hiadlovsky, who was singled out for opprobrium when one of the Clan was despatched to the penalty box for 10 minutes. At it happens, I thought that Hiadlovsky performed heroically throughout the match, notwithstanding the final score (1-5) against his team, plucking any number of powerful shots out of the air and, on one occasion, falling bravely at the feet of an onrushing striker.

The contest was presented with some efficiency: the electronic scoreboard was clear and informative; the four referees were swift in their decision-making and kept the game moving; and the players seemed to accept their (frequent) 2-minutes penalties without apparent dissent or delay. The aural signals to the spectators that a penalty had been incurred were (if I'm not mistaken) some notes from the *Star Wars* theme (for the Clans) and the opening chords of *Dragnet* (for the Capitals). The frequent stoppages in the play were also the cue for snatches of loud pop music – as if the spectators' senses had to be on permanent alert – though I sensed that the orchestrator of that had a nice sense of humour: hence, ELO's "I'm taking a dive" when the Capitals' goalminder was lying prostrate in his net and the theme from *Mission Impossible* when the visitors were 4 goals down with 3 minutes and 9 seconds left to play.

I have observed on previous occasions that the general health of a sports club is often revealed in the quality and coverage of its match day programme. *The Clansman* is impressive, the issue for this match also covering the Clan's other home fixtures in March against the Fife Flyers and Hull Stingrays. In addition to the usual columns by the coach and management, there was a useful summary of the ice hockey basics for newcomers such as me and some interesting articles on past players and matches. Perhaps most significantly, there was also evidence of plentiful sponsorship and advertising.

The Braehead Clan's commercial success was also evident during the play. The last goal (and the best of the evening) was scored by Matt Haywood (sponsored for home fixtures by Action Coach, according to *The Clansman*) after an assist – in effect, a skilful and weaving rush followed by an astute pass – by the impressively speedy Ben Davies (sponsored by Pizza Express). Even the penalty box was sponsored – by The Cathouse, Glasgow (though I am slightly nervous about searching on Google to find out more about this particular benefactor).

For the Clan and the Capitals, the weekend was not over. They met again yesterday evening at the Murrayfield Ice Rink – an echo, it struck me, of the back-to-back fixtures that are often scheduled in American baseball – with the outcome this time being a 2-1 win for the Capitals. As a result, with two fixtures left to play, the Sheffield Steelers (who lost to the Cardiff Devils at the weekend) still have a one point lead over the Clan in the league standings with the Devils now only one point further behind (with the game in hand). However, the Steelers' still have to play the Devils again. There might yet be a twist and turn before the 2014-15 winners of the Elite Ice Hockey League are known.[14]

www.anordinaryspectator/news-blog March 2015

Rugby Union

The Case for Sharing

Much has been made of the climax to this year's Six Nations Championship. The BBC's coverage on Saturday waxed lyrical about the huge number of points being racked up over the course of the afternoon (221 by the close of play) and provided continual updates of the "As it stands" table between and during the 3 matches, before reaching some sort of orgasmic conclusion as England sought (in vain) to score the final converted try that would have made them champions.

It was an afternoon of "What ifs?" What if Wales had taken a late try-scoring chance and then prevented Italy from scoring a converted last-minute try? (Wales would have been champions). What if Stuart Hogg had touched down correctly at the end of the Scotland-Ireland game and the try had been converted? (England would have been champions). What if England had been awarded a penalty try when France collapsed their last minute driving maul? (England would have been champions). What if Ireland had not missed 3 straightforward second half penalty kicks? (Ireland would have been champions more comfortably). In the end, the dice fell Ireland's way.

So, given all the tension and excitement, why do I feel uneasy about the drama that unfolded on Saturday afternoon?

Two reasons.

First, I have a conditioned response against the argument that the honours in sporting contests cannot be shared. It is another import into British professional sport – including both codes of rugby – from America, I suppose. Not only do we feel the need for the US-type branding of the names of long-established clubs (Sale Sharks, Leeds Rhinos *et al*) and the assimilation of the terminology of American sport – with its big hits and turnovers, not to mention the standard requirement for players of all descriptions "to step up to the plate" – but there is now an imperative for there to be a single winner. It is linked to the demands of television, of course: there must be a trophy to present and a winning coach to interview.

In the old days – clearly, this is another appearance of my "grumpy old man" persona – there was scope for the rugby union international championship to be shared. What mattered were simply the games won, lost and drawn: the points differentials did not come into it. In the most famous example – in 1973 – all the teams (five in those days) won their two home games (and, by definition, lost their two away fixtures) and, therefore, all shared the championship. It might be a sporting myth, but I do like the story that, at the beginning of the following season, when asked about his team's chances in the forthcoming campaign, an Irish coach is reputed to have commented: "Ah, to be sure, we won it last year."

Hence, for a supporter of the England team, the pre-match anticipation of an international against (say) France was based around a straightforward question: "Will England beat France?" For the French supporter, it would be the mirror image. And for the last three decades and more, that has been a fairly evenly-balanced query, given the ebbs and flows of each side's successes and failures.

That question was emphatically not what was being asked when the pre-match national anthems were being played at Twickenham. Instead, it was "Will England beat France by at least 26 points?" In my view, that the final game of the championship should boil down to this is wrong on several levels: it ignores the fact that an English margin of victory of this magnitude against France is almost unprecedented (it has occurred once in this fixture in the Five/Six Nations since the First World War); it is hugely disrespectful to the opposition; and, most importantly, it represents a fundamental shift away from the principal objective of playing a rugby international. To win the match: period.

My second objection is based on the practicalities of how the last round of Six Nations matches was organised.

At the start of the day, England, Ireland and Wales had accrued 6 points from their 3 wins and 1 loss from the 4 games played. The respective points differentials were 37, 33 and 12. Because Wales played first, they were effectively in the position of setting Ireland and/or England minimum targets for their subsequent matches against Scotland and France. In the event, the brilliant second half performance by Wales led to a 41 point margin of victory over Italy and set Ireland the target of a minimum 21 point winning margin. Ireland then played exceptionally well themselves against a disappointing Scottish side and won by 40 points to 10. England's target in the third and final game was thus to win by at least 26 points, as noted. The final score in that game was 55-35 and so England fell 6 points short.

Of course, the knowledge that one needs not only to win a game but to build up a considerable margin of victory brings its own pressures. In this respect, the Irish performance was indeed impressive. After racing into an early lead, they dominated for most of the match and their final winning margin of 30 points equalled the largest that they had ever had at Murrayfield.

A key point here, however, is that, by knowing exactly what they needed to do to overtake Wales, Ireland had a considerable advantage. They could manage their game accordingly and they did this very effectively. England's advantage was even greater. When they took the field against France, they not only knew that a 26 point margin would be sufficient, but also that it didn't matter if they didn't go beyond that. (That benefit was not available to Ireland, of course, as they obviously didn't know what score England would subsequently rack up).

The staggered schedule of matches on the last day of the Six Nations Championship means that it is not a level playing field. If the title has to be decided on points difference – and I appreciate that this is always now likely to be the case – then it would be much fairer if the final round of games kicked off at the same time, as they do in the group stages of the soccer World Cup Finals or on the last day of the Barclays Premier League. (I also recognise that the television companies would not find this at all attractive).

That would be my second-best solution, however. In this year's championship, three sides (Ireland, England and Wales) were clearly better than the other three (France, Italy and Scotland), each winning 4 games out of 5 and finishing with 8 points. In the head-to-head confrontations, England beat Wales, Ireland beat England and Wales beat Ireland.

The 2015 Six Nations Championship should have been shared.

www.anordinaryspectator/news-blog March 2015

Cricket

Yorkshire CCC: Branding, Franchising and the Diaspora

The family history research is going well. I have discovered that my paternal grandfather had two older cousins – like him, born in Baldersby, North Yorkshire – who emigrated to the USA in the 1890s, when they were in their 20s. From their families, the number of direct descendants born after 1960 and living in various parts of America, notably Vermont, runs into three figures.

Partly prompted by this, I have returned to a question that has been nagging at the back of my mind for some time. Recent events have increased its relevance, I think.

First, a couple of other (semi-)related facts. One, according to its Department of Alumni Relations office, the University of Cambridge has more than 400 officially recognised Alumni Groups in over 100 countries around the world. Two, I am informed by the Supporter Liaison Officer of Glasgow Celtic FC that the countries in which the club has official Supporters Clubs include the USA, Canada, Australia, Germany, Italy, South Africa, Sweden, Norway, Switzerland, Spain and Sierra Leone "to name just a few."

My question is: *"Would it make sense for the Yorkshire CCC to attempt exploiting the emotional and/or family ties to the county that huge numbers of people around the world might have?"*

Before exploring this theme, let me set out what I am not suggesting. I am not suggesting that the Club attempts to promote itself as a "brand" in order to sell replica shirts – with Andrew Gale's name on the back (!) – to teenagers in Singapore and Sydney. My model is not Manchester United and Wayne Rooney.

What I am suggesting is that, around the world, there will be very many people who retain, however tenuously, an identification with the county of Yorkshire, whether through birth or temporary residence or family history. The vast majority of those will be at least aware – if nothing more – of the significant role that the game of cricket has played in the county over the last 150 years. And some will have a clear understanding of the history of Yorkshire CCC and the way that, over those years, its players have exemplified those characteristics – grit, guts and determination, as my late father used to say – with which Yorkshiremen (and women) are identified, including by themselves.

The two examples given above are not strict comparators, of course. Many of Cambridge University's overseas alumni are foreign students returning to their countries of origin – but not all are. For their part, the external linkages of Glasgow Celtic are tied up with complex issues of nationality and religion. But the underlying thesis holds. Both are clear examples of how – in a world of global connections and the search for one's roots – the emotional attachment to a distant land or institution can be very powerful.

I mentioned that recent events have caused me to reflect on this rather more sharply. I refer, of course, to the debacle of England's woeful performance in the 2015 Cricket World Cup.

The standard call has gone out: "Something must be done." And one of the things that many people are advocating should be done is to reorganise – indeed, revolutionise – the way that one-day cricket is arranged and played in this country. The call for a streamlined franchise system for Twenty-20 cricket in England is being made by a number of voices – some more articulate than others – all of whom seem to be advocating a reduction in the number of teams from the 18 we have now (the first class counties) to somewhere between 8 and 12.

It is interesting that there were no such clamours when England won the World Twenty-20 competition in the West Indies in 2010. But it is also clear that, not only has the most abbreviated form of the game moved on since then, this has had a dramatic effect on the approach being taken to the 50-over version of the sport. The exhilarating batting that we saw in the World Cup from Brendon McCullum and AB de Villiers made the devastation brought about by the previous generation's revolutionary – Sanath Jayasuriya of Sri Lanka in the 1996 World Cup – look almost benign by comparison. And, because McCullum and de Villiers (and Starc and Faulkner amongst the bowlers) have honed their skills in the Indian Premier League and/or Australia's Big Bash competitions, so – the argument goes – that is the model that we must now follow.

I do not offer any views here on whether such a change is needed in England or whether it would be successful. What does interest me is the impact that any change along these lines would have on the status of Yorkshire CCC (and, by extension, the other first class counties). Let me emphasise immediately that this is not because of any reactionary desire of my part to preserve the existing county system in all its faded glory. Rather – and here I will use the word – it is because I think there is a strong probability that at least some of the existing "brands" would become redundant.

We obviously wait to see what form the brave new world of a franchise system for Twenty-20 cricket in England would take, assuming that it does go ahead. What will the teams be called? How many will there be? Who will own them? Who will bear the risks and – if successful – take the profits? How will the counties' revenue streams from the England and Wales Cricket Board be affected? What will be the effects on domestic first-class cricket and test match cricket? And, more parochially, what will be the implications for the name and status of Yorkshire CCC? (It will not have gone unnoticed that, for Twenty-20 purposes, Warwickshire CCC have been the Birmingham Bears for the last couple of seasons).

It is against this background of huge uncertainty about the nature of cricket in England, as played within the county structure, that I think there is an urgent need for a serious assessment of the threats and challenges to the Club in the years ahead with a view to taking anticipatory action. If part of that response involves the Club attempting to reach out to a far bigger target membership (broadly defined) than it currently does, an engagement – emotional, technological, financial – with the Yorkshire diaspora is one (possible) example of how this might be done.

Of course, it would not be easy. There is no database of expatriate Yorkshiremen waiting to constitute a ready-to-use mailing list. This is reflective of national priorities. *The Economist* has reported ("And don't come back," 9th August 2014) that, although 110 of the 193 UN member states have formal programmes to build links with citizens living abroad, Britain is not one of them, even though 5 million Britons are currently living overseas; the Foreign and Commonwealth's database of Britons abroad is described by the newspaper as "patchy."

I recognise that attempting to tap into the Yorkshire diaspora might be seen as a ludicrous idea, requiring far too much imagination and effort for an uncertain reward. Rather like – say – starting the Tour de France in Leeds? In this respect, the expertise of Gary Verity – chief executive of Welcome to Yorkshire and a Board Member of the Club – would be highly significant, albeit that the agency does not focus on family roots and genealogy as a source of tourist expenditure to the same extent as its counterparts in Ireland and Scotland.

It is also clear that any such exercise would necessitate something of a cultural shift within a Club that, for a long period, seems not to have been fully engaged in seeking to cultivate its membership – from within the county, let alone overseas. For many years, the size of the membership – a few thousand from a total population within the county borders of over 5 million – has seemed rather meagre. In the Club's latest accounts, it is shown that less than 8 per cent of income comes from members' subscriptions – it was 44 per cent in 1975 – as other sources of revenue (international ticketing and hospitality, commercial income) have become dominant.

No doubt, most of this relative decline has been attributable to the changes in the overall nature of cricket's finances in England, which have been outside Yorkshire CCC's control. But some of the causes have lain within, as the Club has taken its eye off the membership ball. Even over the last year or so, my own experience of the customer service (when trying to find out exactly what a Club Yorkshire Membership would entitle me to) – unanswered letters and ignored e-mails – has been very revealing.

Two years ago, in an earlier contribution to this occasional series of blogs – "*The Future of Test Match Cricket*" (5th January 2013) – I suggested that the main factor that would prevent Joe Root from becoming the highest test match run scorer for England would be the likely reduction in the number of tests that England played, as that form of the game atrophied or died completely outside England, Australia and South Africa. I speculated that:

> *In 15 years time, instead of chasing whatever test match batting records Alastair Cook leaves behind, the veteran Joe Root would be ending his career playing for the Sheffield Steelers against the Leeds Loiners in the regional play-off of the Global 20-over Big Slog.*

This might seem like an unwarranted concern, given that England are scheduled to play no fewer than 17 test matches over the next 12 months. However, as previously set out, I do have fears – for a variety of reasons – for the medium/long-term future of test match cricket in Pakistan, West Indies, New Zealand and even India.

I would only change a couple of details in the prediction. First, the Sheffield side would have to be called something else because – as noted in another recent blog, "*The Clan and the Capitals*" (16th March 2015) – the Sheffield Steelers are, of course, the city's (very successful) Elite Ice Hockey League club.

Second, I wonder whether, if anything, 15 years might be too far into the future. In any event, another question arises:

If the veteran Joe Root is playing his domestic one-day cricket for the Sheffield Cutlers – a city-based, privately-owned franchise – and the programme of first-class cricket in England has been further reduced, what exactly will be the role and the purpose of Yorkshire CCC?

www.anordinaryspectator/news-blog April 2015

Hockey

I'll Go to the End of Our Street

There are a number of examples of sports events over the years at which my attendance has been based on a straightforward principle: the event was in the general vicinity of where I was living and there was no excuse not to go. I would include in this list the Ryder Cup at Walton Heath in 1981, the Open Championship at Troon in 1997 and the Commonwealth Games swimming and gymnastics in Glasgow in 2014, amongst others.

On Saturday, this maxim was followed to the extreme. At the end of our street – literally – and on the other side of the Auchenhowie Road is situated the Milngavie and Bearsden Sports Club. Along with tennis, archery and shinty, this plays host to the Western Wildcats Hockey Club, which at the weekend had two teams – the Men 1's and Ladies 1's – competing (separately) for places in next year's European Hockey League.

The two teams had both earned the right to challenge for a European spot by finishing in the top four of their respective leagues: the men in third position and the women in fourth. Their respective opponents in the two-legged semi-final play-offs were Grange Mens 1's (the winners of the Scottish Cup the previous week) and Edinburgh University Ladies 1's, who had finished in second and first places, respectively.

At this point, I should perhaps acknowledge that I have form as a chronicler of (field) hockey. In 1976, I was (rather briefly) the hockey correspondent of the main Cambridge University student newspaper – *Stop Press* – and, for my first assignment, was duly requested by the editor to report on a university fixture at Fenner's. Unfortunately, that week's edition of the paper was not published due to some sort of technical problem and so my carefully prepared piece did not see the light of day. By the following week, the editor's interest had moved on – as probably had mine – and so my forlorn attempt to follow in the footsteps of Bob Woodward and Carl Bernstein was strangled at birth.

The Western HC dates from the closing years of the nineteenth century, the club's initial home ground being in Yoker. It has been based at Auchenhowie since 1969 when, according to its website, it was "integrated" with the Milngavie and Bearsden Cricket and Tennis Club. The management of competing sectional interests under such circumstances can be tricky, of course, and so it proved in this case. The cricket section folded 20 years ago.

My neighbour on the touchline for the men's match was a Grange member and supporter. We had a metal fence at our back and so were only about three yards from the side of the pitch. His warning to avoid a misplaced strike of the ball was well-taken: "It would break your shin." My reciprocal alert to him concerned the sporting activity taking place in the field behind us. "I hope those archers know what they are doing," I said.

The men's match was an even contest. Grange took a 1-0 lead into the half-time break, but Western responded with some determination in the second half and were rewarded with a deserved equaliser. The Grange winner was scored with the last shot of the game. I was impressed with the fitness of the participants and the speed of the game; the free hits were taken quickly after each infringement and the continual rotation of players ensured a regular supply of fresh legs.

On the face of it, the Western Wildcats Ladies had the more difficult task. Their opponents, Edinburgh University, had finished top of the league by a convincing margin, having won all of their 18 matches. Moreover, of their squad of 16 players listed in the match programme, 6 were senior internationalists and the other 10 were internationalists at either Under 21 or Under 18 level. "Are they all students?," I naively asked the friendly Western member who had introduced himself as a veteran of the club's move to Auchenhowie in the late 1960s. No, was the answer: it is an open club.

Edinburgh University's status as favourites was fully justified. They emerged as 5-0 winners, the last three goals coming in the closing minutes as the hosts tired in the late afternoon sun. Western did not give up, however, and, having reached their highest-ever league position, can view their season as one of definite progress.

From what my touchline companions were saying – and by casual inspection – it was clear that all the sides on view had a combination of experienced hands and young talent, the latter including several teenagers. This was confirmed in the match programme, which highlighted two Western midfield players: the 18 year-old Joe McConnell and the 17 year-old Ellie Hutcheson. I thought – even with my untrained eye – that both had impressive matches, being neatly skilful and not at all fazed by some of the experienced internationalists around them.

At the conclusion of the matches on Saturday, the two ties were at the half way stage. The second legs were played yesterday, the short turn-round period representing clear challenges to the players' powers of recovery and/or the strength-in-depth of the respective squads. The two Western sides were again defeated – the Men by 2-5 and the Ladies by 0-2 – to put their European aspirations on hold for another year.

It was an interesting afternoon in the sunshine at Auchenhowie. And, when it was over, I didn't have far to go home for my tea.

www.anordinaryspectator/news-blog April 2015

Football

3rd Versus 17th

On Saturday, the cup final was played between the club that had ended the season in 3rd position in the league table and the one that had finished 14 places below them. The former were the pre-match favourites and, having dominated the first half, they took the lead in the 40th minute. At half-time, most pundits probably expected that they would go on to win comfortably against opponents who hadn't lifted the trophy since 1957. And so it proved at Wembley: Arsenal defeated Aston Villa 4-0 to win the FA Cup for a record 12th time.

Earlier in the afternoon, I was at Hampden Park for the Scottish Cup Final. Inverness Caledonian Thistle, third in the Scottish Premiership, played Falkirk, who had finished 14 places (and one division) below them in the end-of-season Scottish club hierarchy. Falkirk had not won the cup since 1957. After an evenly balanced first quarter of an hour, Inverness gained some ascendancy and took a deserved lead in the 38th minute when Marley Watkins finished off a crisp attacking move. At half-time, the neutral pundits (my friend George Farrow and I) seated amongst the Inverness supporters in the South Lower Stand had little doubt that the Premiership side would extend its lead as the game progressed.

It did not turn out that way. Falkirk took the game to their opponents on the resumption of play and retained the initiative for all but a fatal few moments in the second half. After the break Inverness did not seem able to get out of second gear, their play hesitant and inaccurate and, I thought, not dissimilar to the way that they had approached the second half in an earlier round at Firhill against Partick Thistle (see *"The Chances of Success,"* 10th February 2015), though on that occasion they had had a two-goal cushion to protect. Indeed, it was relatively early in the half that my neighbour in the next seat – a young woman from Inverness – sensed that all was not well: "I can't stand this," she told her partner, who cast a less-than-reassuring glance back in response.

Falkirk's attacking threat was enhanced with the introduction of the substitute Botti Biabi, whose close control and neat skills produced a couple of dangerous passes across Inverness's 6-yard box. "I can't stand this, I'm going home," said my neighbour, remaining rigidly attached to her seat.

The drama of the occasion was exemplified in the 76th minute. On a rare foray in attack, Inverness won a free kick outside the Falkirk penalty area. A few seconds later – literally – after the shot had cannoned into the wall and the ball had been hooked upfield by a Falkirk defender, the Inverness full-back Carl Tremarco gifted possession to Blair Alston and then committed a red card offence by fouling his opponent as he sped towards goal.

Falkirk sensed their great opportunity to fill the void that had lasted for nearly 60 years. The tricky footwork of Biabi earned another free kick from which the impressive Peter Grant headed in an emphatic equaliser. It was 1-1 with ten minutes to go and the momentum (and head count) decisively favouring Falkirk.

There was a final twist in the tail, of course. A long solo run by Watkins ended with a fairly tame shot that the Falkirk goalkeeper, Jamie MacDonald, could only divert in the direction of James Vincent, who side-footed the ball into the net. Vincent had only entered the fray as a substitute a few minutes earlier, but his effort to give some support to Watkins – by sprinting fully 90 yards from inside his own penalty area – deserved some reward and he duly got it: the winning goal in a Scottish Cup Final.

My neighbour just about held out during the 3 minutes (and 5 minutes of added time) that remained after Vincent's strike. "I can't stand this," she said for the 48th time, before lightening up a little. "Who scored the goal?" she asked me.

It was an enjoyable afternoon. The weather was bright and dry with a strong breeze enabling the FIFA flag to fly shamelessly on the top of the stand. The crowd was sizeable – over 37,000 – for two sides whose regular attendances add up to barely one-fifth of that and the atmosphere was friendly. And, naturally, there was passion and partisanship. George and I both recognised that, whilst the famous "Hampden Roar" of yesteryear might be a thing of the past, there was an impressive wall of noise continually emanating from the Falkirk support at the far end of the ground.

And so the end-of-season honours are decided. Congratulations to Inverness Caledonian Thistle. And to Arsenal. And – on George's behalf

– to Southend United; following success in the penalty shoot-out that resolved the play-off final with Wycombe Wanderers last week, League 1 football will be played at Roots Hall in 2015-16.

www.anordinaryspectator/news-blog June 2015

Rugby League

An Afternoon in Whitehaven

Two years ago, almost to the day – in *"Scores and values"* (3rd June 2013) – I mentioned that, due to the recuperation programme that I was then undertaking following some surgery, I had been frustrated in my plans to travel down to Whitehaven to watch a rugby league game against the Hunslet Hawks. In that blog, before focusing on its main theme – my response to a particularly distasteful comment by Mr J Clarkson in his *Sunday Times* column about Angelina Jolie's recent double mastectomy – I noted that my trip to the Recreation Ground would have to wait for another day.

I am pleased to report that that day arrived on Sunday.

The fixture has a particular resonance for me. The first live sporting event I was taken to see was the Hunslet vs Whitehaven game at Parkside in August 1961. In the reverse encounter in that season's fixture list – played the following March – Whitehaven defeated Hunslet by 61 points to nil, a gargantuan score in those days.

I was met before Sunday's match by Harry Edgar and Stephen Bowes. Harry is the editor of the quarterly *Rugby League Journal*, an excellent publication which passed its half-century mark earlier this year. He had been present at the 61-0 game as a (very) young supporter of his home-town team: "I was at that game and, like all the other spectators present, could not believe what I was seeing."

Harry's allegiance to rugby league in Whitehaven and Cumberland/Cumbria – and to the sport more generally, notably in France – has spanned over 50 years. This means that the *Journal* provides not only a wealth of nostalgic reminiscence – "for fans who don't want to forget" – but also an informed critique of the current state of rugby league and its governance.

The Whitehaven club – together with their neighbours Workington

Town – are currently placed in the lower half of the Championship, the second tier of professional rugby league. If their positions do not change by the end of July, they will effectively become part of the third tier as, at that time, the top 4 in the division will form a mini-league with the bottom 4 from the Super League to decide next season's Super League participants. The remaining 8 teams in the Championship will continue with their own mini-league (and with the running points totals being carried forward) and seek to avoid being in the bottom two places at the end of the season, as this would bring relegation to League 1.

Further down the Cumbrian coast, the Barrow Raiders are already in League 1. Below that, in the top two divisions of amateur rugby league, are to be found three clubs located in the Whitehaven vicinity: Egremont Rangers, Wath Brow Hornets and Kells. All this would seem to suggest the maintenance of the sport's traditional strength within the region, albeit without a presence in the top flight.

Unfortunately, there are signs of fragility. Both Whitehaven and Workington Town are already caught up (with the Hunslet Hawks and a couple of other sides) in the desperate bid to avoid relegation. Home attendances are often measured in the hundreds: there were 900 present at the Recreation Ground on Sunday according to newspaper reports. As for the amateur game, as Harry Edgar has persuasively written, there are obvious challenges to be faced in attempting to maintain existing levels of player and/or coaching participation, given this year's shift to a summer season and the competition from family holidays and other sporting activities. Moreover, the links between the Whitehaven club and the local amateur teams, once very strong, are now much weaker.

What might be done? During the preparations for the Super League in the mid 1990s, the rugby league authorities proposed that Whitehaven should merge with Workington Town and Barrow (and Carlisle) to form a single Cumbria club. This suggestion was rejected by the clubs and supporters, as was also the case with other proposed mergers, including those between Castleford/Featherstone Rovers/Wakefield Trinity, Warrington/Widnes and Hull FC/Hull KR. The combined forces of the clubs' individual histories and strong local identification enabled the traditionalists to win the day.

Of course, we do not know what would have happened if the Cumbrian Super League entity had been created. Would the club now be competing on equal terms with Wigan and Leeds? Or – to adapt a phrase that has appeared before in this occasional series of blogs – would the merger of two (or more) medium-sized clubs have simply led to the creation of a medium-sized club?

The evidence from elsewhere is mixed. Twenty-plus years on, the merger of the two rugby union clubs which provided the core of my youthful spectating experience in that sport – Headingley and Roundhay – has not produced the Yorkshire-based powerhouse that had been hoped to challenge the game's elite. Moreover, such amalgamations are usually fraught with rivalry and mistrust, as when the Caledonian and Inverness Thistle football clubs combined to form a new club prior to its entry into the Scottish Football League in 1994. On the other hand, Inverness Caledonian Thistle have just finished in third place in the Scottish Premiership and gained a place in next season's Europa League competition. A week ago – as described in my previous blog, "*3rd vs 17th* (1st June 2015) – they won the Scottish Cup.

On Sunday, Harry gave me a copy of *Chocolate, Blue and Gold*, the official publication that he wrote (with a significant input from Stephen) to mark the 50th anniversary of Whitehaven RLFC in 1998. It is a detailed and fascinating read with poignant accounts of the halcyon days of the 1950s, notably the 1956-57 season, when Whitehaven defeated the touring Australians and were within a couple of minutes of reaching the Challenge Cup final at Wembley. The 61-0 game is also covered, of course – "spectators looked on with wide-eyed amazement" – as is Hunslet's visit during Whitehaven's 1957 cup run, when the home side won 7-0. At half-time in that match, two of Hunslet's forwards collapsed with hypothermia. It can probably be said that, during this period, the Recreation Ground was not one of the south Leeds club's favourite destinations.

Whitehaven prevailed again on Sunday in – pardon the cliché – a game of two halves. After a scoreless first 20 minutes, Hunslet gained control through the prompting of half-backs Andy Kain and Danny Ansell and took a 12-0 lead into half-time. However, after the break, with a strong breeze at their backs and urged on from the terraces by a buoyant support that sensed it was going to be their day, Whitehaven scored 28 unanswered points. The second row forward Dave Allen led the way with some strong runs and the opening try. Whitehaven's second try – an 80 yard breakaway when a Hunslet attack broke down near the home side's line – was the critical turning point, I thought. "Dish it to 'em, Haven," cried a voice behind us in the main stand: a satisfied customer at the end of the match, I would guess.

After the match, Harry, Stephen and I adjourned to the neat lounge of a bar overlooking the Whitehaven marina. They explained how the locale had been dramatically transformed; it had once been black with dust from the transportation of coal to Ireland and elsewhere. We talked about Scottish football and rugby union in the south of France and the current state of the rugby league game and politics in Scotland. Later, as I started my bus journey back to Carlisle to catch the train to Glasgow, the bright evening sunlight reflected on the waters of the Solway Firth against the backdrop of the hazy hills of Galloway. I had spent a good afternoon in Whitehaven in some very good company.

www.anordinaryspectator/news-blog June 2015

Cricket

The Unorthodox and the Traditional

I recall a John Player Sunday League cricket match between Yorkshire and Sussex at Huddersfield in June 1969. Rain delayed the start and so the game was reduced to 19 overs per side. Yorkshire batted first and made 89 for 7. I thought at the end of the innings that this total would be sufficient and so it proved: Yorkshire won by 7 runs.

Last Friday, I watched the Yorkshire Vikings play the Nottinghamshire Outlaws in a Twenty-20 match at Headingley. In their 20 overs, Yorkshire made 209 for 4. It is a different game now.

There is much discussion these days about how one-day cricket – in both its 50-over and 20-over formats – favours the batsmen. Fielding restrictions, improvements in bat design, shorter boundaries, immaculate pitches, closely mown outfields…there is no shortage of explanations for why the "par" scores seem to be rising. In the recently concluded 5-match 50-over series against New Zealand, England averaged more than 7 runs per over and scored no fewer than 264 runs in six hits alone.

In a recent television interview, the former England captain, Michael Atherton – a knowledgeable analyst of the modern game – remarked on another factor. He pointed out that, over the last few years, the skill levels of batsmen have been rising, whereas those of bowlers have not. Of course, in saying this, he is not downplaying the skills of the batting greats of yesteryear – Bradman, Hutton, Lara *et al*. Rather, he is suggesting that, prompted by the requirements of the shorter forms of the game, batsmen have responded much more imaginatively in widening their repertoire of shots and their scoring options.

One of the best examples is Glenn Maxwell, a member of Australia's 2015 World Cup winning side. He is playing for Yorkshire this season and on Friday he scored 92 not out from 48 balls. Not everything he attempted came off – and a reverse-sweep or a "Dilshan"-scoop shot can look fairly ungainly when it is not successful – but, by the end of the innings, I doubt that the Nottinghamshire bowlers really knew where to deliver the ball. Maxwell's combination of power, placement and unorthodoxy utterly defeated them.

In the following morning's *Yorkshire Post*, the cricket correspondent Chris Waters reported: "Maxwell's innings...pretty much defied categorisation... [He] was busy not so much rewriting the MCC coaching manual as setting fire to it and dancing on the embers." I can see his point, though I might also add that Maxwell's success is also based on a mastery of the fundamental batting skills: a early six off Samit Patel over the long boundary at extra cover was a shot of exquisite beauty.

Maxwell was supported by the Yorkshire wicketkeeper, Andrew Hodd, who made an excellent 70, again with a mixture of "proper" cricket shots and the type of unorthodox strokes that have now become the norm in one-day cricket. Nottinghamshire lost three quick wickets in reply and did not look like reaching their target, apart from during the partnership between their accomplished captain James Taylor, who was looking dangerous until caught in the deep for 32, and the impressive Patel, who hit a defiant and unbeaten 90. Yorkshire won by 40 runs.

For the Twenty-20 match, there were 8½ thousand spectators present at a cloudy, chilly Headingley. (The match started at 7pm). There were lots of youngsters and families, I was pleased to see, along with the Friday evening office crowd and the rowdy beer-drinkers on the Western Terrace. The presentation of the event was lively and populist with its snatches of pop music, "Dance-Cam" and "Kiss-Cam" close-ups of spectators and a post-match fireworks display. Those following the cricket would have been impressed by the informative MC and the highly efficient scoreboard. And by Glenn Maxwell.

[Postscript: Two days later, the Yorkshire Vikings were beaten by 6 wickets at Edgbaston by the Birmingham Bears. Glenn Maxwell was out second ball].

On Monday, I went to see Yorkshire play Nottinghamshire at Headingley again: this time on the first of the 4 days scheduled for a LV County Championship fixture. The visitors made 169 for 8 in the 47 overs that were possible on a rain-affected day.

It was traditional stuff – with not a fielding circle or a reverse sweep to be seen – and I enjoyed every minute of it. Yorkshire rotated their four fast medium bowlers throughout the day and each was rewarded with two wickets though, in general, I thought they bowled too wide to exploit fully the helpful pitch and cloud cover. Four of the Nottinghamshire wickets fell lbw and I was reminded of that sharp stab of expectation when, before the umpire's decision is made, one senses that the appeal is valid and he is likely to raise his finger.

When the heavy rain set in just after 2.30, I was sitting in front of an elderly gentleman in a corner of the lower tier of the Football Stand. He had been meticulously scoring the match on a huge sheet in his Slazenger scoring book. I was reminded of my own days of scoring, beginning with Geoff Boycott and Phil Sharpe making hundreds for Yorkshire against Pakistan at Headingley in 1967. The man said that scoring books were hard to find these days – my first one had been a *Compactum* purchased from Herbert Sutcliffe's sports shop in Leeds – and that he had had to write off to Slazenger directly in order to obtain the ones he needed.

This suggests that the man took his hobby seriously. I think "very seriously" might be a more appropriate description. He told me that he was a member of the Lancashire, Yorkshire and Nottinghamshire clubs, as well as the MCC, before reeling off the games that he had attended over the last couple of weeks (which, incidentally, had included the Twenty-20 fixture at Headingley on Friday). He said that the first game he had scored had been the famous Old Trafford test match of 1956, when Jim Laker had taken 19 Australian wickets.

The man – I regret not asking him his name – went on to tell me that the first cricket match he had attended was in 1948: Lancashire versus Don Bradman's Australian tourists. A lady behind me to my left chipped in: "1948. I would have been ten. I wasn't interested in cricket then."

I asked if Bradman had played in the match and the man said that he had and that Malcolm Hilton had got him out. (I checked later and he was absolutely correct: the 19 year-old Hilton dismissed Bradman in both innings). Touchingly, he then gave me another detail of that particular occasion. He said that it had been his uncle who had taken him to the game, as his father had been killed in the war.

Perhaps this is part of what still occasionally draws me to county cricket. The honesty and intimacy imparted in the conversations with strangers.

www.anordinaryspectator/news-blog June 2015

Rugby League

The Battle for Fourth Place

Following my trip to Cumbria a couple of weeks ago ("*An Afternoon in Whitehaven,*" 9th June 2015), a long weekend in Yorkshire gave me the chance to attend another rugby league match at a ground that I had not previously visited.

It was a game of some significance, too, in this year's Kingstone Press Championship. Prior to this latest round of fixtures, most sides had only half a dozen fixtures remaining before the 12-team league splits into a top 4 and a bottom 8. The former group will form a mini-league with the bottom 4 from the Super League to decide next season's Super League participants. Two of those places will definitely go to the Leigh Centurions and Bradford Bulls, with the Sheffield Eagles almost certainly taking the third spot. That leaves 4 teams – Featherstone Rovers, Halifax, London Broncos and Dewsbury Rams – separated by only three points in the league table and battling for the final place, as there is then a gap to the other sides in the league. On Sunday, Dewsbury were at home to Halifax.

I never saw a game at the old Crown Flatt ground, which was the home of the current Dewsbury club from its formation in 1898 until 1991 and of its predecessor (the Dewsbury Athletic and Football Club) from 1876. The short move to the current home – also sometimes called Crown Flatt, though Sunday's stadium announcer preferred the Tetley's Stadium in acknowledgement of the club's main sponsors – took place in 1994. The former ground had been the club's home venue in 1929, when Dewsbury played in the first Challenge Cup final to be held at Wembley (losing to Wigan), and in 1973, when they won the Championship play-offs, having finished in 8th position in the regular season. Even earlier, prior to the establishment of the Northern Rugby Union in 1895, Dewsbury had been the first club of the teenage prodigy Dicky Lockwood, who later became the captain of England and the most famous rugby player of his day.

Before the match, I asked the elderly gateman where the old Crown Flatt ground had been; he gave me some detailed directions with a wistful smile.

Unfortunately for Dewsbury, they chose Sunday to incur their heaviest league defeat of the season. Halifax were much quicker out of the blocks and, by mid-way through the first half, had taken an 18-0 lead, the second try the result of an expertly performed training ground move in which a high kick to the corner was palmed back to a supporting player and the third try being allowed after what appeared to be a couple of forward passes. This was a due reward, however: Halifax moved purposefully on to the ball and were more inventive in attack. Nonetheless, Dewsbury did not give up and replied with two tries themselves to reduce the deficit to six points. Another Halifax try followed straightaway: the best of the afternoon, involving a skilful off-load by Luke Menzies, a sprint down the wing by Gareth Potts and an inside pass to the supporting Dane Manning. This took the visitors to a 24-12 half-time lead; by the end of the game, the margin of victory had been extended to 46-16.

The Tetley's Stadium has covered stands down the two touchlines – one of which has seating – but is open-ended behind both sets of posts. I should think that when the wind is blowing from the adjacent fields straight down the pitch, the conditions might be difficult to contend with. As it was, supported by only a stiffish breeze and a long series of bounces on the firm playing surface, one of the Dewsbury drop-outs from under their own posts travelled the full length of the pitch to go out of play behind the Halifax dead-ball line. I'm not sure if I have ever seen this before. It was akin to one of those freak goals by goalkeepers, when they hoof the ball down the pitch and it bounces over their out-of-position opposite number into the far net.

There was a good atmosphere in the North Stand, where the spectators are close to the action. The Dewsbury supporters kept behind their team even with the home side's mistakes and a growing deficit on the scoreboard. They felt that the referee could have been stricter with their opponents' offside and delaying tactics at the play-the-ball. But all such crowds feel that in every game they watch.

In this league, the referees and touch judges are sponsored by Specsavers: a brilliant piece of marketing, I think. At one point, the referee had to halt play for repairs to the communications link to his fellow officials. "You're battery operated, referee," suggested one wag. "Houston, we have a problem," offered another.

For this neutral observer, it looks as if Dewsbury will fall short of claiming a top 4 position to qualify for the end-of-season mini-league. To secure the remaining place, they would probably need to win all 5 of their remaining fixtures during this part of the season, including away trips to Featherstone Rovers and Leigh Centurions.

Whatever happens, they have done well to be in contention for so long into the season. As with so many other sports clubs on which I have reported in the last 12 months – Hunslet RLFC, St Mirren FC, Braehead Clan ice hockey *et al* – budgets are tight and imaginative ways of raising income are at a premium. Clearly, as elsewhere, close links with the local community are vital. In this regard, I noted that amongst the named sponsors of the individual players' are the Hanging Heaton Working Men's Club and the Mount Tabor Church. The local links couldn't get any closer than those.

www.anordinaryspectator/news-blog June 2015

Cricket

The Past and the Present in Roberts Park

In writing about my sports spectating, I am appropriately modest about my own playing exploits – mainly rugby and cricket – largely because there is much to be modest about. However, for three half-seasons in the 1970s – during my student holidays – I did graduate to play in the Bradford League for the Saltaire Cricket Club. 40 years ago today – on 28th June 1975 – I made my first appearance against Bankfoot CC at Saltaire's home ground of Roberts Park. It was not a particularly auspicious start: the fourth delivery of my wily off-spin disappeared into the trees at long on.

Saltaire CC was formed in 1869, 16 years after the opening of Sir Titus Salt's magnificent Saltaire Mills in his new model village. The club joined the Bradford League in 1905, two years after the league's formation. The village of Saltaire, including Roberts Park, became a UNESCO World Heritage Site in 2001; it is a fascinating place to visit.

When I joined the club, I was given a copy of its neat centenary booklet: *Saltaire Cricket Club 1869-1969*. On the brochure's cover is an action shot of the club's wicketkeeper and slip fielder, the latter a young man called Jeff Driver with whom I was later to open the batting on several occasions.

The historic environs within which the cricket club is located are matched by the rich history of the club itself. One of my predecessors as a promising bowler (a 16 year-old in 1938) was a certain Jim Laker who later – in the 1956 test match at Old Trafford – took 19 of the 20 Australian wickets to fall. During the Second World War, Saltaire's bowlers included the former England test players Bill Voce of Nottinghamshire (who had been a partner of Harold Larwood on the 1932-33 Bodyline Tour to Australia) and Tom Goddard of Gloucestershire, amongst several other county and international players.

In an earlier period, between 1915 and 1923, Saltaire's bowling attack was led by one SF Barnes. It is difficult to know where to start on Sydney Francis Barnes: perhaps by suggesting that there is a strong case to be made that he was the greatest bowler of all time. He took 189 wickets in 27 test matches for England between 1901 and 1914 – including 17 in one match against South Africa at Johannesburg – at an average of 16.43 runs per wicket. In its 100th edition in 1963, the *Wisden Cricketers' Almanack* listed him as one of the "Six Giants of the Wisden Century."

By the time that he first played as a professional for Saltaire, in 1915, Barnes was 41 years old. According to the centenary booklet, in the nine seasons to 1923 he took 904 wickets at an average of 5.26. (This followed the nine seasons he had played in the North Staffordshire League, when his record had been almost identical: 893 wickets at an average of 5.28). These are astonishing figures. On one occasion – against Baildon in 1915 – Barnes took wickets with 5 consecutive deliveries. Not surprisingly, Saltaire won the league 4 times between 1917 and 1922 and again in 1926.

It might be noted that Barnes was not just playing against ordinary club cricketers. The Bradford League attracted many famous players during the First World War years (when first class cricket was suspended), including Jack Hobbs of Surrey and Frank Woolley of Kent as well as Yorkshiremen such as Schofield Haigh and Wilfred Rhodes. At the same time, Barnes knew his worth, given the thousands of people who would flock to see him play: 6,400 in the case of Saltaire's fixture at Bowling Old Lane in 1923, the league record. The centenary booklet reports that Barnes "drove a hard bargain in his negotiations with our club officials." His initial fee of £3 10s per match had risen to £18 15s – plus expenses, talent money for his performances and an annual benefit – by the time he left the club during the 1923 season. (In the latter year, average earnings in Britain were less than £3 per week).

Last weekend, I walked around Roberts Park during Saltaire's first division fixture with Bradford and Bingley CC. Given its protected status, it is not surprising that a great deal seemed unchanged from my brief time there as a player. The River Aire flows by next to the boundary path; on the other side of the ground, the gentle banking of grass provides a good vantage point for the casual spectator; the outfield is deceptively undulating in places; the row of tall trees remains behind the bowler's arm at the pavilion end.

However, whilst a superficial inspection suggests that not much has changed at the ground, the Bradford League's website reports that that there have been considerable efforts to upgrade the club's facilities in recent years: a refurbished clubhouse, a new electronic scoreboard, better practice facilities, a redesigned tea-room. The website notes that these improvements have been brought about "under the inspired leadership of the chairman, Jeff Driver."

There are obvious changes on the pitch as well. Some of these reflect the evolution of club cricket in general since I was a lad – fielding circles, protective helmets, the touching of batsmen's gloves between overs, and so on – but the most radical difference is undoubtedly in the composition of the Saltaire team. When I played, we had a useful West Indian professional called Gordon McLennon supported by a team of white players. Last weekend, there were 9 players in the side of Pakistani or other descent from south Asia: an impressive reflection of the determined efforts that the club has made in recent years to ensure that it draws upon – and represents – the whole of its local community.

I met Jeff Driver – now the club president – by the pavilion and re-introduced myself. He was kind enough to say that he remembered me and to give me a tour of the extended pavilion with its refurbished changing rooms and proud photograph display. He also introduced me to Richard Spry, the cricket captain, and pointed out Julian Young, who, like Jeff, has been a member of the club for over 50 years. In all cases, the warmth of greeting was very touching.

On this occasion, Saltaire came off second best. Batting first, a promising position of 90 for 1 was not maintained and the score had only reached 151 when the last man was out. In the early evening sunshine, the target was confidently reached by first three Bradford and Bingley batsmen, the visitors winning by 9 wickets with plenty of overs to spare.

Later, I looked at the match programme. It contained supportive advertisements from a dozen local businesses – a healthy sign – one of which was for The Shuttle of Baildon Bridge in Shipley: "for the finest selection of fabrics by the metre in Yorkshire." I compared it with the programme for the match against Bankfoot CC in 1975 in the centre pages of which could be found an advertisement for The Shuttle of Baildon Bridge in Shipley and Cavendish Street in Keighley: "for real value in fabrics by the yard." Good for them, I thought.

The main commentary in the match programme was written by Richard Spry who, after reviewing a couple of recent performances by his side, took the opportunity (as the following day was Father's Day) to pay tribute to the encouragement and support that his own father had given him when he was learning the game. It was a nice piece which, I'm sure, would have echoes of acknowledgement from many other – if not most – club cricketers.

The last time that Saltaire were champions of the Bradford League was in 1943. It has been a long wait to repeat the feat and the intervening years have been characterised by the highs and lows that are familiar to most sports clubs. In my first season, we were relegated to the second division and we did not succeed in achieving promotion in either of the two subsequent years prior to my permanent move down south (and the different challenges to be faced in the Thursday XI of Camden CC in Cambridge and, later as a guest player, with the Old Paulines CC in the Surrey Cricket League). Saltaire have been promoted and relegated half a dozen times since 1975 with the most recent promotion (in 2014) now placing them back in the top tier. As last weekend's defeat in Roberts Park confirmed their position at the foot of the league table, the continuation of the recent "yo-yo" status is distinctly possible.

But, no matter. I wish the club all the best for the rest of the season. And, in 2019, I look forward to the souvenir booklet celebrating Saltaire CC's 150th anniversary.

www.anordinaryspectator/news-blog June 2015

Speedway

The Eye of the Tiger

A welcome characteristic of several of the blogs that have followed the publication of *An Ordinary Spectator: 50 Years of Watching Sport* has been that they have featured sports that were not covered in the book: women's football, Gaelic football, swimming, gymnastics, ice hockey, field hockey...

Yesterday, I added another sport to this list.

The Glasgow Tigers compete in speedway's British Premier League, which is the second tier below the Elite League. Their home has been at the Ashfield Stadium in Possilpark since 1999, though the Tigers nickname dates from 1946 and the original club was formed in 1928.

The Premier League has 13 teams, of whom six will qualify for the end-of-season play-offs. Before yesterday's meeting, the Tigers were in 5th place with their opponents – the Berwick Bandits – in 7th, so there was much to play for.

The speedway season is demanding – the regular league fixtures run from early May to September with the play-offs to follow – and irregular, as the Tigers also had away meetings on the three consecutive days before yesterday. It struck me that the demands on the teams' resources and the individuals' powers of recovery were not dissimilar that those I had noted (in May) in connection with the schedule faced by the Braehead Clan ice hockey team.

There are other similarities with the ice hockey. One is the cosmopolitan nature of the teams. At the beginning of the 2015 season, the 7 names on the Tigers' roster comprised three Australians, two Englishmen, a Swede and a Frenchman, of whom only one rode for the Tigers last year. This suggests that there is also a high turnover of personnel between seasons, which must in part be due to the league rules which, in the commendable attempt to create a competitive division, impose maximum levels for the combined points averages of the 7 riders during the previous season.

Within the season, the further turnover of riders is undoubtedly due to the hazardous nature of the sport: 3 of the Tigers' original roster for 2015 were absent yesterday for injury-related reasons. Fortunately, the league has a liberal attitude to filling gaps with guest riders. Indeed, one of the Berwick successes yesterday – the Dane, Thomas Jorgensen – had guested for the Tigers as recently as last Friday at a fixture in Somerset.

I attended the meeting as a speedway novice. I was familiar with its basic principles – the absence of brakes on the bikes and the technique of broadsiding the corners on loose dirt – but my familiarity with the sport did not extend much beyond occasional glimpses on television. And, as I expected, television does not provide the whole picture. In particular – as with the tennis ball passing over the Wimbledon net or the swimmer surging down the Commonwealth Games pool – it does not fully capture the speed of the spectacle.

I picked this up from my initial vantage point amongst the spectators on the lower level towards the end of the back straight as the riders passed me for the first time in the first heat. As, at the same time, I received a light stinging on the face – accompanied by a disconcerting clatter on my spectacles – from the shower of loose shale thrown up by the skidding riders, I decided to make a tactical retreat to the upper level for the second heat. It was the 5-1 points advantage that the Tigers gained in this race (3 for the win and 2 for second against the Bandits' single point for third place in the four-man race) that took the home side into the lead for the first time. By the end of the meeting, the margin had been comfortably stretched to 58-34.

The Glasgow Tigers club makes every effort to welcome visitors. The main entrance to the stadium took me through the club shop where – to the accompaniment of "Tiger Feet" – I could peruse not only the usual array of branded clothing and other merchandise, but an interesting array of old programmes and other speedway memorabilia. I waited in vain for a few minutes for "Eye of the Tiger." The same room also contained the main bar, which complemented the rudimentary hospitality sites elsewhere in the stadium. Perhaps it was the timing of the meeting – a Sunday afternoon – but, as far as I could see and hear, there was to be no hint of any anti-social behaviour. Or perhaps it was just a speedway crowd respectfully enjoying some skilful and bravely supplied entertainment.

The club is also targeting a family audience. The MC flagged this up at an early stage when he referred to the races that would take place later for the Under 8s and Under 12s. I did wonder about this: was not the age of 6 or 7 a little young for skidding around the corner on a speedway bike? I needn't have worried: the races involved chasing Roary the Mascot (on foot) around the final bend to the finishing tape.

In common with many of the other sports that I have observed over the last year – county cricket at Headingley, gymnastics at the Glasgow Hydro, ice hockey at Braehead – the speedway meeting has its elements of ritual. These range from the grandstanding in front of the main stand by the home side's heat winners on their victory laps to the painstaking recording of the results by spectators in the (excellent) match programme and the ground staff's manual raking of the shale from the top of the banking back down on to the main body of the track after each race (akin to Sisyphus pushing the boulder, I thought). Indeed, the rituals began before the meeting had started, when the riders were paraded around the track on the back of a lorry. It was not quite the tumbril on the way to the guillotine, but if the riders' waves to the spectators were somewhat half-hearted, this would have been completely understandable, given the risks and challenges that they were shortly to face.

I counted four heats in which riders came off their machines, fortunately on each occasion without any apparently serious mishap. On two occasions, the races were halted with – and this did seem to add insult to (potential) injury – the fallen riders being disqualified for having been the primary reason for the heat being stopped. Rules are rules. The meeting was efficiently officiated and, even with a couple of breaks for track maintenance and the lottery draw, the 15 heats were completed in a little under two hours.

For one of the later heats, I made my way back through one of the small covered stands, where the modest band of Bandits supporters, initially loudly supportive of their team's efforts, were coming to terms with the meeting's inevitable outcome. They fell into silence as the Tigers riders swept past on the heat's last lap to complete another 5-1 sweep of the points. Then, for the last two races, I stood near the starting line. By this time, the track at that point had been heavily churned up and, as the clock counted down, I could see the riders wrestling with their machines to establish a firm base for take-off. When the tape was raised, there followed the furious dash for supremacy at the first bend with only the slightest margins of error in the jockeying for position. A heady cocktail of fumes and noise trailed in their wake.

As ever, my interest in the afternoon was in the whole sporting event: its presentation, the environs of the stadium, the nature of the crowd, the evolving outcome of the contest. But the riders were the main focus, of course – jumping out at the starts, fighting for (and occasionally losing) control of the skids, searing down the straights, checking out the positions of their team-mates and opponents. At speed.

After the last heat, as I prepared to make my exit, the Glasgow Tigers' tumbril appeared again to do a lap of honour, this time containing the team manager and mascots and presentation girls as well as the riders. The latter – young lads some of them – were smiling this time. And, over the loudspeaker, came "Eye of the Tiger."

www.anordinaryspectator/news-blog July 2015

Cricket

"Match Drawn (Pitch Violated)": 40 Years On

Next Wednesday, it will be 40 years to the day since one of the major anti-climaxes of my sports spectating career.

It was on the early morning of 19th August 1975 that the groundsman at the Headingley cricket ground arrived at work to discover that the pitch, on which the first four days of the third test match between England and Australia had been played, had been vandalised. The combination of holes dug in the wicket and oil poured on its surface meant that the match would have to be abandoned.

It was immediately apparent from the accompanying graffiti at the ground that the damage had been caused by the friends of a man called George Davis, who was in jail for an armed raid on the London Electricity Board in 1974 – a crime, they argued, that he did not commit.

Four decades on, it is interesting to reflect on this episode and to consider some of the features that, even today, make it unique.

First things first: the cricket. It had been an utterly enthralling game up to the close of play on the Monday: Dennis Lillee and Jeff Thomson tearing into the England batsmen; the two brave half-centuries from David Steele; Phil Edmonds's 5-wicket haul in his first test match; the stunning catch by Thomson at mid-off to dismiss Alan Knott in England's second innings…

At the end of the fourth day, Australia, chasing the huge target of 445 to win, were making more than a reasonable fist of it at 220 for the loss of three wickets. One of the men dismissed was Ian Chappell, the Australian captain, who was given out leg before wicket to Chris Old. It can reasonably be said that Chappell disagreed with the decision. He stormed off and, having rushed up the pavilion steps and entered the door directly opposite our vantage point on the Western Terrace, slammed it so ferociously that the whole building seemed to shake. The taunting laughter of the crowd around us who witnessed this dissent was no doubt cheered by the reassurance that the full width of the cricket ground separated us from the irate perpetrator.

It was on the Tuesday morning, just as I was setting off to meet my friend Andrew Carter to catch the bus to Headingley, that my mother suggested that I might wish to listen to the latest news broadcast on the radio. It was announced that, as the pitch was unfit for play, the match would have to be called off. Mum queried this: surely they could just move a little further along the square and set up the stumps there?

I rang Andrew to cancel our plans for the day. By the time I had put the receiver down, the sense of anti-climax was strongly taking hold. All these years later, the recollection is that my immediate feelings were not so much of anger or resentment, but of an overwhelming sense of void and emptiness. What I cannot recall is the weather. It was not until many years after the event, when I read Ken Dalby's *Headingley Test Cricket 1899-1975*, that I realised that "steady rain would almost certainly have prevented play in any case."

The campaign organised on Davis's behalf was successful. He was released from prison in May 1976, the Home Secretary (Roy Jenkins) having formed the view that his conviction was unsafe. Davis rewarded his family and friends with his involvement in an armed robbery in 1977 for which he was sent to jail the following year. After his release from that sentence, he was jailed again for another crime in 1987.

The passage of time allows one to put the 1975 Headingley test match "outrage" – as it was described in the following year's Yorkshire CCC *Annual Report* – into some sort of context. Within the UK sporting environment, I think it remains highly unusual for two reasons: the motive for the protest and the impact on the event being targeted.

First, the motive. I would hazard a guess that the vast majority of protests at sporting events in Britain are related to one of the individuals or teams participating at the event itself, usually reflecting disgruntlement about management and/or ownership. Examples during the last football season included the boycott of attendance by some Newcastle United season ticket holders and the pitch invasion on the last game of the season by disgruntled supporters of Blackpool FC. (For completeness, I make a clear distinction between my definition of "protest" – to which I give a fairly wide interpretation – and naked football hooliganism as evident at, for example, Luton Town vs Millwall in 1985 or Ireland vs England in 1995).

In cases in which the causes of the protests are non-sporting, they have often been for reasons that concern politics or religion, albeit with some variations in the clarity of objective. The most famous example is that of Emily Davison throwing herself in front of the field of the 1913 Derby in the cause of female suffrage. More recent instances of individual protest include a former Roman Catholic priest Neil Horan proclaiming that the end of the world was nigh as he ran across the Silverstone track waving a banner during the 2003 British Grand Prix and Trenton Oldfield's wail against "the culture of elitism" in British society after he had been fished out of the Thames at the 2012 Boat Race. (That both Horan and Oldfield avoided the fatal consequences that befell Davison is a minor miracle).

Local grievances have also been a cause of protest. There are several examples of disgruntled locals objecting to the closure of road networks for cycle events by covering parts of the routes with carpet tacks and drawing pins, including the Etape Caledonian in Perthshire in 2009 and the Etape Cymru in North Wales in 2013. However – with the striking exception of the continual disruption of the 1969 South African rugby tour by anti-apartheid demonstrators – the occurrence of any sizeable political protest at sporting events in Britain has been absent.

By contrast, the George Davis case remains a rare example of direct action being committed with the aim of disrupting or bringing to an end a major sporting event in Britain for what are essentially *personal* reasons relating to an individual's or family's circumstances. Other instances are hard to find, though one such case occurred in 2012 when a man called John Foley handcuffed himself to the goalpost during an Everton/Manchester City match in protest at his daughter's dismissal by a budget airline. As far as I am aware, the only example of the Fathers 4 Justice campaigners encroaching on a sporting event was when two protesters climbed on to the roof of the Crucible Theatre in Sheffield during the Embassy World Snooker Championship of 2005; the main targets of F4J have tended to be prominent civic sites such as the Houses of Parliament, Buckingham Palace and Tower Bridge.

Second, the action of George Davis's supporters had the effect of ending the test match. Play was not resumed (notwithstanding my mother's suggested action). This was unlike the other examples referred to here: the 1913 Derby ran its course; the Grand Prix drivers were slowed down by a safety car before resuming the race; the Boat Race was only temporarily halted; at Goodison Park, the football match was delayed for a few minutes; the snooker was not affected; the cycling in Scotland resumed after an hour and a half; the 1969 Springboks completed their itinerary in full.

By contrast, the England/Australia scorecard in the Yorkshire CCC *Annual Report* of 1976 was soberly headed "Match drawn (Pitch violated)."

The *Annual Report* argued that: "It is easy to be wise after the event and plan the security devices which might have been employed. It is less easy to anticipate the actions of the mindless few who will go to any length to draw attention to a cause, however good or bad." This was a fair standpoint, I think, though I would offer one caveat. I am not sure that "mindless" fitted the bill: Davis's supporters knew exactly what they were doing.

The main lesson from the test match pitch episode of 1975 was to confirm that – should a small group of people so wish – significant damage could be wrought by those armed with a straightforward plan, simple tools and a perverse imagination. It was ever thus and it remains the case. It is a corollary of living in a liberal democracy in which civic conduct is based on mutual trust.

The damage caused at Headingley was significant in the context of an Ashes test series. But it was still only a cricket match. 40 years on – in the higher realms of the geopolitical sphere rather than the lower level sporting one – the stakes are different, but the lesson still applies. The cruel havoc that some others seem to wish upon us – with their corresponding combination of plan/tools/imagination now allied to their perception of a clear political/religious agenda – means that we must ensure that, next time, our wisdom does indeed not only come after the event.

www.anordinaryspectator/news-blog August 2015

Rugby League

The Spectacular and Thrilling "Boy Hero"

Those of us who have attended live sports events over many years might sometimes ask ourselves the question: why do we bother? What draws us back to watch our preferred sports – for me, rugby and cricket – time and time again, when we could spend our time (and money) doing other things?

The answers will vary from one person to the next. For many, it will be the identification with a home-town side or the sense of camaraderie with our fellow supporters or the reflected glory from a consistently successful team. On the pitch, we might be looking for the specific qualities of particular players: their skills or courage or unpredictability. Any of these reasons – or none – might be appropriate.

In my case, I am unquestionably drawn to sport's capacity for providing drama. The sports arena is a theatre and for the players on the field – the actors on the stage, if you like – there are the ever-present possibilities of glory and despair, of success and failure, of hubris and nemesis.

At one level, there is the drama of the full stage: the complete event, with its surrounding hype and atmosphere and gladiatorial engagement. Examples are not hard to find within the sporting calendar: the Ryder Cup, an Ashes cricket test match, the Challenge Cup final...

However, there is also another type of drama, which occurs less frequently and is experienced over a much shorter time frame. It is the drama of the moment – possibly even of the micro-second – in which the defining characteristic of the contest is revealed. In some instances, the particular detail can determine the whole memorised experience years after the event.

Nor is this the full story. In many cases, the key to these dramas of the moment is not the incident itself – or the actual observation of the incident – it is in that split-second before the event occurs. It is in these moments that sport really makes the heart pound and causes the sharp intake of breath to be made. In short: it is often in the *anticipation* of the incident that the ultimate drama lies.

In a book published a couple of years ago, I identified a number of such "nano-dramas" that I had seen over half a century of watching sport. Some of them are very well-known – the stroke that brought up Geoff Boycott's 100th first class century in a test match against Australia at Headingley in 1977, for example, or Martin Offiah breaking into the wide open spaces of Wembley for the first of his tries in the Challenge Cup final of 1994 – whilst others are more personal to my own spectating experience and will have long departed from the collective memory.

One such nano-drama occurred exactly 50 years ago – on a Monday evening in September 1965 – in the Yorkshire Cup semi-final between Hunslet and Castleford at Parkside.

At 10 years of age, I was already in my fifth season of supporting Hunslet, my dad's team. It had been a productive period, given the Yorkshire Cup and Second Division championship successes in 1962-63 and, of course, the Challenge Cup final appearance against Wigan the previous May. All seemed to be well at the club – 11 of the Wembley team took the field against Castleford – with no immediate signs of its subsequent and sad decline.

The visitors' side included Roger Millward, who had come to a modest fame playing for the Castleford and District Under 17s in a series of televised junior rugby matches that the commercial channel had shown at Sunday lunchtime a couple of seasons earlier. Now, having just turned 18 – and at his full height of five feet four inches – he was in the first team of his home-town club. The match-day programme bracketed Millward with Alan Hardisty, the Great Britain international, in Castleford's stand-off position. However, although Hardisty was injured and did not play, it was Derek Edwards who wore the number 6 shirt for this game.

On paper, the semi-final teams were evenly matched. Although only sitting in mid-table in the league – Castleford had won 3 out of 6 league games and Hunslet 3 out of 8 – each side had supplied four players to the Yorkshire team that had defeated New Zealand the previous week in the first match to have been played under the Wheldon Road floodlights. Indeed, the whole of the Yorkshire pack – Hartley, Ward, Eyre, Bryant, Ramsey, Taylor – was on display at Parkside. Following his rapid promotion from the Castleford "A" team, Roger Millward was now taking the field in some illustrious company.

On the day after the semi-final, the front page of the *Yorkshire Evening Post* reported that Clara Bow – "The 'It' Girl" of the 1920s – had died at the age of 60. I was more interested in the sports section, where Arthur Haddock gave his assessment of a "...splendidly fought Yorkshire Cup semi-final [that] had just about everything...the superb tackling, resolute forward play, a fightback by both teams, a boy hero and the right result."

The "boy hero" was Millward, of course. My memory is of him playing on the wing and being absolutely mesmeric. As reported by Haddock: "It would be difficult to imagine anything more spectacular and thrilling than his two wonderful tries and touchline goal in the space of three minutes just after half-time that put Castleford ahead 8-7."

My father and I stood in the covered stand behind the goalposts at the Dewsbury Road end of the ground. After Millward's heroics at the beginning of the second half, Hunslet responded by regaining the lead. Then Castleford pressed again. As they did so – and each time the ball was passed across the back line in Millward's direction – the sizeable visitors' support in the large crowd roared with anticipation. They – we – could not wait to see what the outcome would be when he next touched the ball. The noise echoed from the roof and back of the stand. What drama this was. I held my breath: captivated, transfixed and almost overwhelmed.

Of course, for me – the young Hunslet supporter – Millward was an opposition player and I wanted his team to lose. I willed the Hunslet defence to close in on him and eliminate the attacking threat. At the same time, I also knew the significance of what I was seeing. With his speed (described as "bewildering" in the following day's *Yorkshire Post*) and agility and devastating changes of direction, this was clearly a wonderful and unusual talent.

The rest of the crowd – home and visiting – thought so too. Arthur Haddock again: "Every one of the 9,753 spectators, friend and foe alike, gave him an ovation in a great spontaneous gesture that warmed the heart."

On this occasion, Millward's efforts were in a losing cause. The home side's pack – with Geoff Gunney and Bill Ramsey prominent – gradually took control. Two tries by Barry Lee and one from Kenny Eyre, plus four Billy Langton goals, took Hunslet to a 17-10 win and a (losing) Yorkshire Cup final appearance against the recently resurrected Bradford Northern at Headingley the following month.

My assessment of Millward's talent was not a difficult one to make, even for a 10 year old. Within 6 months, he had won the first of his 29 Great Britain caps and, in Australia in 1970, he was the linchpin of the last British side to win an Ashes series. I followed his career with interest and, as it happened, was present at some of its significant moments, including his debut appearance for Hull KR at Parkside in 1966, his first try for Great Britain (against Australia at Headingley in 1967), the touchdown in his last test match in 1978 (also against Australia at Headingley) and the crude jaw-breaking assault on him at Wembley in the Challenge Cup final of 1980.

It is half a century since I watched the Yorkshire Cup semi-final of 1965, but my recollection of the crowd's excitement at watching the young tyro on the Castleford wing – and, in particular, of the nerve-racking sense of anticipation about what might shortly happen, as the ball got closer to him – remains absolutely fixed. The moments were described then – and are headlined again here now – as "spectacular and thrilling" and yet that somehow seems hopelessly inadequate.

The Castleford backs passing the ball towards the young Roger Millward on their left wing in a cup-tie at Parkside. It sounds routine, of course: and, at one level, it was. This was a professional rugby league side transferring the ball skilfully across the pitch and, as it did so, being challenged by a resolute defence. I can only report that the action can be conjured up again in my mind's eye in an instant. And when it is, there is an immediate frisson of excitement, as well as the painful pang of nostalgia.

It was an exquisite sporting nano-drama, the memory of which will remain with me for ever.[15]

The Rugby League Journal Autumn 2015

Cricket

Headingley and Hove

> *They confirmed to an impressionable boy that, by watching Yorkshire and wanting them to do well, I was engaging with a sporting entity that had a noble tradition and a successful history. I knew that the club had been a touchstone for successive generations of cricket followers across the county, who had shared in the feats of the great players and teams and taken a pride in their achievements. I can read the same passages in Headingley today and still feel moved. [OS, page 53]*

This paragraph refers to John Marshall's *Headingley*, which I read, as a teenager, shortly after its publication in 1970. The book – copies of which are still occasionally to be seen on the second-hand stalls at Headingley – is a straightforward chronological description of the feats of Yorkshire CCC and its players through to the end of the 1969 season. (A propitious time to stop, as it happened). It is written in a neat and simple style which, in my view, adds to the drama of the story it is telling.

Next Tuesday, Yorkshire CCC will begin the final match of their 2015 County Championship season – against Sussex at Headingley. It is this encounter that has reminded me of the book – for reasons that are set out below.

It is a fixture with a rich history. Since 1899, including this year's game, Sussex have been Yorkshire's final opponents in the championship season on no fewer than 29 occasions. The difference this time is the venue: this is the first time it has been a home fixture for the White Rose. On all the previous occasions when it has been the last game of the season, the Sussex/Yorkshire encounter has taken place on the south coast: twice (before the First World War) at Hastings, the others at the County Ground in Hove.

The main reason for the fixture's frequency over the years was that, in the four decades up to the Second World War, Yorkshire's county championship season ended with a tour of the southern counties. The precise itinerary varied from year to year but, between 1899 and 1939, Sussex versus Yorkshire at Hove was the final game 20 times. (On another 12 occasions, it was Yorkshire's penultimate fixture, often to be followed with a game against Hampshire). However, even in the post-war period, Hove has been the venue of Yorkshire's county championship finale in 8 seasons, most recently for a high-scoring draw in 2008.

There is a further connection with 2015, of course. In the last century, Sussex were Yorkshire's final opposition in 11 championship-winning seasons, although the most recent example dates back to 1959. Often – as this year – the title had been won by the time the game took place. 1959 was an exception. In that year, Yorkshire – under their last amateur captain, JR Burnett – had to win the final game and, in the fourth innings, that meant reaching a target of 215 in the 105 minutes that were available. They did so with seven minutes to spare, thanks largely to a rapid century opening partnership between Bryan Stott and Doug Padgett, to register one of the Club's most famous triumphs. [An aside. To their credit, Sussex were in their 29th over when the target was reached: an over-rate of 17½ per hour].

Not surprisingly, the fact that Sussex was the last game of the season meant that, for some of Yorkshire's greatest players, the fixture was their final bow in the county championship before their retirement. This was the case for Schofield Haigh in 1913 and George Herbert Hirst in 1921, for example. Other championship careers for Yorkshire came to an end at Hove, but were resumed elsewhere. In the post-war period, these range from those of John Hampshire (in 1981 following more than 450 first class matches for Yorkshire) to Gary Keedy (in 1994 after his only appearance).

However, the match in Hove was also the last appearance for some whose lives were to be cut short. Major Booth took the last couple of his championship wickets in the drawn fixture of 1914; he was killed on the first day of the Somme offensive in July 1916. Roy Kilner scored 91 not out and took 8 wickets in a comfortable Yorkshire win in 1927; he died at the age of 37 the following April of a fever contracted in India.

And, of course, there is Hedley Verity, who died of the wounds suffered serving in Sicily in 1943. Four years earlier, after Sussex had amassed 387 and Yorkshire had replied with 392, he took 7 wickets for 9 runs in the second innings, as the home side was skittled out for 33 and Yorkshire won by 10 wickets. (It is reasonable to assume that the great bowler enjoyed playing in Sussex: he also took 13 wickets at Hove in 1931 and 14 at Eastbourne in 1937).

It was in John Marshall's *Headingley* that I first came across these exploits of Yorkshire players at Hove – and elsewhere. Following Verity's triumph, there is a poignant description of the team's return from Sussex at the beginning of September 1939: the journey that marked the break-up of the great Yorkshire side of the 1930s – "Final handshakes were exchanged in the Leeds City Square."

In *An Ordinary Spectator*, I noted that such passages in *Headingley* registered profoundly with me when I first read them. They still do.

www.anordinaryspectator/news-blog September 2015

Football

Legends

> **Legend** n...[2] an extremely famous person...
> *Oxford English Dictionary.*
>
> **Legend** n...[4] a person whose fame or notoriety makes him or her a source of exaggerated or romanticised tales...
> *Collins Concise Dictionary.*

The significance of sporting tradition has been an important theme in my spectating career. Most recently, I noted the rich heritage of the Yorkshire versus Sussex cricket fixture as the final game of the county championship season. Last week, I had the opportunity of reflecting on the impressive traditions and successes of another sporting institution – Arsenal Football Club – when I went on an official tour of the Emirates Stadium.

The tour can be done in two ways: as a self-guided walk with the aid of an audio cassette or in a group hosted by a "legend" from Arsenal's past. Fortuitously, the timing of my arrival at the stadium allowed me to take one of the last places on a legends tour guided by Perry Groves. (Charlie George and Nigel Winterburn are the other main hosts for these types of tour).

Groves played 155 times for Arsenal between 1986 and 1992, scoring 21 goals. There is no doubting his respect or passion for the club, nor his knowledge of both its history and current status, and he was an excellent guide. It helped also, I think, that he was willing to make some revealing comparisons between what is expected of Premier League footballers today and the accepted norms – including those off the field – of his own playing era.

I came away from the stadium tour with three strong impressions, none of which was a particular surprise, but each duly confirmed. The first was the obvious sense of scale: the stadium's 60,000-plus capacity, the 9 year waiting list for season tickets in the favoured Club Level middle tier of the stands, the eye-watering financial commitment required to become a member of the exclusive Diamond Club... The clear sense of corporate power and financial muscle was encouraged, no doubt, by beginning the tour in the Directors' Box. Here, on the right hand side of the entrance, stands the unique Invincibles Trophy commemorating Arsenal's unbeaten Premier League season in 2003-04.

Second, there was the attention to detail. Perry Groves made this point emphatically when we reached the home changing room, the surface of which is of a fabric specifically designed to prevent players – assets worth tens of millions to the club, of course – slipping over on a wet floor. The room itself is a horseshoe shape, recognising a concept that the manager Arsene Wenger picked up during his time in Japan relating to the ways in which the right-angled corners of conventional changing rooms encourage the formation of cliques and inhibit communications within the group as a whole. (It was noticeable that the away dressing room had neither of these features). More details were given as we took our places on the cushions situated on each player's bench (designed to increase blood-flow during half-time!): the mineral-enhanced water used in the showers, the specific items that the players are required to consume in their post-match meals, the foot-warming facilities used on the substitutes bench...

My sense is that these high standards are sought throughout the club. Certainly, within the large club shop – the Armoury Store – I was met by courteous and smartly attired staff who seemed genuinely keen to help. I have been in club shops elsewhere, where, confronted by closely-packed racks of merchandise and disinterested assistants, I have felt as if I were an unwelcome intruder. Here, the atmosphere was friendly and airy and – I did not fail to recognise – conducive to the casual purchase: in addition to the ticket for the legends tour (£40), I bought a tour brochure (£5), a coffee mug (£8) and a photograph of me with the FA Cup (£10). The last of these reminded me of being photographed with the family (and Mickey Mouse) many years ago at Disneyland (and duly parting with my ten dollars) but, as also on that occasion, I did not regret the investment.

Finally, of course, there is the tradition. In this respect, the relocation to the Emirates Stadium might have provided something of a challenge for Arsenal, notwithstanding that the previous ground is only 500 yards down the road, as Highbury had been the club's home venue for the 93 years to 2006. However, the clever move was to draw on the supporters' close identification with the club as an integral part of the migration process. The individual inscriptions on the granite paving stones around the outside of the stadium bear eloquent witness to the role of the club within the lives of so many. Similarly, on a series of large panels at the base of the exterior stadium wall, each of the images and details of 32 of Arsenal's most famous players is accompanied by a fan's particular memory of that player. I was glad to see that this line-up – whilst excluding Perry Groves, alas – not only included representatives from the Invincibles side, but members of Arsenal's first double-winning team of 1971 (whose league defeat to their nearest rivals Leeds United at Elland Road I witnessed at first hand) and famous names from the pre-Second World War period such as Ted Drake and Alex James.

As with the attention to detail, the recognition of Arsenal's tradition and sense of history is all around: the marble floor of the old Highbury entrance provides the way in to one of the executive suites on an upper level; a larger version of the famous Arsenal clock is located on the top of the stand behind one of the goals; and, in the nearby museum, one of the cabinets neatly displays a nineteenth century cannonball made at the Royal Arsenal Munitions factory in Woolwich next to a chunk of the terrace from Highbury's North Bank.

Perry Groves drew attention to one of the action photographs on the wall near the stairs leading up to the Directors' Box. It showed the moment when Michael Thomas scored the extra-time goal at Anfield in the last league match of the 1988-89 season, thereby giving Arsenal their first First Division Championship title since 1971 (at the expenses of their hosts on that evening). It was highly unusual for league matches to be televised in those days, but when the TV executives of the time noted the viewing figures for this encounter (nearly 18 million, according to Groves), the mental light bulbs started flashing. It was the first year of Sky TV. The rest, as they say, is history.

Thomas's goal completed the 2-0 victory (Arsenal had needed to win the game by at least two clear goals) that is one of the most famous in the history of the club. Apart from him, all the other players in the photograph are from Liverpool, with the exception of a peripheral and slightly blurred figure on the extreme left of the scene some way from the action. When Perry Groves modestly stated that that second Arsenal player was him, I immediately saw how it all fitted together. From the perspective of Arsenal FC – and their supporters – the "legends" concept extends far beyond the 32 players identified on the panels on the outside of the stadium (or the shorter list of 10 named in the stadium tour brochure). The legends are a much wider group: a collective entity, whose individual components might be relatively small, but each of whom is nonetheless a legitimate part of the whole.

www.anordinaryspectator/news-blog October 2015

American Football

Friday Night Lights

This year marks the 25th anniversary of H G Bissinger's *Friday Night Lights*, which is widely regarded as the best book written on high school football (American Football to British readers, of course) in the United States. Arguably, because of the hugely significant role that football plays in the State, it is also the most informative primer for understanding the culture and psyche of Texas, especially in the rural areas and the smaller towns and cities. A critically acclaimed feature film based on the book was released in 2004, whilst a fictional version was adapted in 5 television series between 2006 and 2011.

A recent family holiday in Texas has enabled me to explore the phenomenon of high school football at first hand. I went to see the Jefferson Mustangs play the McCollum Cowboys in the Alamo Stadium in San Antonio. The number 8 bus took me on a 20 minute ride from the stop near my downtown hotel directly to the stadium on the north side of the city with, I was assured, the last bus due to return some time after the game had finished. I knew that this was not small-town Texas, of course – San Antonio is the 7th largest city in the United States – but I still reckoned that the evening might give me a flavour of what Bissinger had richly described. I was not disappointed.

Afterwards, when thinking about how I might summarise what I had experienced, I decided that three particular words would go at least part of the way: energy, commitment and choreography. This applied not only to the action on the pitch, of which more below, but to the wider spectacle as a whole.

And it was definitely a spectacle, not least because, throughout the evening, the sides were vigorously supported by their respective marching bands, both numbering well into three figures, in the bleachers. The signature tune for a McCollum touchdown was "Hey Look Me Over," though this was sometimes accompanied – rather uncomfortably for British ears – by the chant from a Gary Glitter hit of the 1970s. Both bands also gave impressive half-time displays which – responding to three different conductors and accompanied by their sides' cheerleaders, dancers and flag-bearers – added to the overall sense of exuberance and fun. The actions of American marching bands – with their rotating shoulders and stiff-legged movement and sudden changes of direction – are quick and urgent: an unlikely combination of the precise and the spontaneous. They are a long way removed from the Grenadier Guards on Horse Guards Parade.

Built in an abandoned rock quarry, the Alamo Stadium is owned and operated by the San Antonio Independent School District and is used by several of the local high schools. Jefferson played Corpus Christi high school in the first match to be held there in 1940. Following its refurbishment last year, it has a seating capacity of over 18,000 with long clean rows of terraced benches rising up on the three sides of a horseshoe shape; there were several hundred fans present to see the Mustangs and Cowboys. The stadium is open to the elements which, on this occasion, simply meant the darkness of a warm evening at the end of a hot October day. The floodlighting swamped the field: Friday Night Lights indeed.

An early score took the visitors into a 7-0 lead. To my untutored eye, it looked as if, in the opening exchanges, McCollum had a quicker snap of the ball and a stronger defence. On the other hand, the Jefferson quarterback, General Gonzalez, displayed a strong left-armed throw and one of his accurate missiles enabled his side to draw back to 14-14. Unfortunately for the home supporters, just before the half-time break, the McCollum running back, Mike Ramirez, surged down the sideline to give his side the lead again. Ramirez's was the dominant performance of the evening as he registered five touchdowns.

When the McCollum quarterback, Jordan Ortega, extended the lead to 28-14 by running unopposed for a 40 yard touchdown early in the second half, I did wonder if the floodgates might open. (Many of the other high school scores relayed at half time had been very one-sided). But this was not the case. Jefferson stuck to their task and, whilst they could not cope with Ramirez's power and pace, they scored two more touchdowns themselves and were not disgraced in the final outcome of 28-48. Even with only seconds remaining – and the result beyond doubt – Jefferson competed enthusiastically for a on-side kick that might have given them possession and the chance of a final offensive play.

There was plenty of effort and commitment, therefore. The on-field choreography comes with the sport itself, I think, and its carefully prepared repertoire of plays in both offence and defence. I was struck – and this is certainly not intended to be patronising – by how clearly both sides knew what they were doing. They appeared to be well-coached with their prepared routines being carried out as planned, though not always with success. What did surprise me was the number of penalty yards conceded, particularly in the first half: both sides were to lose valuable field positions because of these indiscretions.

Towards the end of the game, when I had moved up to stand at the top of the terracing to the side of the main entrance, I struck up a conversation with a charming man who introduced himself as Curtis and whose daughter played in the Mustangs Band. He told me that, across San Antonio as a whole, there were probably around 25 such high school football games being played on this particular Friday evening. It was a revealing comment. Each match would have its starting teams and back-up players and coaches and assistant coaches and cheerleaders and majorettes and the dozens of musicians on the different instruments in the marching band. And programme sellers and fast food vendors… And a supporting contingent comprised of parents and friends and school staff and former players… And *ad hoc* neutrals, such as a captivated observer from Glasgow.

I was reminded of the brilliant line in *Friday Night Lights*, when Bissinger describes the incongruous visit made to a high school football game in Marshall, Texas, by a delegation of Russians who had been visiting a nearby US Air Force base: "[T]hey don't understand a lick of football, but…their understanding of America by the end of the game will be absolute whether they realise it or not."

For me, this was also a Friday night in Texas and I certainly felt that I had learned a little more about the place I was visiting. There were clues everywhere. To take one example: one of the sentences in the opening paragraph of the impressive match programme read "[Thomas Jefferson High School]'s mission is to be the best urban high school in the US preparing all graduates for college, leadership in the military or job skills in growing industries." I would be surprised if an explicit reference to the military appears in the mission statement of any secondary school in Britain. But this was Texas.

There is a postscript. At the bus stop outside the stadium, a young woman waiting for a lift informed me that the last number 8 had already headed back downtown. As I watched the car park quickly empty of the supporters' cars and the team buses and the police vehicles – and remembering that I did not have a phone on me – I asked her which was the best route to walk back into the city centre. She gave me a pleasant smile which, I realise in retrospect, might well have been disguising a look of pity for the village idiot. Then, without any prompting on my part, she rang for a Yellow Cab, carefully explaining on the call back from the driver exactly where I was waiting. He duly arrived about 15 minutes later.

My thanks to Stephanie: the kindness of strangers.

www.anordinaryspectator/news-blog October 2015

American Football

The Alamodome

The evening after my exposure to Texan high school football ("*Friday Night Lights*," 26th October 2015), I graduated to the college version of the sport: the University of Texas at San Antonio (UTSA) Roadrunners versus Louisiana Tech Bulldogs at the Alamodome (not to be confused with the previous night's Alamo Stadium) in San Antonio.

This time, the family came with me. I attempted – fairly unsuccessfully, I suspect – to impart to them my rudimentary knowledge of the objectives of American Football. But their collective confusion about the action that unfolded in front of them did not seem to matter. Later, we were to agree unanimously that those moments early in the second half – as we were sitting in our row of comfortable Club Level seats, level with the end-zone line, and consuming our hot dogs (three with tomato sauce, one without) and beers/cokes – had been amongst the many highlights of a great vacation.

I wrote earlier this month ("*Legends*," 4th October 2015) that the capacity of the Emirates Stadium in London – the home of Arsenal FC, one of Europe's elite soccer clubs – is about 60,000. The Alamodome's is somewhat larger – 65,000 – and this for a football team that represents one component of The University of Texas System.

For the Roadrunners/Bulldogs confrontation, the Alamodome was under half-full – 24,392 was given as the official attendance – though, at times, under the enclosed roof, the noise of the crowd made this difficult to believe. In the second half in particular, the Bulldogs' offensive snaps were accompanied by a cacophonous roar, as the home supporters attempted to frustrate the communications between the quarterback and his offensive line. (This took me back to the Washington Redskins/Tennessee Titans game I had seen at the FedEx Stadium in Maryland in 2006; during a Redskins defensive set towards the end of that match, the roar from the crowd was probably the loudest that I have ever heard at a sporting event). The following day's *San Antonio Express-News* neatly described the Alamodome crowd as "getting rowdy."

In its preview of the game, the newspaper had reported that "UTSA sophomore walk-on Dalton Sturm is expected to get his first career start at quarterback following an injury last week to starter Blake Bogenschutz." It seemed to be a classic case of "Go out there and come back a star." Would he be up to the challenge?

It did not start well. Sturm's first pass was intercepted, leading to the opening score for LA Tech: 0-7. His team's first 4 running plays all resulted in a net loss of yards and this was followed by an underthrown (and dropped) pass. Then, Sturm was intercepted again.

It took some courage on the quarterback's part, therefore, for him to attempt another tricky pass, but this time the outcome was much more favourable: a touchdown which, with the extra point, tied the game at 10-10. By the end of the evening, Sturm had 4 touchdown passes to his credit, a record for a UTSA quarterback on debut. His bravery also extended to the physical side of the game as, on several occasions, he attempted to rush for valuable yards himself only to receive some heavy tackles by the Bulldogs defence.

Sturm's last throw of the game was a speculative "Hail Mary" from near the half-way line into the Bulldogs end-zone, hoping that one of his wide receivers would make a catch or take a lucky rebound. Had it succeeded, it would have given the Roadrunners the lead for the first time in the game – and that after the stadium scoreboard showed that the last seconds had ticked down during the course of the play. However, it was not to be, as the ball was tipped away by a Bulldog. This was something of an anti-climax for the Roadrunners fans, who had seen their team fight back from 17-31 down to level the score at 31-31 only for the Bulldogs to skilfully run down the clock – aided by a couple of outstanding catches by the wide receiver, Carlos Henderson – before landing a 32-yard field goal with 10 seconds left to play.

As with the previous evening's high school football game, the event was full of movement and colour. Not surprisingly, this was sometimes on a larger scale: the UTSA marching band must have had at least 200 members, though their half-time performance was relatively short. The extra curricula activity was imaginative, though not all of it was planned. There was a collective gasp when the euphoria of charging on to the field at the start overcame one of the young UTSA flag-bearers, who stumbled and fell (and then got up again and carried on). Later, some of the frequent stoppages in play were occupied by competitions for individual fans: an attempt to throw the ball to a target receiver (narrow failure) and an effort to kick a field goal (complete hash). Each UTSA score was greeted by the arrival in the end-zone of a group of college athletes, who would perform the number of press-ups that matched the points that their team had then accumulated: a task that, by definition, became more onerous as the evening progressed.

As anticipated, given that it is only just over 20 years old, the Alamodome is a well-appointed stadium with clean lines of sight, an instantly updated scoreboard and, as noted, the facility to create a vibrant atmosphere. The only downside was that, in our seats, the stadium's acoustics were poor – in marked contrast to those in the Alamo Stadium – and it was difficult to discern the announcements of either the match referee or the stadium announcer. Incidentally, for all the sport's incorporation of the modern means of presentation and analysis, I do like the way that American Football – even at the highest levels – retains some aspects of the low-tech: the chains to mark the 10 yard target for the 4 downs and the quaint little board held on the side line to show which down it is.

Football at the University of Texas is big business. A new book by Gilbert Gaul (*Billion Dollar Ball*, reviewed in *The Economist*, 5th September 2015) reports that, in 2012, the university's football programme had an income of $104 million from ticket sales, broadcasting rights and merchandise licensing and a profit of $78 million, all of which remains within the athletic departments (rather than subsidising the academic side of the university). Later in our vacation, when we had moved on to the State capital, I took a walk past the Darrell K Royal-Texas Memorial Stadium, the home venue of the University of Texas at Austin Longhorns football team. This has a capacity of just over 100,000: far in excess of any sports stadium in Britain and, according to Wikipedia, the 12th largest stadium in the world.

The Longhorns are the university's flagship football team. According to a detailed article in *USA Today* published at the time of our visit, their head coach has a total pay package of $5.1 million with a further bonus of up to $1 million depending on the team's results. (The total pay packages of the UTSA and LA Tech head coaches are $427,000 and $517,000, respectively). This is only exceeded by the total pay packages of the head coaches at the University of Alabama and the University of Michigan, which are in excess of $7 million plus bonuses.

Of course, I knew before setting out on the vacation that football is ingrained in Texan culture. But it was fascinating to see the confirmation of this and the many ways that it is represented. Can it be a coincidence that the traffic barriers in Austin are painted in orange and white, the colours of the Longhorns? Likewise, it can only be reader demand that results in the scores of over 600 of the State's high school games from Thursday and Friday being listed in the Sunday edition of the *Austin American-Statesman*. By contrast, it took me a week to find out some of the results of the Rugby World Cup being played in England – and only then, taking advantage of a chance encounter outside the Austin Visitor Information Center, by asking a well-built middle-aged man wearing an Australian rugby shirt.

My perception of Texan football was complete, therefore. I had confirmed that the locals were not only hugely knowledgeable about their sport, but besotted with their team and passionate about every detail. The only doubt set in just before the Roadrunners/Bulldogs encounter, when I asked a barman at the Alamodome whether he fancied the home side's chances that evening.

"I don't know," he replied. "Who are they playing?"

www.anordinaryspectator/news-blog October 2015

Cricket

"Death of a Gentleman"

In an earlier contribution to this occasional series of blogs – "*The Future of Test Match Cricket*" (5th January 2013) – I set out some reasons why I was concerned about the long-term prospects for this version of the sport. A follow-up piece – "*The Future of Test Match Cricket: Feedback*" (15th February 2013) – summarised some of the responses I had received via the Members' Forum of Yorkshire CCC.

The original blog suggested four main reasons for concern: the pull of highly-paid one-day cricket on the best players' commitment and availability; the diminished "mystery" attached to international cricketers; the poor results obtained in recent series played in Australia/England/South Africa by the other test playing countries; and the apparently ambivalent status being given to test match cricket by some of the national or international authorities.

It was with some interest, therefore, that I attended a recent one-off showing of *Death of a Gentleman* (2015, certificate 12A) at the Glasgow Film Theatre. This is a full-length documentary (directed by Sam Collins, Jarrod Kimber and Johnny Blank), the central theme of which is that test match cricket is being sold short by the relevant cricket authorities, who are more interested in the vast riches to be gained through the promotion of one-day and Twenty-20 cricket. The showing had been arranged by Neil Clitheroe, a local cricket enthusiast, and he was rewarded with an audience of about 40: not bad for a damp Bonfire Night with Glasgow Celtic playing a European tie elsewhere in the city.

Death of a Gentleman is really two interwoven films. The first concerns the Australian batsman, Ed Cowan – a friend of Kimber's – who played in 18 test matches between 2011 and 2013. We learn about his late breakthrough with Tasmania, his euphoria at being selected by his country for his first test match against India, the pride of his father and wife, a century against South Africa and the appalling vitriol posted in the social media when a poor shot led to a first-ball dismissal in an Ashes test match. Cowan's own summary of how he will have been perceived by the average Australian cricket follower – "not good enough" – is genuinely poignant.

It is not clear how Cowan's story relates to the film's larger theme, which concerns the governance of cricket by the International Cricket Council (ICC) and the national boards, particularly the Board of Control for Cricket in India (BCCI), England and Wales Cricket Board (ECB) and Cricket Australia (CA). The dominant role – reflecting the massive following for (and resultant finances of) the one-day and Twenty-20 versions of the sport in India – is that of the BCCI.

The film's arguments about the conduct of the ICC and BCCI will be familiar ground to those who have followed the diligent examination of the former by Lord Woolf, the impressive journalistic investigations by Gideon Haigh and others and the accounts of the occasional whistle-blowers. Woolf and Haigh are interviewed for the film, though their contributions are not as extensive as one might have wished. However, whilst the contents of the rap sheets are well-known – poor governance, conflicts of interest, lack of transparency, use of threats and intimidation, lack of pastoral care for the sport as a whole – the film provides a service to cricket followers in setting them down via this particular medium.

The documentary style pays homage to the approach used successfully many times by Nick Broomfield: hand-held camera, urgent phone calls in hotel rooms, taxi rides through unfamiliar and brightly illuminated cities. And, in the same way that Broomfield landed interviews with the likes of the Hollywood madam Heidi Fleiss and the far-right Afrikaaner Eugene Terre'Blanche, Collins and Kimber are successful in sitting down with their own key targets: Narayanaswami Srinivasan (ICC and BCCI), Lalit Modi (the marketing genius behind the Indian Premier League – "I created a monster") and Giles Clarke (then Chairman and now President of the ECB). By letting Clarke's demeanour and responses speak for themselves, the directors have no difficulty in casting him as the pantomime villain.

The film reaches a proper climax: the meetings in 2014 which re-allocated the ICC's huge income in favour of the BCCI, ECB and CA to the relative detriment of the other test playing countries and the associate members. By this stage, the door-stepping of Clarke in the latest 5-star hotel is less productive and – in their roles as mere supporters of test cricket – Collins and Kimber could have been in no doubt about their places in cricket's pecking order. As Haigh states, it is the fan's role simply to be "monetised and exploited" by those – national boards, sponsors, elite players, broadcasters, corporate interests – higher up the food chain.

If I were to be critical of the film, I would point to two missed chances. The first would have been to read across from test match cricket to the status of first class cricket as a whole in the respective countries. In England, Clarke has overseen the hollowing out of the summer season in which half the 4-day county championship matches are played in either April/May or September leaving vast tracts of the most suitable cricket playing/watching months devoted virtually entirely to the one-day and Twenty-20 competitions. Has the same undermining of the first class infrastructure happened elsewhere? It would have been interesting to have explored this.

Second, the film needed more evidence to support its central argument – that test match cricket is worth preserving. From a personal perspective, I would much rather spend my time watching the brilliant skills of the Pakistani spin bowlers on a wearing test match pitch (even if it is at England's expense) than Kevin Pietersen bludgeon the nth six of yet another Twenty-20 innings in yet another Big Slog competition somewhere in the world. But if a battle to save test cricket is indeed necessary – and is to be won – it is up to the film's directors (and to me and other like-minded folk) to make the case emphatically and persuasively that both forms of the game have their place, not simply to state that test cricket is better.

Ironically, I thought that this case was actually being made when the film showed Ed Cowan opening the batting with David Warner for Australia in a test match against India. When Warner, whose reputation and status has been built on his exploits in the one-day game, reached his century, Cowan had made 30-odd. One batsman the dashing product of the modern age, lofting shots and treating every ball as a boundary-scoring opportunity; the other, a traditional gritty accumulator of runs; together, a rich combination that confirmed that test cricket is the many-faceted and intriguing version of this wonderful game.

Afterwards, in the GFT bar, I had a good chat with Neil Clitheroe and thanked him for arranging for *Death of a Gentleman* to be shown. For anyone with an interest in test match cricket, it is a film worth seeing.

www.anordinaryspectator/news-blog November 2015

Rugby Union

What's in a Name?

In the 20 years or so since the creation of the Super League of the rugby league elite clubs in the UK and the official move to professionalism within rugby union, I have been consistently interested in the branding of rugby teams.

    For some of the Super League sides, it has been a question of succumbing to various forms of dangerous wildlife: Tigers, Wolves, Wildcats, Rhinos. However, the geographical location of the respective clubs – Castleford, Warrington, Wakefield and Leeds – has remained firmly fixed in their official names. Hence, whilst the seven-syllable Wakefield Trinity Wildcats does not exactly trip off the tongue, at least the location and origins of that particular club (founded by a group of men from the town's Holy Trinity Church in 1873) are still respected.

    There is a revealing contrast to be found on the official website of the 2016 Super Rugby (union) competition – which will be comprised of 16 state/provincial/regional teams in Australia, South Africa and New Zealand plus sides representing Argentina and Japan – which lists the fixture schedule for the first weekend (at the end of February) and the subsequent weeks.

    With one exception – the not-so imaginatively named Argentina Super Rugby – all the teams listed have generic names. Hence, the Crusaders will play the Chiefs, the Stormers will play the Bulls, the Blues will play the Highlanders, and so on. A little detective work on the site yields a couple of the geographic identifiers – the Queensland Reds and the Melbourne Rebels, for example – but these are in the minority. For most of the teams, there is little or no indication of what their home bases might be: even the Japanese side is called the Sunwolves. Whilst this locational anonymity might seem irrelevant for the southern hemisphere rugby *aficionado*, it is something of a frustration for this casual observer.

Super Rugby is a highly competitive tournament, the honours of which will be fought for furiously next season. It is also clearly successful, having expanded through phases of being Super 10 (from 1993), Super 12 (1996), Super 14 (2006) and Super 15 (2011). Far be it for me, therefore, to decry the branding and presentation of its teams. For one thing, the arrangements make it relatively easy for a major sponsor to attach its own name to a particular side. Hence, the Cheetahs are also known as the Toyota Cheetahs which, I have to admit, does prompt a recollection for me of Harvey Smith riding a horse called Sanyo Music Centre in the televised show-jumping of the early 1980s. It was only after further research – and the discovery that yet another name is the Toyota Free State Cheetahs – that I had any sense of place for this particular rugby team.

In December 2004, I visited the Hughendon ground, just off Glasgow's Great Western Road, to see the Llanelli Scarlets narrowly defeat Glasgow Rugby in a Heineken Cup match, noting in particular the impressive performances of Dwayne Peel at scrum half and Chris Wyatt in the second row. On Saturday, I watched the two sides meet at Scotstoun Stadium in the group stage of the European Rugby Champions Cup. The difference this time was that the home side was the Glasgow Warriors and the visitors were called the Scarlets.

The Llanelli Scarlets entity was created by the Welsh Rugby Union in 2003 as part of its drive towards promoting regional rugby in Wales as the means of meeting the competitive challenges presented by the wealthy clubs of England and France. The provincial/regional model had also found favour in Ireland and Scotland. The core of the initial playing and coaching staff of the Llanelli Scarlets was provided by the existing Llanelli RFC: the obvious starting point, of course, given the club's high standing in British rugby. Twelve years on, the Scarlets are one of the four Welsh sides in the Guinness Pro 12 competition, two of which – the Cardiff Blues and the Newport Gwent Dragons – retain a local identifier. The Swansea-based Ospreys have followed the Scarlets' model.

For some time, I had wondered why, following the dropping of the Llanelli name at the beginning of the 2008-09 season, there appeared to have been a distinct effort to move away from a direct association with the town in order to promote the broader Scarlets concept. After all, the Llanelli "brand" has its own rich history: three victories over Australia dating from 1908, the famous 1972 win over the All Blacks, Lewis Jones, Carwyn James, Ieuan Evans, *et al*... And it was not as if the current links were hard to find. In addition to the inheritance of the playing and coaching resources from Llanelli RFC, noted above, one of Llanelli and Wales's greatest players – Phil Bennett – is the Scarlets' president, whilst the traditional (from 1884) colour of the Llanelli club shirt is reflected in the very name.

It turns out that I have answered my own question. I am informed – by a good friend who is hugely knowledgeable on matters relating to Llanelli, Scarlets and Welsh rugby – that the team was popularly known as the Scarlets long before the professional era began and the modern branding managers were twinkles in their mothers' eyes. As he put it, the press might have reported on the Llanelli matches but the fans, even those born and bred in the town, went to watch The Scarlets. When I learned this, I thought immediately of the last line of the famous Max Boyce poem – entitled "9-3" – which was written to celebrate the win over New Zealand. The clue was there all the time – on the *'Live' at Treorchy* album that I had added to my vinyl collection over 40 years ago – "When I went down to Stradey and I saw the Scarlets play."

It is clear, therefore, that the Scarlets' designation is not the casual result of a brainstorming session in some sports marketing agency. Yes, it has a simplicity and easy identification which the brand managers will like. But it is also firmly anchored in rugby history and, crucially, explicitly recognises a traditional association between the side and its support base. (Meanwhile, of course, the original name is sustained through Llanelli RFC in the SWALEC Premiership).

On Saturday, the Glasgow Warriors won comfortably: 43-6. The visitors, missing several of their key players through injury, were second best in the set scrum, overwhelmed by the aggressive Glasgow defence when they did have the ball and, in particular, unable to cope with the rampaging runs of the Fijian-born Australian international, Taqele Naiyaravoro, who scored three tries.

But no matter. I went down to Scotstoun and I saw the Scarlets play.

www.anordinaryspectator/news-blog December 2015

Cycling/Cricket/Corruption in Sport

Seeing and Believing

> *The fact that the issue is raised [by me] at all – and that any doubt might exist about the legitimacy of the sporting action that thousands of spectators paid to see – is only one of the unpleasant after-tastes that remains, following the revealed corruption in international cricket at this time. [OS, page 287]*

I must admit that, over the years, I have had a confused attitude to professional road race cycling. I am certainly not an expert, but I have had a grudging admiration for the skill and stamina of the participants as they haul themselves up the sides of mountains or sprint through urban streets on the way to the finishing line. There is certainly a poetic beauty in the televised pictures of the progress of the *peloton* through the French countryside.

At the same time, I have not been naive enough to overlook the fact that, for many cyclists and their teams, performance-enhancing drugs have long been – or, at least, were – an essential part of the medical kit. Indeed, I am of an age to remember (vaguely) a television interview conducted with the British cyclist Tommy Simpson in the 1960s when he showed the pills he was taking and admitted that he did not know exactly what effects they had. It was Simpson's death on Mont Ventoux during the Tour de France of 1967 that prompted the cycling authorities to take some action on the use of amphetamines and other stimulants.

I have just finished *Seven Deadly Sins: My Pursuit of Lance Armstrong* (2013) by David Walsh. It's a story of cheating, intimidation and bullying by the cyclist and his entourage and of pusillanimity by most of the cycling media. It made this reader angry. Set against that are admiration for the dogged determination of Walsh and a handful of other journalists and the courage of sources who were prepared to go on the record. The Afterword – which reports on Armstrong's admission to Oprah Winfrey that he had taken banned substances or blood-doped in each of his seven Tour de France victories – is a delight, notwithstanding that some held the view that Winfrey did not pursue some lines of questioning vigorously enough.

Reading Walsh's book has led me to consider – not for the first time – whether my ambivalent attitude towards cycling is acceptable. Can I really have it both ways? Can I legitimately admire the sport and its participants for the reasons outlined above when there is a suspicion that some of those participants – even in the post-Armstrong era – might be cheating? Some participants, not all: that is the key point, I think. As the *peloton* inches up the mountainside or thunders down into the next valley, is there really a level playing field?

I take it as axiomatic that most spectators want the competitions they are viewing – in whatever sport, at whatever level – to be fair and honest. If not, what's the point? One of the saddest aspects of *Seven Deadly Sins* is the way that Walsh – a cycling and Tour de France fanatic in his youth and early adulthood – appeared to have completely fallen out of love with this sport and its premier event.

In *An Ordinary Spectator*, I report on two incidents involving South African international cricketers that, years after they occurred, set me thinking. The first was in the Headingley test match of 1994 when the captain, Hansie Cronje, missed a straight delivery and was bowled first ball by Philip DeFreitas. The second was in a group stage match of the 1999 World Cup, when Herschelle Gibbs dropped a sitter of a catch early in Steve Waugh's innings; Waugh's century was instrumental in seeing Australia to victory and keeping them in the competition, which they subsequently went on to win.

At the time, my responses to these incidents were clear and unambiguous: elation at Cronje's dismissal on DeFreitas's and England's behalf and astonishment at Gibbs's ineptitude. It was only the perspective of time that introduced the complications as we learned, later, of the captain's role in match-fixing in the 1990s and of Gibbs's suspension for his involvement in the scandal.

As far as I am aware, there has never been any suggestion that anything untoward occurred in the conduct of the 1994 Headingley test match or that particular 1999 World Cup cricket match. But, as I reported in the book, I was asking myself in retrospect: "could we believe what we were seeing?" That is a very uncomfortable question.

Of course, the history of sport is littered with contamination: the

Chicago White Sox at the 1919 World Series, the infamous "phantom" punch from the then Cassius Clay that floored Sonny Liston in 1964, the match-fixing of some Sheffield Wednesday (and England) players in the 1960s, Ben Johnson at the Seoul Olympics of 1988, the Tour de France victories of Armstrong… The list is lengthy. And growing. In *The Sunday Times*, David Walsh's investigations have moved on from Lance Armstrong and the Tour de France to the athletes of Russia, the London Olympics of 2012 and the International Association of Athletics Federations (IAAF).

Nor, it should be emphasised, is it just at the highest levels of elite sport that the cheats have been exposed. In recent days, there have been only the latest in a series of reports of match-fixing – of cricket in South Africa, India and Sri Lanka and in lawn tennis – which, in the case of the latter, include corrupt practices in relatively low-grade satellite tournaments. Unfortunately, it seems that the combination of the human weaknesses of players and coaches, the greed of betting syndicates, the reach of modern technologies and inadequate policing by the authorities will now always produce circumstances in which this type of activity can occur.

An unstated assumption underpinning the sporting competitions on which I have written was that they were indeed fair and honest. I shall continue to watch sport on that basis, though I shall also reserve the right to be sceptical if I think it appropriate. To reach the alternative conclusion – after more than half a century of sports spectating – does not really bear thinking about. If I were to do so, what indeed would have been the point?

www.anordinaryspectator/news-blog January 2016

Rugby Union

No New Kitchen

It is one of the most common pub quiz questions: which British soccer team plays at Rugby Park?

The answer is Kilmarnock FC, of course. The club has played at the venue since 1899, the name of the stadium having been inherited from a nearby ground that had hosted rugby and cricket as well as soccer during the previous 20 years.

Through a nice circularity of circumstances, I was there on Saturday to watch a rugby match: the Glasgow Warriors vs Racing 92 in the last of the group games in this year's European Rugby Champions Cup. The pitch at Scotstoun has been unplayable since the torrential rains of December and early January and, not wishing to risk another postponement, the Warriors management wisely decided to opt for the reliability of Kilmarnock's artificial surface. (A happy bi-product was that the crowd capacity was increased by over 2½ fold to Rugby Park's 18,100).

In the event, just over 9,000 turned out on a wet and chilly evening. No doubt, the attendance would have been higher had Glasgow not already lost three of their previous five group fixtures, thereby – in the absence of a highly improbable combination of results in the final matches in the other groups – falling short of qualifying for the quarter-finals. By contrast, Racing 92 had not only already won the group, but had registered enough points to guarantee a home fixture in the next round.

There appears to be a great deal of money sloshing around the elite clubs within French rugby. Racing 92 are a good example, their budget extending as far as enticing the great All Black fly-half Dan Carter to join their ranks after his successful 2015 World Cup exploits.

No doubt it was to protect their expensive investment from mishap in what for them was a dead rubber that Racing 92 took the field without the record international points scorer. Indeed, the French side included only seven of the side that had comfortably defeated Glasgow in the reverse fixture a couple of weeks earlier. Not only no Carter, but no captain Szarzewski, no Nyanga, neither of the first-choice prop forwards…

Before the game, I did wonder about this combination of circumstances: Glasgow needing a bonus-point win to sustain their chances of quarter-final qualification; the home side also keen to show its supporters that it could legitimately compete at this level; a playing surface conducive to open rugby and a high-scoring game; the visitors perhaps resting on their laurels, their team selection signalling their overall approach to this particular contest. Notwithstanding the respective positions in the group table, could this end up as a comfortable Glasgow win? At the very least, the match would be a test of Racing's strength in depth, as none of the players on the replacements bench had been in their squad for the first game.

I checked out what the experts thought. The pre-match odds from Ladbrokes offered 25 to 1 for a Warriors win by between 21-30 points and 150 to 1 for a points margin of 31-40. A successful wager of £10 on the odds for a margin of 41-50 points – had that outcome occurred – would have funded a new kitchen.

The prospect of a high-scoring match did not really come to fruition in the first half: Glasgow led 3-0 at half-time. Nor, from the outset, was there any doubt about the visitors' resolve. The opening Glasgow attack passed through no fewer than 22 phases of possession all of which Racing defended strongly and successfully. Later in the half, Racing's own dangerous attacks near the Warriors line were undermined only by the visitors' inaccuracy – a couple of forward passes and some inaccurate line-out throws – in the testing conditions. And so through to the last minute of the match, when Glasgow were looking to extend their lead to a margin of victory of some interest to those punters who had taken the odds of 25 to 1. The ferocious assault on the Racing line was again determinedly repulsed, leaving the final score at 22 points to 5.

"Could have…would have…" the gambler's lament. Mr Ladbroke always wins in the end.

www.anordinaryspectator/news-blog January 2016

Football

Allegiances

On Saturday, the early afternoon train from Milngavie to Edinburgh filled up quickly with rugby supporters on their way to Murrayfield to join the 67,000 attending the Calcutta Cup match. The seats opposite me were taken by two middle-aged ladies proudly wearing replica Scottish shirts under their open jackets. At Queen Street a large young man took a corner seat, resplendent in his full kilt and with the whole of his face painted as a saltire. "The bad news is, he's the referee," I whispered to my two unresponsive companions.

My destination was different, however. I was resuming my occasional and haphazard tour of the football grounds of western and central Scotland and I got off the train at the half-way point. I was to join the crowd – 717 in total, as it turned out – in the Jack Dalziel Stand at the Excelsior Stadium in Airdrie for the Ladbrokes League 1 clash between Airdrieonians and Cowdenbeath.

The result accorded with the respective league table positions. Airdrie won 2-0 to consolidate their 4th place – a play-off position as things currently stand – though they are some distance behind the sides above them. Cowdenbeath remain in 8th position in the 10-team league, one place above the relegation play-offs and nervously flirting with a second successive demotion.

As is so often the case, the scoreline did not quite reflect the flow of the match. After Airdrie opened the scoring after a quarter of an hour, when Marc Fitzpatrick nudged the ball home after a flick on from centre-forward Jim Lister – just about the only goalbound attempt that either side produced in the first half – the visitors enjoyed the bulk of possession for most of the remainder of the match. Unfortunately for them, their tidy efforts in midfield did not yield any clear-cut chances until the closing stages when

Airdrie's defensive line was pushed continually back into its own penalty area. The line held, however – Airdrie have a couple of resolute centre-backs and an impressive left back in the newly acquired Kieran Macdonald – and the siege was lifted in the 89th minute when Lister ran away to score a fine solo goal.

I enjoyed the afternoon. The steward outside the entrance turnstile, the man behind the counter in the club shop, the young girl serving my pre-match hot chocolate: all were friendly and polite, a couple of them also enquiring about my non-local accent. In the stand, the place a couple of seats away was taken by an elderly man who nodded to me and asked – slightly oddly, I thought – if my bag had been searched. In conversation, it was clear that my neighbour was a keen and knowledgeable supporter of Airdrie, his long allegiance considerably pre-dating the former club's slide into bankruptcy and liquidation at the turn of the century. After a while, his friend joined him and he also looked at me somewhat inquisitively. It turned out that they thought me a *Doppelgänger* for a third friend, who usually attended but was not present on this occasion. It was not clear which of us thought this situation the most bizarre, but this did not detract from their friendly welcome once they had identified that I was indeed a stranger in their midst.

On the train journey home, I had a look through the match day magazine, which included a forthright interview with the Airdrie chairman. Tom Wotherspoon took over the reins 6 months ago and already there have been appointments of a new chief executive and a new manager, a streamlining of the playing squad, and announcements about new training facilities and the resumption of the club's full-time status. The disturbing part of the interview was Wotherspoon's reference to the abuse that he and his daughter had received on social media following the Scottish League Cup tie between Airdrie and Rangers in August, when the latter had appeared as the mascot – for Rangers.

Wotherspoon stated that he had made "a schoolboy error." Perhaps he had, given that, while his long-standing support of Rangers had been well-known, his formal responsibilities now clearly exist elsewhere. But really – who are these trolls that would direct on-line abuse at a 9-year old girl?

The face-painted foot-soldier and the rugby-shirted women preparing to belt out "Flower of Scotland"; the friendly individuals at the Excelsior Stadium; the permanently embittered on social media… These various allegiances and behaviours – national, local, tribal – make Scotland a complex and intriguing and, at times, unsettling place.[16]

www.anordinaryspectator/news-blog February 2016

Rugby Union/Rugby League

Overlaps and Skills

Dad pointed to Shelton as the basic role model to illustrate the skill of taking the ball, drawing the man and giving the pass. It is one of the most fundamental of all rugby skills – in either code – and Shelton was the expert, to the considerable benefit of his winger and the team. [OS, page 10]

My father introduced me to the various skills shown by the professional rugby players at the Hunslet ground at Parkside in south Leeds in the early 1960s. As noted, one such player was the centre three-quarter, Geoff Shelton, who was the master of the timing of taking and giving a pass.

The reason this skill is so important is that, when a side in possession of the ball manages to create an overlap – 2 attackers facing 1 defender, or 3 on 2, or 4 on 2, etc – the swift transference of the ball should allow the outside man (usually a speedy winger) to have a clear run for the try-line, subject to eluding any other opponents covering behind the first line of defence. It represents an excellent try-scoring opportunity which – far more times than not – a professional rugby side should take. As noted above, this applies in both codes of the game.

Let us consider a couple of incidents from the first weekend of this year's Six Nations rugby championship earlier this month:

- Scotland vs England at Murrayfield. The 42nd minute with the score 6-7. Scotland have a 4 on 3 overlap on the left hand side of their attack only 15 yards from the England line. The first player, Mark Bennett, runs straight into an England defender. Scotland are penalised at the subsequent ruck and England clear the ball into touch. Final score: Scotland 9 England 15.

- Ireland vs Wales in Dublin. The 6th minute with the score 3-0. Wales have a 4 on 2, again on the left hand side, 35 yards from the Ireland line. The man in possession, George North, drifts slightly to the touchline forcing the next man, Taulupe Faletau, to run behind him on an inside line. North is then tackled. After several more phases, Ireland win possession and clear their lines. Final score: 16-16.

And so on to the second Saturday of the championship:

- France vs Ireland in Paris. The 11th minute with the score 0-0. From a scrum in the middle of the pitch about 30 yards from the Ireland line, France create a 4 on 3 on the left hand side. The outside-half, Jules Plisson, drifts across with the ball so far that he almost collides with the man two places away, the winger Virimi Vakatawa, who had run on a good straight line. The forward momentum thus lost, the ball is shuffled on at walking pace to Maxime Medard and then to Jonathan Danty, who drops it just as he is confronted by two Ireland defenders. Final score: 10-9.

These were not the only examples in these particular games, but they serve to illustrate a highly significant issue which, I think, has been evident for some considerable time. There is a chronic inability at the top level of rugby union – at least in the northern hemisphere – to take advantage of overlaps when in possession of the ball. As a result, there is a huge profligacy in spurning try-scoring opportunities in important matches which, as in all these cases, are usually very closely contested on the scoreboard.

Of course, scoring a try when having an overlap is dependent on executing a number of skills. It requires the ball-carriers to run straight and commit their opposite numbers to the tackle; it requires the release of the ball at exactly the right time, as well as accuracy in its transfer; it requires the supporting players to get their timing right when taking the pass; it also requires them (obviously) not to drop the ball; it requires the whole exercise to be done at full pace.

As an example of all these conditions being fully met, I refer to a try scored by the Wigan Warriors against the Leeds Rhinos at Headingley in June 2012. This might seem to be a somewhat dated reference, but such was its excellence – and, no doubt, also reflecting my fascination with the skills in question – I made a note of the details at the time. Wigan had a play-the-ball about 5 yards from the Leeds line to the left of the posts with Michael McIlorum in the dummy-half position. Outside McIlorum, Wigan had 4 attackers – Brett Finch, Sam Tompkins, George Carmont and Anthony Gelling – to 3 Leeds defenders. The ball went swiftly through each pair of Wigan hands, each Leeds defender was committed, and the extra Wigan man – Gelling – touched down in the corner.

Clearly, there are very many other successful examples of more recent vintage to which I could refer. In this case, however, what was even more impressive was that the move had begun so close to the Leeds try-line, as this had allowed the defenders to start from positions closer to the Wigan players than they otherwise would have been. Finch and his colleagues had to conduct their manoeuvre with pinpoint accuracy and at top speed. And they did. It was – unquestionably – a thing of beauty.

I should make it clear that I am not particularly seeking to make this a union versus league discussion. Whilst there might indeed be a case to be made for the generally greater proficiency in this skill in the latter code, there is evidence, of course, that the top union players can indeed take advantage of a 3 on 2 or 2 on 1, just as the league practitioners can fail to take such opportunities.

What does continually surprise me, however, is the number of occasions on which international or elite club rugby union players either seem not to recognise these opportunities when they occur or are simply unable to take advantage of them. This is even more perplexing, given the league background of so many of union's top coaches. Moreover, it is evident that union (and league) players are proficient in the creation of overlaps in the first place: the current Wales side, for example, is particularly adept at this in its "short side" attacks.

I wonder if it is something to do with modern-day coaching methods and, perhaps, the emphasis on seeking advantage through power and physicality at the expense of practising other – complementary – skills. The latter would include the development of spatial awareness in order to identify overlaps and take advantage of them.

For a clue on this, whenever I attend a top-level union game between elite clubs, I am always interested in seeing how the players warm up on the pitch in the minutes before the match. In most cases, this preparation time will include groups of 4 or 5 players running back and forth some 25 yards or so and passing the ball across the line.

I have to say that I am invariably struck by how poorly this is done. For any repeated set of such exercises, it seems almost inevitable that a high proportion of the passing sequences will be flawed, usually by a player having to reach up or back to catch the ball and thereby breaking his stride, or taking an extra pace before passing the ball or, even, dropping it. All done at a jogging pace with no opposition. It is no wonder that the necessary skills tend to be absent in the frenzy of an actual match.

The skills needed to exploit an overlap do seem to come naturally to some players – Geoff Shelton, who won 7 caps for Great Britain between 1964 and 1966, was one of them – but they can also be developed by the less technically gifted. Needless to say, for this to happen, they require countless hours of intense practice, so that the muscle-memory and thought processes are suitably honed and the necessary actions and timing become second nature. The pre-match warm-up would then be a final and brief confirmation that they are in place. At present, the evidence too often suggests that the current generation of elite rugby union players – on their six-figure salaries – are not paying them sufficient attention.

www.anordinaryspectator/news-blog February 2016

Rugby League

Two Cumbrias

At the time that my father introduced me to the sport – in the early 1960s – there were 30 teams in the Northern Rugby League. Of the grounds on which those sides played, there were – until last Sunday – 3 currently still being used that I had not visited.

I have to admit that my progress on this rather esoteric bucket list is not quite as impressive as I initially imply. Although I did visit the grounds of 2 of the 3 teams that are now long defunct (Blackpool Borough and Bramley, though not Liverpool City), there are a total of 16 other grounds that are no longer used, their former playing surfaces now the sites of various housing estates, warehousing complexes or supermarket checkouts. Of these, I visited just four, missing my chance to watch rugby at famous venues such as Thrum Hall, the Boulevard and Knowsley Road. Given that there are 8 grounds still in use at which I have seen games, that left the three on the "to do" list.

The professional rugby league club in Barrow-in-Furness – known as the Barrow Raiders since 1997 – has played at Craven Park since 1931. In his authoritative *The Grounds of Rugby League* (1991), Trevor Delaney noted the half dozen occasions between 1933 and 1951 on which Barrow's home matches attracted over 20,000 spectators, including the record figure of 21,651 for the Salford fixture on Good Friday 1938.

Those days are long behind us, of course. The Barrow's club last period of sustained success was in the 1950s, when it reached the Challenge Cup final at Wembley on three occasions, winning that trophy (and also the Lancashire Cup) in 1954-55. Craven Park's current capacity is 6,500. The attendance for Sunday's match against the Hunslet Hawks in the Kingstone Press League 1 was officially announced as 1,003.

The ground can best be described as functional with its basic facilities being…basic. However, the view of the action from the main stand is good and – in exactly the same way that I found on my visit to the soccer at Airdrieonians last month, as reported in *"Allegiances"* (8th February) – there was a uniformly friendly welcome from the various volunteers and staff (stewards, programme sellers, lottery ticket vendors) whom we met.

For my wife and I, the visit to Barrow was part of a long weekend in Cumbria – based at Grasmere – that mainly took in some of the attractions offered to the early-season tourist in the Lakelands and fells: a walk along part of the Coffin Trail towards Ambleside, Cumbrian tea bread at Rydal Mount, a stroll through the Wordsworth daffodil garden, dinner in the Red Lion, and so on. Who cannot but have their spirits raised by the view through the mist of the swans swimming in formation across Rydal Water or, early on the following morning, the sight of a squadron of Canada geese flying across the clear blue sky above St Oswald's Church?

The most direct route from Grasmere to Barrow takes one back to Ambleside and then down the winding A-road next to Coniston Water. By the time that Ulveston is reached, the Lake District National Park has been left behind and a different Cumbria entered. I learned from Wikipedia that Barrow's long industrial heritage includes the building of the *Mikasa*: the flagship of the Japanese Imperial Fleet in its emphatic victory over Russia in the war of 1905. That heritage has now extended through to the massive BAE Systems complex, in which Britain's twenty-first century submarines are built and maintained. There are not too many daffodil gardens dedicated to Romantic poets in this town.

The home supporters would have been pleased with their team's performance on Sunday, especially in the first half. Barrow were the sharper side in attack and much more aggressive in their tackling and, by half-time, had taken a 28-0 lead. The prop forwards Joe Bullock and Oliver Wilkes made the consistent hard yards as the first receivers, with the latter's off-loading skills an added feature of the side's attacking prowess. In this sport, a couple of dropped passes, compounded by a missed tackle or two, can lead to a serious deficit being faced, as Hunslet found to their cost. As I watched the visitors take their places behind the try-line waiting for another conversion attempt to be made, my attention wandered past the goalposts and the row of houses running up the hill and over to the impressive spire of St James' Church in the middle distance.

The size of the crowd might have been somewhat smaller than in the club's halcyon days, but there was no lack of passionate support for the Barrow team from those in attendance. I was also struck by the regular name-checks that the club's various sponsors were given by the stadium announcer whenever the opportunities arose. The crucial network of local connections – a necessary condition for a vibrant club – seems to be in place.

Hunslet rallied after the resumption and scored a neat try of their own at the beginning of the second half. However, Barrow resumed control and the final score of 40 points to 6 told the story of their comfortable win. Curiously, a fixture between the two sides in South Leeds only a fortnight earlier had resulted in a Hunslet victory by 46-12: exactly the same substantial margin. I will leave the experts to explain how such a turnaround could occur.

In the meantime, that's another traditional rugby league ground successfully ticked off the list. Only two more to go: the Select Security Stadium (formerly Naughton Park) in Widnes and Derwent Park in Workington.

www.anordinaryspectator/news-blog March 2016

Cycling

Cycling Nun Raises Irish Hopes for Rio Olympics

News Release
Embargoed until 00.01am on 01.04.2016

As the 2016 Olympics Games in Rio de Janeiro draw near, hopes are being raised of an unexpected potential success for Ireland in the women's cycling road race. The unlikely heroine is the 28 year-old Sister Mary O'Malley – the "Cycling Nun" – whose performance in the recent national trials has delighted the Irish team management.

Sister O'Malley is a familiar figure on the roads around the tiny west coast village of Flairpool. Sitting atop her state-of-the-art bike – designed by her famous father, Thomas – she presents a wondrous sight as she careers around the tight bends and then accelerates along the short stretches of straight road.

Sister O'Malley's only concession to modern cycling gear is her bright green helmet, worn for safety purposes. Otherwise, she retains the nun's conventional habit, her long flowing garment billowing out in the wind but, seemingly, not providing any handicap to generating high speeds over great distances. It remains to be decided, however, whether this outfit would be permitted in Rio, if she were selected for the Ireland team.

Bishop Alf O'Ploir, the Church's head of community relations in the west of Ireland, stated:

> *Sister O'Malley is an inspiration to us all. Not only is she a humble and devoted servant, she is bringing joy to all around her through the use of her extraordinary talents. I am certain that her father is especially proud, having made his own significant contribution to human understanding.*

Note for Editors
Thomas O'Malley is Professor of Mechanics and Design at the West of Ireland Institute of Practical Sciences. Last year, he won the distinguished La Rio Flop Prize for his pioneering work on the development and use of small silent motors.

Contact
www.anordinaryspectator.com

www.anordinaryspectator/news-blog 1st April 2016

Football

The View from the Milburn Stand

These are difficult times for Newcastle United FC. Prior to last Saturday's home fixture with Swansea City, they were in 19th position in the Barclays Premier League – one of the 3 relegation places – with only 6 games left to play. The side residing in the safety of 17th place (Norwich City) had 6 more points to their name in the league table, albeit having played an extra game.

It is widely stated by football scribes that relegation from the Premier League, whilst a painful and depressing outcome at any time, will be especially traumatic this year, given the additional billions that the new television deals will make available to the top tier participants from next season. For this (very) detached observer of England's elite teams, however, there is only mild indifference to this: I'm not particularly concerned about which of the top players (and their agents) will be able to add a couple of noughts to their already bloated wages.

What is of far more interest is the effect of the prospective demotion on a club like Newcastle, with its rich tradition and passionate support. The loss of esteem and status would be keenly felt. This is a club that is still located – at St James' Park: "the cathedral on the hill" – within a few minutes walk of the central railway station, not on a greenfield site next to a suburban motorway. The team's weekly fortunes have a significant impact on the local mood. The stalls of the match-day programme sellers take their places amongst the bustling Saturday lunchtime shoppers in the city centre.

This is a club with a pride in – and, perhaps, a longing for – its past.

It is the case, of course, that the tradition with which Newcastle United is associated has not been accompanied by any notable success for many years. The last majority trophy to be lifted was the Inter-Cities Fairs

Cup in 1969. Since then, there have been three losing appearances in FA Cup finals and two runners-up positions in the Premier League, none of which have been in this century.

Unlike Glasgow Celtic's European Cup-winning side of two years earlier, the Newcastle team that lifted the Fairs Cup was not composed of local lads. Indeed, of the 12 players who took part in the two-legged final, only three were from the north-east of England and only one (Frank Clark) from Tyneside. The others were from across the UK – 4 from Scotland and 2 each from Wales and Northern Ireland – supplemented by the Dane, Preben Arentoft. What did characterise the side, however, was its stability and cohesion: 8 members of the squad were each to play at least 180 times for the club, with the goalkeeper (Willie McFaul) and two full-backs (Clark and David Craig) amassing over 1,150 appearances between them. They were readily identifiable – by home and opposition supporters alike – as Newcastle United.

Reflecting the modern game, the catchment area of the present generation of Newcastle players is much wider: the 14 who played against Swansea on Saturday came from nine different countries across Europe and Africa, although 5 were English, a higher proportion than in the Fairs Cup-winning side. However, it is widely agreed that the more important difference, compared with 1969, is the players' attachment to the club. For some of the current squad, this is generally regarded as being – to put it mildly – much weaker.

I had been struck by the way this point was emphatically made in the match report by Martin Hardy following Newcastle's 1-3 home defeat by Bournemouth last month (*The Sunday Times*, 6 March 2016). Hardy is a knowledgeable and respected commentator and the report contained more than the standard description of the game's course, with its goals and bookings. In addition, there was a sad summary of the home side's technical deficiencies – "Newcastle were…poor. They could not defend and they did not look like scoring" – as well as a vitriolic condemnation of the lack of commitment: "It was an X-rated afternoon for anyone with black and white blood. There was none given for the cause by [the] players… It is a football club without a heartbeat. A team without character."

The following week, Steve McLaren was dismissed as manager. His replacement – Rafael Benitez – was brought in with 10 league matches to play as the final throw of the dice to maintain Newcastle's premier status. His first four games had yielded one point.

And so it was that, on Saturday, I took my place in the Milburn Stand at St James' Park. This was another reference to Newcastle's history, of course: its tradition for talismanic centre-forwards – Jackie Milburn (who scored goals in two of the three 1950s Cup Final victories), Malcolm Macdonald (121 goals in 228 appearances), Alan Shearer (the club's leading scorer with 206 goals) *et al.* This season's top marksmen – Georginio Wijnaldum and Aleksanar Mitrovic – have notched six goals each.

I had a good view from the stand, as I would have had from anywhere in this fine stadium. As the kick-off time approached, I watched the ground fill up – the attendance would be just under 49,000 – the mid-afternoon sunshine filtering through the transparent roof which swept around high above me and over to the Leazes Stand behind one of the goals. A blast through the loudspeakers of the Animals and "It's My Life" was followed by a spirited live on-field rendition of "Blaydon Races." I thought the crowd's response to these local anthems was somewhat muted, however; there were clearly some nerves about what might follow.

In some respects, it was a strange game. What struck me about Newcastle's approach was the lack of an upbeat tempo: there just didn't seem to be any urgency. I mentioned this to the middle-aged man sitting next to me, who responded that it had been the apparent lack of effort that had most aggravated him and his fellow supporters during the season. "A waste of a shirt," he muttered to himself, as one of the players was substituted in the second half. For their part, Swansea played a neat passing game without seeming likely to threaten the Newcastle goal. Then, a couple of minutes before half time, from a corner kick on the left hand side, Jamaal Lascelles was allowed to head the ball into the Swansea net from a distance of about two yards.

There was a period midway through the second half when Swansea were in complete control. A couple of timely substitutions sparked their attacking threat and, over the course of 10 minutes or so, led to the creation of 3 clear goal-scoring opportunities, all of which were wasted. On another day, the home side would have found itself seriously in arrears. Instead, with a few minutes left to play, from another Newcastle corner on the left-hand side, the ball fell to Moussa Sissoko, who crashed it home. (My footballing acumen detects that Swansea might have a problem defending corners). A neat finish towards the end by Andros Townsend – Newcastle's best player, in my view – gave the scoreline an emphatic 3-0 polish.

Sunderland's earlier victory at Norwich meant that it had been a very good day for Newcastle United. They were still in 19th place in the league, but the gap with Norwich had been reduced to 3 points with Newcastle still having that game in hand – against Champions League semi-finalists, Manchester City, at St James' Park tomorrow evening. The view from the Milburn Stand – or, at least, from my neighbour – was that Newcastle should put in a couple of hefty challenges in the first two minutes to test the water.

Earlier, on my way to Johann's coffee shop in the Fenwick department store – another local landmark – I stood back on the stairs to let an elderly lady walk down slowly with her stick. "I used to be able to dance down these stairs in my high heels," she told me wistfully. In our different ways, perhaps we all have a pride in – and a longing for – our past.[17]

www.anordinaryspectator/news-blog April 2016

Football

The Bully Wee

Prior to last Saturday's fixtures – the final round in the regular 36-match season – 4 sides were in the running for the 3 play-off places for promotion from the Scottish Professional Football League Two. (The 4th play-off spot would be taken by the side finishing second bottom of League One: Cowdenbeath as it turned out). East Fife had already won the division and gained automatic promotion.

For Clyde FC – in 4th place going into the last game – a win at home to Stirling Albion would guarantee a play-off place. A draw or even a defeat might still be sufficient, but that would depend on how Annan Athletic (in 5th place) performed in their match with Queen's Park. For Stirling, there was nothing at stake, other than disputing the bragging rights of 6th place with Berwick Rangers.

It could have been a tense afternoon for Clyde. In the event, it was reasonably straightforward. They took a lead through David Marsh after a quarter of an hour and the same player extended this advantage with a fine header before half time. A swift counter-attack made it 3-0 on the hour and, with Stirling having a player red-carded shortly afterwards, there was little danger of Clyde's immediate mission not being accomplished. The home supporters could even acknowledge the best goal of the game – a perfectly struck volley from outside the penalty area by one of the visitors' substitutes, Scott Burns – five minutes from time.

Clyde have been based at the Broadwood Stadium on the outskirts of Cumbernauld since 1994 – some distance from both the club's 19th Century Glaswegian origins at Barrowfield Park and the Shawfield Stadium that was the home ground for almost 90 years. The informative Wikipedia entry provides three possible explanations for the club's nickname – well-known in Scottish football circles – of "The Bully Wee," of which the one most widely accepted refers to the Victorian idiom "bully" as meaning "of a high standard." Hence, it is argued, "Bully Wee Clyde" was an early acknowledgement of a first-rate small club. Sounds plausible to me.

For a routine League Two fixture such as Saturday's, all the spectators at Broadwood are located in one of the covered stands on one side of the ground. This has the advantage of providing a sense of intimacy for a modest attendance – 704 on this occasion – but it also means that it is difficult to distance oneself from the continual swearing and coarseness of the couple of dozen or so hard core supporters at the back of the stand. Late in the game, as this group droned through another of its repetitive chants, an elderly man behind me remarked to his neighbour that even Gareth Malone would have difficulty creating anything worthwhile out of that particular choir. His friend reflected on this for some time before replying; "Who's Gareth Malone?"

Not for the first time, my attendance at a sporting event provided me with a host of indicators of the wider society in which that sport is contested. With my senior pass, I obtained a two-thirds discount on my train fare from Milngavie to Glasgow and then free bus travel for the return journey on the X3 from Buchanan Street bus station to the Craiglinn Interchange. A journey that would otherwise have cost £8-70p set me back £1-30p: a discount of 85 per cent. Such are the travel concessions that have been made in Scotland to those of retirement age, irrespective of their particular circumstances: gratefully received nonetheless.

On the return bus journey, a group of 8 or 9 boys – aged 12 or 13, I would guess – joined some young girls sitting in the front half of the upper deck. One of the boys threw an empty plastic bottle down to the front of the bus. Another made his way through a takeaway meal in a polystyrene container and casually deposited the items he didn't fancy – cucumber, onions, lettuce – on to the floor; when he had finished his meal, he dropped the retrieved bottle out of one of the upper windows as the bus turned on to the motorway. For the (several) other passengers in the latter half of the bus, there was almost audible sigh of relief when the party alighted at Muirhead. No-one said or did anything, however, other than take care where they were treading on leaving the bus later. As noted: the wider society in which we live.

I prefer to retain more pleasant recollections of the afternoon: the friendly response by the turnstile operators when I inadvertently attempted to enter the part of the ground allocated to the Stirling Albion support; the solid display in the Clyde defence by the 40 year-old Mark McLaughlin; the excitement of a couple of middle-aged supporters calculating which side would be Clyde's play-off opponents, as we waited for the Glasgow bus.

Elgin City in the answer. The first leg is at Broadwood tomorrow (Tuesday) evening. Good luck to the Bully Wee.[18]

www.anordinaryspectator/news-blog May 2016

Rugby League

Humiliation, Tactical Offside and a Wonder Goal

It is widely recognised that the decision to take the Challenge Cup final to Wembley in 1929 was one of the most far-sighted ever made by the rugby league authorities. Since then – apart from the years of the Second World War and, later, of the venue's redevelopment – the stadium has been a prized destination for successive generations of players, officials and supporters.

My first visit to Wembley was 50 years ago this month for the 1966 encounter between St Helens and Wigan. In common with other schools in Leeds, St Matthew's C of E primary school in Chapel Allerton ran a trip every season for boys in their final year. Thus it was that, on the third Saturday in May, my dad dropped me off at the city's railway station, my bag laden with sandwiches and pop, to meet up with my friends and my teacher – Mr Somes – in time to catch the early morning train to King's Cross.

As I had been captain of the school team, I was regarded by my friends as the resident expert on the game and, accordingly, I was asked on the train which side was going to win. I confidently predicted that, since Wigan had been good enough to defeat the team that my dad and I supported (Hunslet) in the previous year's final – and that the bulk of that side remained – they would retain the trophy. But what did I know? The final score was St Helens 21 Wigan 2, at the time the second biggest winning margin since the war. The credibility of the expert had disappeared long before the St Helens captain, Alex Murphy, led his team up the Wembley steps to receive the trophy from the Prime Minister, Harold Wilson.

On arriving in London, before the match, we had a coach tour of the capital. It was a cloudy, drizzly day and, as we shared the crowded bus with children from three or four other schools, the interior windows soon misted up. I remember that I actually saw very little, apart from fleeting glimpses of Buckingham Palace and the Tower of London. (The latter was not at all what I had expected, my experience of towers being limited to a couple of holiday visits to the tall structure on the Lancashire coast).

I also recall that the site in which our tour guide was most interested was Highbury Stadium, where, later the same day, Henry Cooper would challenge the then Cassius Clay for the World Heavyweight Championship. I thought that if Cooper could reproduce the left hook that had floored Clay on their previous meeting, he would take the title: another of my less successful sporting predictions, as it turned out.

I used the spending money that I had saved up in the previous weeks on match memorabilia: a programme (price: one shilling), of course, and a series of Wigan rosettes. I bought four of these altogether. I can vividly remember wearing one on my coat, as we walked into a throng of spectators near to the Twin Towers, and then coming out of the throng on the other side with it having disappeared. Another rosette was stolen from my table on the train coming home by someone walking down the aisle. I do not know what became of the third, but the fourth remains in my possession, its cherry and white ribbons now somewhat faded but still proudly identifying their team's colours.

Before the kick-off, there was the announcement of the teams to the crowd. My dad had always thought that one of the most dramatic aspects of any Challenge Cup final was the peeling off of the players, one by one, from the team line up that had been introduced to the dignitaries, as their names were announced over the stadium's loudspeakers. I agreed with him entirely and, as I watched the Wigan and St Helens players go through this ceremony, I thought how thrilling it must have been for all the players concerned. Whatever the confusion of the team battle that was to follow, this was each individual's particular moment of recognition by the watching multitude.

Years later, I read what it had actually been like on this very day. In *My Kind of Rugby: Union and League*, Ray French, who played in the second row for St Helens, recalled the moment: "'Watson, Sayer, Halsall, Warlow...' the voice boomed out with its southern accent, so foreign on the northerners' day out. 'French'. I was jolted into action and strode to our side of the pitch, impatient to get started." It was fascinating to read this passage in French's book and to recapture the excitement of this part of the pre-kick off ritual. It is a great shame, I think, that it no longer features in the match preliminaries.

We did not have much of a view of the game itself. The schoolboys were given the rows of wooden benches near a corner flag and at ground level. The lack of elevation meant that any three-dimensional perspective on the game was lost – and this to someone initiated in his rugby viewing, some years earlier, from the lofty perch of his father's shoulders at the back of the stand at Parkside. Worse still, a group of grown-ups then came along to stand right in front of us. I can remember shouting at them to move. Surprisingly enough, they ignored the squeaky voice coming from behind them and, to be honest, I was rather glad at the time that they did not seek to find out whose voice it was.

Ultimately, however, I don't think I was that concerned that I could not see much. I was attending a Challenge Cup final in this famous stadium, after all, and I was entranced by the sheer vastness of the Wembley bowl. By the time of the kick-off, the mass of spectators stretched out into the distance as far as I could see. This was by far the largest crowd I had ever been in – and, indeed, as I have reported in my memoirs of more than half a century of sports spectating, that remains the case: the official attendance was 98,536. I looked across the vast army with a combination of trepidation and excitement. The far side of the ground looked a long way away – it was a long way away – and it was difficult to take in the obvious point that the distant spectators were about to watch the same match as I was.

For those spectators that had a better view than we did, the afternoon was a disappointment – the St Helens supporters excepted, of course. Not only was the outcome very one-sided, but the general standard of play fell far short of that expected by those who had recalled the excellence of the Hunslet-Wigan encounter 12 months earlier. The headline to Harold Mather's report in the following Monday's *Guardian* summed things up: "Wigan humiliated by St Helens in a poor final."

Mather did note the areas of the Saints' superiority – "the strong running of French, the thrust of Halsall and Watson and the fine backing-up by the side as a whole" – though, even here, there was an element of faint praise: Tommy Bishop, he remarked, "controlled his feelings better than usual." For their part, however, Wigan were "dreadfully disappointing" giving "a display which…was hard to believe." Overall, Mather could not resist an analogy with the later events at Highbury: "the game…was so poor it might even have been declared 'no contest' by a boxing referee."

The most controversial aspect of the 1966 Challenge Cup final was St Helens's apparent use of what Arthur Haddock in Monday's *Yorkshire Evening Post* labelled as "tactical offside." Harold Mather noted the same point: "persistent offside tactics at play-the-balls…caused annoyance to the spectators." The reasoning, of course, was that Wigan – without their first-choice hooker, the suspended Colin Clarke – would be at a disadvantage at the scrums that followed any penalty kicks to touch. (The St Helens hooker, Bill Sayer, had been signed from Wigan just before the transfer deadline). Interestingly, Mather pointed out that Wigan did win more than a third of the scrums; moreover, on more than one occasion, the penalty kicks failed to find touch in the first place.

The St Helens tries were scored by John Mantle, Len Killeen and Tommy Bishop with Alex Murphy adding a drop goal to 5 goals from Killeen. Laurie Gilfedder kicked a first-half penalty goal for Wigan.

The match programme had presciently described "Leonard M A Killeen" as "an exceptional kicker even at long and awkward distances." This was emphatically confirmed with St Helens's second penalty goal which, in retrospect, was probably the most significant score of the match. In his Saturday match report for the *YEP*, Arthur Haddock stated that it had been taken 2 yards inside the St Helens half and 10 yards in from touch, "so to carry to the posts, the kick must have been around 70 yards."

There might have been a slightly dodgy application of Pythagoras's Theorem in this on-the-spot estimate, but Haddock was not too far out. Harold Mather reckoned it was 5 yards inside Killeen's own half, so a carry of 70 yards looks about right. "It was a beauty" said Haddock. The score might only have taken St Helens to a 4-0 lead but, I suspect, the psychological impact on their opponents would have been considerable.

And so to the train journey home. Here I must report a stroke of genius by Mr Somes, who was clearly drawing on his years of experience of this occasion and his proven methods for dealing with a group of tired and yet boisterous 11 year-old boys. Sitting in the carriage, four to a table, we were instructed to write an essay about our day out. The bulk of the return journey was passed this way. I composed three or four sides in the best handwriting that I could manage on the jolting train. In my match report, I included a reference to the Lance Todd Trophy and offered the view that, whilst I had not heard who had won it, my choice would have been Len Killeen. After reading each essay carefully, Mr Somes then announced that I had won three shillings for writing the best one. I have to say that this was a prize worth winning – the equivalent of three weeks' pocket money – so I was suitably pleased.

When I got home, the day's entry into my Lett's Schoolboy's Diary took its usual parsimonious form: "Arose at 5.30. Went to Wembley to see St Helens 21 Wigan 2. Toured London. Smashing experience. Bed 12.05." It was not exactly Samuel Pepys, but it captured my day. (And in fewer than 140 characters: Twitter users, please note).

It was many years later that I thought about the full context of the primary school trip to Wembley. This was prompted by a delightful letter I received from Harry Jepson, the President of the Leeds Rhinos, after I sent him a copy of my book. He mentioned that his first visit to the stadium had been the trip organised by the Leeds and Hunslet Schools in 1934 when, appropriately, his beloved Hunslet had defeated Widnes.

It occurred to me that, for a huge number of schoolboys from the north of England, over very many years, the Wembley trip organised for primary schools would have been an extraordinary and eye-opening adventure. As far as the rugby was concerned, it would have been their first opportunity to attend the iconic sporting occasion that is the Challenge Cup final. How many of them, as a result, were hooked on the sport and the day out and were to return to Wembley in later life with their families and friends?

Even more significantly, for many, it must have been their first visit to London and their first sight of the famous landmarks that I had glimpsed through the steamed-up coach windows. In the period before family saloons and motorways and Inter-City travel, the capital city was otherwise a very distant place for the Leeds schoolboy, whose narrow horizons might usually be extended as far as Bridlington or Filey once a year for a week's family holiday. The organisers of the Wembley trips – and the teachers who supervised them – had both courage and imagination.

I have to report the postscript to my day at Wembley, of course. The following morning, I read about the Challenge Cup final in my dad's Sunday paper. It reported that Len Killeen had won the Lance Todd Trophy. In my mind, at least, some element of expert credibility was restored.

The Rugby League Journal Summer 2016

Cricket

Bank Holiday Monday

Last Monday – 30th May, the bank holiday – I attended the second day of the Roses match in the Specsavers County Championship at Headingley.

I might only see one day of first-class cricket this year, so this was undoubtedly the one to choose. It was exactly 50 years ago to the day (Monday 30th May 1966, a bank holiday) that, at the age of 11, I saw Yorkshire play for the first time – the second day of the Roses match at Headingley.

The strong memories of that occasion are crystal clear: sitting between my father and my uncle on the packed wooden benches of the sun-drenched Western Terrace; being enthralled by the supporting cast of scorecard and newspaper sellers and ice-cream vendors; Yorkshire declaring their first innings with a sizeable lead; Freddie Trueman charging in from the Kirkstall Lane end; John Waring, a second team bowler, taking 7 Lancashire wickets; Yorkshire sending out Jimmy Binks and Don Wilson – not Geoff Boycott, to my dad's dismay – to knock off the 6 runs needed to register a 10 wicket victory.

I was absolutely captivated.

This year's play was keenly contested. Following the fall of the last Yorkshire first innings wicket shortly after the start of play, their seamers bowled with admirable discipline to take the first 7 wickets before Lancashire had reached three figures. Adil Rashid then bowled more loosely, but wrapped up the tail to give the home side a first innings lead of over 100. Yorkshire's second innings progressed to 79 for 3 by the close, based on a watchful knock by Adam Lyth. (Yorkshire went on to complete a 175 run win on the final afternoon).

I shall resist the temptation to make a series of "then and now" comparisons over half a century for the game of cricket as a whole – even this blog must have a limitation on its length. Still less shall I offer any broader philosophical reflections on the inexorable passage of time, though the occasion has undoubtedly prompted these.

Instead, I simply offer some observations on the respective Yorkshire sides of 1966 and 2016.

Perhaps the most striking characteristic of Yorkshire's 1966 XI was its test match pedigree. (This was before the advent of one-day internationals, of course). Nine of the side had played for England, although for four of them (Binks, Padgett, Taylor and Trueman), their test careers were over by that stage. Three (Boycott, Close and Illingworth) played for England in 1966 and two others (Sharpe and Wilson), whilst not playing in that year, won test caps both before and afterwards. That left John Hampshire, who was to make his test match debut in 1969, and Waring.

Of the XI who took the field this week, 5 have played test cricket – with Tim Bresnan the most experienced at 23 caps – though it is reasonable to expect that a couple of the others will also do so before their careers are over. Of course, this is not a strict like-for-like comparison, as this year's Roses match overlapped with the second test match against Sri Lanka at Chester-le-Street. However, the modern-day central contracts effectively preclude the participation of some of Yorkshire's key players in mid-season with the result that, even had England not been playing, it is doubtful that Joe Root and Jonny Bairstow (and James Anderson for Lancashire) would have been on show at Headingley.

The comparison of the test match experience of the two sides does not reflect their respective ages. The average age of the 1966 XI was 30, ranging from Waring at 23 and Boycott and Hampshire at 25 through to Close and Trueman at 35. Six of the side was aged 30 or over.

The current Yorkshire side is slightly younger in terms of average age – by just under a year – but actually has 6 players aged 31 or 32; the mean age is brought down by the youthful Jack Leaming and Alex Lees at 22 and 23, respectively. Tricky things, averages.

Notwithstanding the age range of the 1966 side, that was not yet a team in decline. Indeed, after winning the championship in 1966, the first-choice Yorkshire XI remained almost unchanged for the next two years (with Tony Nicholson as the first choice opening bowler in support of Trueman) when the title was retained on both occasions. It was 1968 that represented the high-water mark for the Club's championship success; after that came the long barren period that was to last for the rest of the century.

Unlike in 1966, the Yorkshire side of 2016 went into the May Roses match as the current county champions, following their emphatic successes in 2014 and 2015. Indeed, in last year's final table, the points difference between Yorkshire and Middlesex (in second place) was greater than that between Middlesex and the bottom-placed side (Worcestershire).

The side entered this year's Roses match in 4th position in the first division of the championship, 19 points behind the leaders. A major difference with 1966 was that those leaders were Lancashire, newly promoted from the second division, whose fine start to the season had seen them win 3 of their 5 matches. 50 years ago, there was little doubt that Lancashire were the weaker of the two sides – notwithstanding that 6 members of their team were (or were to become) test match players – and they were to finish the season equal 12th of the 17 in the championship table.

What of the composition of the respective Yorkshire sides? In 1966, there were five specialist batsmen, two all-rounders (Close and Illingworth), a wicketkeeper (Binks) and three specialist bowlers. This gave a 5-man bowling attack with Brian Close operating as the first-change third seamer. In the event, 17 of Lancashire's wickets in the match fell to Trueman (7) and Waring (10) with Close, Wilson and Illingworth picking up only two between them in their combined 60 overs. (The other wicket was a run out).

The designation of players is rather more difficult these days, as there are generally far fewer genuine tail-enders in county cricket. However, if I (perhaps harshly) judge Liam Plunkett, Steve Patterson and Jack Brooks to be the specialist bowlers, the Yorkshire line-up is not too dissimilar to that of 50 years ago with 5 specialist batsmen, a wicketkeeper (Andrew Hodd) and two all-rounders. (It was the century sixth-wicket partnership between the last of these – Rashid and Bresnan – on the first day of this year's match that was instrumental in Yorkshire reaching a total in excess of 300. Between them, the pair also took 8 of Lancashire's second innings wickets). If I ignore Adam Lyth's capabilities as an occasional off-break bowler, the main difference between the two sides is the replacement of the second spinner by the fourth seamer – but that takes us into cricket's general shifts over the last half century, which I have promised to put to one side.

The style of management of the Yorkshire team has changed radically, of course. In 1966, although the Club was notionally governed by a General Committee of almost 30, the main figures off the field were Brian Sellers as Chairman of the Cricket Committee and Arthur Mitchell, the county coach: two formidable individuals.

I have no inside track on the current Yorkshire changing room, but I sense that Martyn Moxon and Jason Gillespie have a more modern approach to man-management, although some of the decisions they have made in the last couple of years – omitting players for certain matches, for example – reveal that an element of discipline has been retained.

As for the management of the game on the field, Andrew Gale is in his seventh season of captaincy and has the two championship successes as notches on his belt; between them, Lyth, Rashid and Bresnan have made over 420 appearances in first-class cricket; Ryan Sidebottom (absent from the Roses match) is in his 20th season. In the current team, therefore, there is no shortage of the type of knowledge that can only be generated through experience. However, in terms of sheer cricketing nous, it is difficult to believe that any side through the years – of any county – had the collective wisdom that the triumvirate of Close, Illingworth and Trueman brought to the Yorkshire team of the mid-1960s.

I leave the most obvious comparison until last. In 1966, Yorkshire fielded 11 players born within the county; the corresponding figure this year was seven.

I think that it is this final statistic that captures the overall change in the Yorkshire team that I am seeking to identify. It is a different Yorkshire, but not radically so. Most importantly, it is still one to which I can relate – though with the regional pride of an exiled 60-something, rather than the 11 year-old's enthralled captivation.

On Monday, I watched some of the day's closing overs from a vantage point near to the edge of the Western Terrace. The shadows were lengthening in the early evening sunshine. I reminded myself again of the anniversary. And I thought of absent friends.

www.anordinaryspectator/news-blog June 2016

Cricket

Six and Out

Rather belatedly, I have recently come across an article by Mike Selvey in *The Guardian* of 23rd June: "Rein in the size of cricket big bats and allow the best to be the best." It covers an issue which has been around for some time, not least in Selvey's columns, and which I think is of some significance in the current development of the sport.

Selvey reports, with some enthusiasm, that the International Cricket Council's cricket committee will recommend to the cricket committee of the MCC (which has responsibility for the Laws of Cricket) that there should be new legislation to rein in the influence of the modern bat. His argument is that technological advances in bat production – particularly with respect to the thickness of the edges and the depth of the "spine"- have had a disproportionate (and damaging) effect on the way that cricket is played.

In Selvey's view, the "massive expansion in the 'sweet spot' hitting area of the bat (research estimates this to have increased from 3 inches vertical to 8 inches)" now means that "moderate and even mediocre batsmen are able to hit sixes with shots that would otherwise have brought about their dismissal." In addition, many more top-edged shots that would previously have fallen short of the boundary are now clearing the ropes for six. "Mis-hits should bring wickets not reward."

I have to say that I have some sympathy with Selvey's argument. I think that it is a flaw in the modern game that a bowler can entice a batsman into a woefully false shot – say, a top edge or a lofted strike that does not come out of the (proper) meat of the bat – that, instead of landing in the field of play, still manages to carry the boundary. In Selvey's words: "This is just wrong."

However, although the article prompted a healthy and informed on-line response that was broadly supportive – with no fewer than 265 comments before the discussion was closed – it is clear that matters are far from straightforward.

Perhaps the first thing to note is that virtually all sports are continually subject to some form of technological progress which, in most cases, it is unrealistic to expect to be disinvented. Formula 1 motor cars, golf clubs, tennis rackets, racing bicycles, swimming costumes…there is no shortage of examples of designers seeking to (legitimately) exploit a new idea for the benefit of their sporting clients. The key point is that, where such innovations have been made within the framework of that sport's existing regulations, it is a relatively short step to the designer's legal argument of "restraint of trade," if the authorities were to decide that the changes should not be permitted. Golf clubs and tennis rackets provide case studies here.

There is little doubt that the incidence of six-hitting has increased in the modern game of cricket, even within the Twenty-20 format. In a slightly nerdish – and, admittedly, far from scientific – exercise, I looked at the scorecards of Yorkshire's Headingley-based fixtures in this competition in 2005 and 2006. The 8 matches produced a total of 2455 runs by Yorkshire and their opponents combined, of which 15 per cent were the result of sixes. By contrast, in 2015 and 2016 (to date), in which 10 matches have produced 2952 runs, the proportion of runs scored in six-hits has risen to 22 per cent.

At first sight, this finding seemed to be consistent with my gut feeling that, compared with a decade ago, much more of the modern batting style in Twenty-20 cricket – even on grounds that are as big as Headingley – comprises a "stand and deliver" philosophy that results in either a big hit or, if unsuccessful, a scrambled single or dot-ball. In this perspective, some of the traditional subtleties of batting – for example, the quick single or the careful placement and swift running that allows a single to be transformed into a two – are being squeezed out of the game completely.

However, the data from my statistical exercise suggest that this is not quite the case. In 2005 and 2006, the proportion of the runs in Yorkshire's Headingley Twenty-20 games that came from ones, two and threes was 39.1 per cent. In 2015 and 2016, it was actually marginally higher: 39.9 per cent. The increased propensity for six-hitting has been at the relative expense of striking fours: these accounted for 41 per cent of the runs in 2005/2006, but only 33 per cent in 2015/2016. (The remainder of the runs in both periods – 5 per cent – were extras).

Of course – unless you are the bowler's mother – the striking of a six is usually a notable incident in any cricket match. I have referred elsewhere specifically to the blows struck by Don Wilson for Yorkshire in the Gillette Cup semi-final at Scarborough in 1969 and by Viv Richards for Somerset in a John Player Sunday League match at Park Avenue, Bradford, in 1975:

each massive and majestic and firmly retained in the memory. And some six-hits undoubtedly have significance in cricket folklore: Mike Selvey reminded us that it is well over a century since Albert Trott struck a ball over the pavilion at Lord's. But, as we watch the ball land in the stands for the nth time in an innings, the laws of diminishing returns must set in.

I do recognise that it is not only cricket bat technology that is at work here. The athletic frames of modern batsmen are much more likely than in previous times to feature the powerful upper arms and shoulders produced by serious weight-training. It is also clear that many more batsmen these days have the positive intent – or necessity – to score their runs quickly, not only in Twenty-20 matches, but in other forms of the game.

And, not least, there is the question of where the boundary ropes are actually laid. How often do we see the full playing area not being used, but the boundaries set several yards in from the fence? This provides the clear indication of what the preferences of the cricket authorities are. They recognise that the majority of the modern support base like to see a "maximum" – to use the awful description favoured by the authorities' cheerleaders in the media – being struck. (No matter that it might come off the top edge of the bat and land on the opposite side of the ground to which the shot was being played). For those one-day competitions that involve the direct sponsorship of six-hits, the alliance between the commercial interests and those charged with maintaining the game's integrity is presented in even starker relief.

The sensible placing of the boundary rope is one – relatively minor – contribution towards redressing the imbalance between bat and ball that concerns Mike Selvey and others. For many grounds, it would be irrelevant, of course, and it obviously does nothing to deal with the thorny issue of bat technology. For the reasons summarised, this will be a far harder battle to win.

One final thought. Last Friday, when Lancashire were (unsuccessfully) chasing a target of 142 to beat Yorkshire in the Twenty-20 match at Headingley, 6 sixes were struck, three of which were by Liam Livingstone off successive deliveries. However, eight of the Lancashire batsmen were caught on the boundary or in the outfield. At least two of those blows would have gone for six had they not been caught. The Yorkshire catching was outstanding and the first catch – by Adam Lyth – was stunningly brilliant. It occurred to me that had the carrot of the "maximum" not been present – albeit made easier than in years gone by for technological and other reasons – we might not have seen this thrilling demonstration of one of the other fundamental cricketing skills.

I did say that matters were not straightforward.

www.anordinaryspectator/news-blog July 2016

Golf/Homelessness

Income Levels

One of the responses I received to my previous blog – on the impact of technological developments on cricket bat design (*"Six and Out,"* 4th July 2016) – was from Neil Clitheroe, whom I met at the Glasgow Film Theatre last autumn after he had arranged the showing of a documentary film about the threats posed to test match cricket (*"Death of a Gentleman,"* 8th November 2015).

Neil mentioned that he had recently walked part of the golf course at Troon that was to be used for this year's Open Championship, which concluded yesterday. He had been concerned that some of the traditional par 4 holes would have their standing undermined by the much greater distances that professional golfers are now able to generate from the tee – again due to technological progress, this time in club design.

Last Friday, I attended the second day of the Open. During the afternoon, I spent some time at the top of the spectator stand behind the tee on the 8th hole – the famous Postage Stamp. The green of the 7th hole – 401 yards, par 4 – was below me to my right. In quick succession, we saw the tee shots of Bubba Watson and Rory McIlroy emerge from the far distance, land on the fairway and roll up to within 10 yards of the edge of the green. As forecast, I thought.

Of course, there are actions that the tournament organisers can take to swing the odds back in the course's favour. One concerns the positioning of the pins. At the first hole, I watched 7 groups of 3 (and one pair) for the first hour and a half after I arrived (beginning with the group including Ernie Els and the first round leader, Phil Mickelson). There were one or two close shaves – Dustin Johnson managed to miss from about two feet – but no-one registered a birdie, due principally to the positioning of the hole near the front edge close to two deep bunkers.

The other key factor is the weather, of course. During the period I was at the 8th, a strong wind was blowing across from the firth – left to right – making judgement of the tee shot particularly difficult, albeit on a hole that was only 123 yards in length. A succession of caddies arrived at the tee and checked the conditions by throwing loose bits of grass into the air before offering final pieces of advice. A succession of their employers then proceeded to watch their balls drift off the right hand side of the green down the slope and into the bunker.

One of these was Watson. McIlroy avoided this fate; he pulled his shot into the "coffin" bunker on the left. Both players then extricated themselves, in turn, by playing exquisite bunker shots – Watson to within six inches of the flag – and then putting safely to secure their pars. There might be power in their play – as we had seen at the previous hole – but there is also skill and finesse and, not least, the ability to keep a cool head when it is most needed.

Earlier, I had spent another 90 minutes standing at the edge of 15th green, which was in an attractive hollow and also guarded by some testing bunkers. Throughout this period, there was a torrential downpour. The play continued, however – the benefit of being on a links course with its natural drainage – and I watched a succession of previous (and, as it happened, American) Open champions trudge soggily through: Todd Hamilton, Mark Calcaveccia, Ben Curtis, John Daly. And Justin Leonard, who won on this course in 1997. Their best days have gone, though: none of them made the half-way cut.

One of my favourite locations on the Troon course is the distant 11th hole – The Railway – which is a 482 yard par 4 with a blind tee shot over thick gorse, more gorse on the left of the fairway and an "out of bounds" marked by a low stone wall on the right, on the other side of which is the railway line from Troon to Ayr. Most of the time, the hole is thinly populated by spectators and it is a good spot in which to find some personal space to watch the passing parade.

I asked one of the marshals where the best place to stand might be. He recommended the other side of the fairway, where there would be a good view of the second shots to the green. "But be careful," he warned, "A lot of them are landing over there." Sure enough, to the sound of "fore right" from the man with the red flags standing on top of a nearby lookout tower and the sight of the spectators bracing themselves in cowering anticipation of painful bombardment, Bubba Watson's drive landed squarely on the railway line and headed off in the direction of the town centre. It is amazing how high a golf ball can bounce when it lands on a railway sleeper.

The following day – Saturday – I spent an hour or so in George

Square, Glasgow: as the crow flies, about 30 miles from Troon. It was the last day of Homeless World Cup – an annual event which was first held in Graz in Austria in 2003. I caught the second half of Wales versus Zimbabwe and – as pure chance would have it, as I turned up without knowing the schedule – Scotland versus England.

The week-long tournament took place across three artificial pitches – each the length of a tennis court and about twice as wide – in the most prominent public space in Glasgow. 48 men's and 15 women's teams represented their countries in their respective competitions with over 400 matches being played. Each game lasted 14 minutes with 4 players per side on the pitch at any one time, including the goalkeeper, though rolling substitutions were allowed. Around each pitch, there were banks of temporary stands and so, for Scotland-England, there was a crowd of several hundred.

It will take some time, I think, before the full implications of the juxtaposition of these two sporting events – viewed on successive days – fully sink in with me.

It is an obvious – and fairly trite – starting point to compare the (literal) fortunes of the respective participants. The ten golfers I have name-checked above have, according to sources accessed on Wikipedia, combined career earnings from tournaments of approximately $375 million – ie even before income from sponsorship and endorsements. The players at the Homeless World Cup had a catalogue of experiences which included substance abuse, gambling and alcohol addiction, mental health problems and street-gang violence as well as homelessness. The case studies recorded in the official tournament programme provided some sobering reading.

However, I was struck by how much the two events had in common. Not least, for the spectator, they were both very well organised. At Troon, there was a continually operating bus service from the railway station to the course and back; the signage on the course was very clear; the electronic scoreboards were excellent; and the refreshment and restroom facilities were plentiful. In George Square, the volunteer guides gave a friendly welcome and, most impressively I thought, the MC introducing the Scotland-England game gave a short introductory request for spectators "whatever their usual feelings" to refrain from booing the England team or their play. His plea was met with a warm round of applause. I made a point of going up to say well done after the match had finished. "No worries," he replied as we shook hands.

I am tempted to say that, in the Homeless World Cup, the results didn't matter: it was the occasion and what it meant for the players (motivation, self-esteem, recognition) that was more important. I am sure that is right, but I couldn't help but notice the joy shown by the Wales players and their entourage on winning their match, which gave them the Shield (for winning the group of teams ranked 25th to 31st in the tournament). Likewise, Scotland's win over England (by 6 goals to 4 for the record) meant that they finished 21st overall (and their opponents 22nd), but was greeted with a similar enthusiasm.

And for the spectator? At Troon, I had a great day, notwithstanding the weather, as I always do when watching elite sporting performers at the top of their profession. The masters of the previous generations – Bobby Moore, Gareth Edwards, Sachin Tendulkar *et al* – have been duly followed by the likes of Mickelson and McIlroy.

That part is easy. At Troon, I knew beforehand that I would have a great day. When approaching George Square, I had been worried. Would it not just be patronising to watch the homeless play football? Will their temporary place in the sun simply be followed by a return to the shadows of the street? In the event, I was won over by the players' commitment and pride and by the Glasgow crowd's sympathetic identification, not only with their own national representatives but with all the teams in Wales's Shield group – from Hong Kong to Norway and others – as they lined up to collect their commemorative medals. This is a hard city, but also a compassionate one.

In my writing on sports spectating, I make repeated references to my (unoriginal) view that sport generally tends to reflect the broader world around it. Henrik Stenson's Open Championship success yesterday was the result of thousands of hours of practice and dedication to his craft coupled with the consummate skill and ice-cool nerve that he demonstrated at Troon. His rewards will be high – quite apart from the £1.175 million prize money – due to the economics of globalisation, given the vast reach of his sport and its commercial and media "partners."

Meanwhile, the weekend's sporting itinerary also reminded us that many of the most significant political issues of current times – the distance between the haves and have-nots, the problems of the marginalised and downtrodden, the opportunities for mobility and progression, the remoteness of the ruling elites – are relatively easy to articulate, but very difficult to address. If the hosting of the Homeless World Cup in Scotland encourages us to try harder, that will be something.

www.anordinaryspectator/news-blog July 2016

Rugby League

Eights

And so to the Big Fellas Stadium (or Post Office Road, as we traditionalists still prefer to call it) for last Saturday afternoon's opening encounter in the First Utility Qualifiers – or "Middle Eights" – between Featherstone Rovers and Leeds Rhinos.

The nomenclature indicates that the 2016 professional rugby league season has now entered its second phase. The arrangements are slightly complicated, so bear with me.

The top 8 teams in the Super League are playing each other – in the "Super Eights" – to determine which four sides will contest the competition's semi-finals. Meanwhile, the bottom 4 are competing with the top 4 in the next division – the Kingstone Press Championship – to decide which four sides will remain in (or enter) next year's Super League: this is the Middle Eights competition. The other 8 sides in the Championship play each other to decide which two teams will fall into the third division, which is confusingly called League 1.

League 1 has its own Super Eights competition, as the leading 8 teams are also meeting each other again. After that round of matches, the two sides finishing at the top of the pile will play each other (yet) again to decide on the automatic promotion into the Championship; the loser of that game will have another chance for advancement by playing off for the second promotion spot with the sides finishing between the third and fifth places. (With the exception of the Middle Eights competition – which starts from scratch – the clubs carry forward the points accrued in the season to date in their respective league tables).

I think there are both pros and cons with these arrangements, which are only in their second year of implementation. On the downside, they make the spectator's advance planning of matches in this part of the season rather difficult. It was not until 12 days ago that the specific dates for the Middle Eights fixtures were known: something of a frustration for the casual visitor – travelling from, say, Glasgow to Yorkshire, to give a hypothetical example – looking to arrange his spectating itinerary.

On the plus side, the new schedule is designed to ensure that interest in the season is maintained by teams that, under other circumstances, might have achieved a mid-table comfort (with nothing else to play for) with several fixtures still to play. In the event, this did not happen in this year's Super League, where the 4 teams destined for the Middle Eights (Leeds Rhinos, Salford Red Devils, Hull KR and Huddersfield Giants) were known some time before the end of the first phase of the season and those placed just above them (Widnes Vikings, Castleford Tigers and Wakefield Trinity Wildcats) knew likewise that they were safe from the threat of relegation.

The main positive feature of the system is that it honours the concept of promotion and relegation. In my view, this is essential to the integrity of a competitive league structure (though I do appreciate that other highly successful sporting competitions – notably the National Rugby League in Australia and the National Football League in the USA – seem to cope perfectly well without it).

However, I do wonder if the promotion/relegation net is being cast too widely. Theoretically, prior to the Middle Eights and League 1 top 8 play-offs getting underway, it would have been possible for Leeds, who finished 9th in the Super League, to be relegated to next year's Championship, where they could have met London Skolars, hypothetically promoted after finishing 8th in the first phase of this year's League 1. Very highly unlikely, it must be said – but not impossible. The gap between these two sides was no less than 23 places in the rugby league hierarchy: a huge range, given that there are only 39 teams across the three divisions.

Undoubtedly, the most striking feature of this year's Super Eight/Middle Eight split is the presence of the Leeds Rhinos in the latter group. This is the club that achieved a treble success in 2015 – Challenge Cup, League Leaders Shield and Super League – but which has had a wretched season this time round, mitigated only marginally by victories over two of Super League's top three clubs (Hull FC and Wigan) after its Middle Eights fate was sealed.

The rugby league historians have had a field-day. The last time that Leeds competed outside the top tier of British rugby league was in the 1902-03 season, when they finished second (to Keighley) in the Second Division. This was three years before teams were reduced to 13-a-side and four years before the introduction of the play-the-ball rule. The competition in the same division that season included teams from Millom, South Shields and Morecambe.

A second historical throw-back for the match at Post Office Road – albeit one that was generally less remarked upon – was that it was scheduled to kick off at 3.00pm on a Saturday afternoon. This was the norm for most rugby league games in the early 1960s – when I was cutting my spectating teeth – before the advent of Sunday afternoon sport or the (much more recent) phasing of evening kick-offs over the long weekend. It brought back memories of being driven home from Hunslet's matches at Parkside in my dad's little green van to have my tea and watch William Hartnell in the latest instalment of *Doctor Who*.

In general, it is to be expected that the greater resources – in some cases, far greater resources – of the existing Super League clubs will mean that they will prevail in the qualifying competition for next year's Super League. But the Championship sides' places in the Middle Eights sun have been hard-won – this year by the Leigh Centurions, London Broncos and Batley Bulldogs as well as Featherstone – and none were to be taken lightly, notwithstanding that the last two of these squads comprised part-time professionals who also held down "day" jobs during the week.[19]

This was reflected in Saturday's game. Featherstone found it difficult to deal with the speed and power of the Leeds attacks, particularly down the latter's right hand side, where the skilful distribution of Danny McGuire and the swift intrusions from full-back of Liam Sutcliffe repeatedly created the openings from which Kallum Watkins could profit. Although a breakaway try reduced Featherstone's deficit to 4 points at one stage, a crucial score just before half-time took the visitors to an 18-6 interval lead. Thereafter, Leeds were in complete control, even playing up the slope, the final tally being 62-6 with Watkins registering 4 tries and the impressive Sutcliffe 26 points with two tries and nine goals.

However, despite the result, the Featherstone club enjoyed a good day in the warm sunshine. The attendance of over 6,600 was the largest for a home fixture since the introduction of summer rugby league in 1996; the supporting entertainment ranged through the generations, including an excellent local male-voice choir (for many of whom the rendition of "When I'm Sixty-Four" might well have required the good Doctor's time-travelling skills) as well as half-time mini-rugby matches that reached down as far as the Under 7s; and the home team was given rousing support throughout the match by their loyal supporters. (I also noticed that since my only previous visit to the ground four years ago – reported in *"No Trains to Featherstone,"* 5th September 2012 – there had been the addition of two new covered stands).

On the evening before the Featherstone-Leeds encounter, I was at the South Leeds Stadium for the League 1 Super Eight match between the Hunslet Hawks and Doncaster. The home side had had a good recent run – 8 wins in 10 matches, including the first two of the top 8 fixtures – and, as a result, had a reasonable expectation that they could squeeze into at least fifth place in the final standings and secure a promotion play-off spot. Those hopes received a setback, however, as a strong first half performance took Doncaster into a 24-6 interval lead that the visitors had consolidated to 36-24 by the close of play.

The attendance at the South Leeds Stadium was announced to have been 501. I met another of them the following day when, changing trains at Wakefield Kirkgate on my way from Leeds to Featherstone, I had a brief chat with the driver as he was loading up what he described as the "Leeds Rhinos Express" (albeit comprising exactly two carriages). He happened to mention that he had been at the Hunslet-Doncaster match and we duly compared notes. I think he appreciated my line about how – were the results in the Middle Eights and League 1 top 8 matches to go certain ways – Leeds and Hunslet could be playing in the same division next season.

Again, it's still not impossible. After all, this time last year, what were the odds on Leicester City winning the Barclays Premier League title? However, on this occasion – given the balance of probabilities – I will probably resist the temptation to test the market with Mr Ladbroke.

www.anordinaryspectator/news-blog August 2016

Rugby League

Mr Jepson

I have referred previously (*"It makes me realise what I had without knowing it,"* 24th October 2013) to the kind response I received from Harry Jepson, the President of the Leeds Rhinos rugby league club, after I had sent him a copy of *An Ordinary Spectator*. He wrote to me on first receiving the book and then again having read it with some very complimentary comments and some fascinating reminiscences of his lengthy attachment to – and love for – the sport of rugby league.

In later correspondence (September 2013), he mentioned that that year's Challenge Cup Final had been the first he had not attended since 1946. However, he was looking forward to the 2014 reunion of the Hunslet club's ex-Parkside players, at which the 80th anniversary of the 1934 Challenge Cup success would be celebrated. Later still, in October 2014, I introduced myself to him when we met at the opening of the "Hunslet Rugby League Remembered" Heritage Room at The Garden Gate public house in south Leeds and we had a nice conversation (*"The Garden Gate,"* 27th October 2014).

Harry Jepson died last month at the age of 96. There have been many fine obituaries and tributes, including on the Leeds Rhinos website and by Phil Caplan, editor of *Forty-20* magazine, in the *Yorkshire Post*. After Second World War service in North Africa and Italy, he trained as a teacher before taking up the secretarial responsibilities at Hunslet and then moving to Leeds in the early 1970s. The obituaries refer, amongst other things, to his role in the development of Colts rugby, his involvement with French rugby league and his role as chairman of the Rugby League Council at the time of the foundation of Super League in 1995.

On Thursday, I caught the short tribute on Premier Sports' *Backchat* programme, in which Garry Schofield, the ex- Hull, Leeds and Great Britain international – and former pupil – referred repeatedly and respectfully to "Mr Jepson." Phil Caplan noted the remarkable fact that Harry Jepson had been personally acquainted with some of the club officials who had been responsible for the establishment of the Northern Rugby Union in 1895.

I can date exactly the previous occasion on which I met Harry Jepson: Tuesday 29th March 1966. It was the last week of the school term at Chapel Allerton Primary School in Leeds and we were playing two rugby league matches against Rodley County Primary School. Two matches: a fixture backlog meant that the two halves of the scheduled game were deemed to count as separate fixtures. My recollection is that our teacher, Mr Somes, refereed one match and Mr Jepson refereed the other. The day's parsimonious entry in my "Letts Schoolboys Diary" records that Chapel Allerton won both games and that I scored a try in the second match.

At that time, in addition to fulfilling his teaching duties, Harry Jepson was also the Secretary/Manager of Hunslet RLFC. The previous evening, Hunslet had begun a run of 4 successive games in 12 days at their home ground of Parkside (which was to culminate, the following week, in a 7-6 victory over Leeds). At the end of the second Chapel Allerton/Rodley match, I nervously approached Mr Jepson to inform him that my dad and I were Hunslet supporters. He said that we should look him up and say hello the next time we were at Parkside. In the event, to my later regret, my shyness got the better of me and I did not take up the offer.

Not immediately anyway. I did eventually catch up with him – at The Garden Gate nearly 50 years later – to thank him for taking the trouble to write to me about the book. I'm glad I did.

Harry Jepson OBE, 1920-2016. RIP.

www.anordinaryspectator/news-blog September 2016

Football

Blue Ribbons and a Talented Sportsman

In its usual upbeat fashion, the "It wasn't all bad" feature of the 19th December 2015 edition of *The Week* reported on a positive story, following the devastation wreaked by Storm Desmond across northern Britain earlier that month: "three koi carp were reunited with their owner after being spotted swimming in the goalmouth of Carlisle United's flooded football pitch."

Good news for the koi carp and their owner, no doubt. However, I'm not sure that the recovery of these fish would have constituted much in the way of compensation for the many households and businesses in Carlisle who were dealing with the aftermath of Desmond, which left large tracts of the town – including the Brunton Park ground – under several feet of water.

Reflecting the response to the floods across Cumbria as a whole – stoical, determined and, no doubt, (justifiably) embittered – the football club rolled up its sleeves and set about getting back to normal: removing the tons of silt and debris from all parts of the ground, re-establishing its office and other facilities and completely replacing the turf on the pitch. On the playing side, "home" fixtures in December and the New Year were switched to Blackburn, Blackpool and Preston. The normal home programme was resumed with a fixture against York City at the end of January. The following week, the team's good FA Cup run, which had seen them reach the fourth round, was rewarded with a visit from Everton and a capacity attendance of over 17,000.

I had intended to attend a Carlisle United match last season by way of offering some (very modest) support to their recovery process. In the event, circumstances prevented that, but, last Saturday, I did go to their home Sky Bet League 2 fixture with Hartlepool United.

It was a good one to choose. For one thing, in a division in which 14 of the other 22 clubs are situated below the Severn-Wash line, this match – whilst, I would have thought, not exactly a local derby – constituted something unequivocally northern. (This season, the die-hard travelling supporters of Carlisle and Hartlepool are faced with expeditions to places as distant as Yeovil, Newport and Exeter). In addition, the home side entered the game having made an excellent start to the season: unbeaten after 12 league fixtures (albeit with 7 draws) and standing third in the table. Hartlepool had made a more solid start, sitting in mid-table, though also with 7 draws (plus 3 wins and 2 defeats) from their opening games.

The sense of history is not hard to find in Carlisle. After my lunchtime scone in Café Zest on the second floor of the House of Fraser store in the city centre, I set off on my walk to the ground past an elegant three-storey building noted as "The Site of Highmore House." On the left hand side of the façade was inscribed "Here Prince Charles Edward Stuart had his quarters 1745" and on the right "Here the Duke of Cumberland had his quarters 1746." For anyone who might not have known, the difference in dates provided a clear indication of the outcome of an earlier northern battle, held in the latter year at Culloden. The building now houses Marks and Spencer.

As I walked down Warwick Road, I passed a phalanx of about 200 Hartlepool supporters making their slow and halting progress towards the ground, cordoned off by a considerable police presence. Indeed, "considerable" would probably be an understatement and "significant" more appropriate: officers, cars, vans, dogs. The visitors were escorted past a reception committee of their home-town counterparts at the main entrance to the ground and on to their designated section in one of the stands where, it was later announced over the tannoy, they would be held for ten minutes at the end of the game "in the interests of health and safety."

Warwick Road was badly affected in last December's floods. I struck up a conversation with a young steward, mentioning – hopefully without wishing to appear a disaster-tourist – that I was trying to get a sense of what had been experienced. He patiently pointed out to me the blue ribbons that were tied on various items – drainpipes, door frames – on the front of some of the nearby houses at the height that the water level had reached. They were slightly above the top of my head. His older colleague chipped in: "We had floods in 2005. They said then it was something that happened once in a thousand years." His tone reflected a combination of bitterness and resignation.

On the way to my seat in the Pioneer Foods Stand, I walked through the Chris Balderstone Bar. Of course – I remembered – Chris Balderstone: one of those talented all-round sportsmen who, before the overlap of the seasons, played two sports at a professional level: cricket in the summer and football in the winter. I looked up his details later: he played in 68 first-class cricket matches for Yorkshire without being capped, but found success at Leicestershire and played test cricket for England against the West Indies in 1976. His football career included 117 matches for Huddersfield Town and, in the ten years to 1975, 376 games for Carlisle United, where he is obviously remembered with some affection. He died in 2000 at the age of 59.

It was a really entertaining game played in the bright sunshine of a crisp autumnal afternoon. Carlisle took the lead after 20 minutes – slightly against the run of play, I thought – when a brilliant cross from Shaun Miller was forcefully met by the centre-forward Jabo Ibehre. Miller then turned villain. After missing a chance to extend the lead by blazing over the bar from about ten yards, he was booked for kicking the ball away after being caught offside and then, early in the second half, he collected a second yellow card (and an automatic red) for deliberately handling the ball when lying on the ground. Hartlepool sensed their chance and an equalising goal duly came. At this point, with about 25 minutes to go, I would have been tempted to place a small wager on the visitors going on to win the match.

A superb strike by captain Danny Grainger restored Carlisle's lead, but Hartlepool, prompted by the influential Josh Laurent in midfield, fought back to level again. Even when Michael Raynes took Carlisle into the lead for a third time with a powerful header from a Grainger corner, the visitors did not give up. But Carlisle held on for the 3-2 win and another notch on their unbeaten opening run. The 7,000-plus crowd – easily Carlisle's largest home attendance of the season – roared them home: "United, United."

In the meantime, whilst this enthralling match was unfolding in front of us, a separate confrontation was taking place throughout the game further along the stand to my right. At the far end were the Hartlepool contingent – white, male, mainly aged between about 16 and 35, though with some older (though possibly not wiser) heads; in front of them and to their left, a hard core of their Carlisle *Doppelgänger*; between them, a platoon of hi-vis jacket-attired peacekeepers; and, across the divide, a continual stream of obscenity and invective.

At one point, our attention from the football was diverted by what appeared to be a potentially serious scuffle. A number of people in front of me – mainly not of my generation, it has to be said – stood up to record the action on their phones. The more significant recording was being made, quite openly, by a young police officer on his camera, I noticed. "Don't look. It only encourages them," shouted a woman sitting a few places behind me.

Later, passing the time before my train, I sat on a bench across the road from the entrance to the railway station to read the match programme.

The Carlisle United chairman's introduction referred to their visitors having "made the journey across from the North East to compete in what for all of us is called a local derby." So that was me corrected.

The extensive police convoy – cars, vans, dogs *et al* – appeared at the top of The Crescent escorting their cargo down to the Newcastle train and out of the city. An elderly man nodded to me sagely: "How much is this costing? I'd lock every f***** one of them up." (I assumed that he meant the fans, not the police). I asked one of the officers whether it was like this for every match; he carefully explained that Carlisle was the only major football team in Cumbria and that the Hartlepool supporters had bought 800 tickets for the game. (There were far fewer than that in the escort party, I thought; most of them must have travelled – peaceably – by car or coach). Another casual observer – one of the local station employees – mentioned that the Carlisle fans had previously caused damage in Hartlepool. And so it goes on.

Sport as a reflection of the society around it: the well-worn them of *An Ordinary Spectator* and these subsequent blogs. In this case, though, I wonder if it's quite as straightforward as that. During the course of the afternoon, it had seemed as if I had been an observer of two separate worlds: in one, several thousand people were engrossed in watching two well-matched football teams; in the other, there was a ritual of hot air and posturing and latent aggression involving two competing (but effectively identical) small tribes. These worlds had been occupying the same space, but – notwithstanding the overall footballing context that they had obviously shared – I'm not sure there was anything much in the way of a connection.

I had left Brunton Park with nice memories, however. As I departed through the Chris Balderstone Bar, by then closed, the tannoy blasted out some Bob Marley: "Don't worry about a thing. 'Cos every little thing's gonna be alright." For Carlisle United, as matters currently stand – third in the table with just over a quarter of the league season now completed – things are indeed all right.

www.anordinaryspectator/news-blog October 2016

Rugby League

Elite Sportsmen at the Top of Their Game

> *The game was one of unremitting ferocity, notwithstanding the stern discipline imposed by the referee, Eric Clay from Leeds, who sent off two Australians and the British prop, Cliff Watson. I remember sitting in the stand and being awed – and, it has to be said, somewhat frightened – by the violence of grown men. [OS, page 25]*

It is appropriate – for three reasons, I think – that the last in this series of post-*An Ordinary Spectator* blogs should be on last Sunday's England-Australia rugby league international in the Four Nations Tournament at the London Stadium.

First, the event. It was a rugby league match between Great Britain and Australia – at Headingley in November 1963 – that was the first international sporting contest I attended. As noted above, it was a violent affair, which left a deep impression on the 9 year-old boy.

Second, the venue. An early entry in this collection of blogs – "*Olympic Games Football: What Do I Know?*" (August 2012) – recognised Glasgow's contribution to the 2012 Olympics by reporting on two of the matches in the football tournament played at Hampden Park. This blog completes an Olympic circle by ending the collection at the main venue of that successful Games.

[An aside. It is under some sufferance that I refer to the venue as the London Stadium. For me, it remains the Olympic Stadium, which, let us not forget, was funded by taxpayers across the UK, not just in the capital. However, it does now seem to have been fully colonised by its football tenants – West Ham United FC – as evident in the external signage, the Bobby Moore and Sir Trevor Brooking Stands, the listing of club honours on the balcony and the use of claret and blue colours throughout the stadium].

But, back to the rugby. This year's Four Nations Tournament has been contested by New Zealand and Scotland, as well as Sunday's combatants, the England/Australia match being the last in the round-robin stage. Following the earlier matches – which, crucially, included England's one point defeat by New Zealand – the hosts had to avoid defeat (ie to win or draw) in order to qualify for next Sunday's final in Liverpool.

England were still in the game at half-time, trailing by only 6-10, having earlier taken the lead through a well-worked try by Jermaine McGillvary on the right wing. However, Australia were too good after the break, when a lethal combination of power, skill and precision produced 18 points in one 12 minute spell. Three of their five second half tries could be attributed to the strength and technique of individual players close to the England line. England scored a couple of good tries of their own through Gareth Widdop and Ryan Hall, but succumbed to the continual pressure exerted by their superior opponents. The final score of 36-18 properly reflected the contest.

It had been over 20 years since I had seen the Australian rugby league team in the flesh: a test match with Great Britain at Elland Road in 1994. Throughout this period – as also for the 20 years before that – they have generally been the sport's dominant international team, albeit with some occasional dents in their crown from New Zealand. In the second half on Sunday, the game having been effectively decided, I was able to sit back and admire the excellence of the team – its accuracy, cohesion and relentlessness – and the individual players within it.

And so to the third reason for this being an appropriate juncture at which to draw this collection of blogs to an end. At various times in the last five years – as during the half-century before that captured in the book – I have been reminded of the pleasure in watching elite sportsmen at the top of their game. Throughout this long period, I consider myself fortunate that, even when the side I had been supporting – whether Yorkshire CCC or the European Ryder Cup team or the England rugby union side – have been second best, I have been able to recognise the brilliance of their opponents: Alvin Kallicharran and Jack Nicklaus and Gareth Edwards *et al*.

In terms of the rugby league players of Australia, this acknowledgement of excellence stretches back to seeing the great Reg Gasnier in that turbulent match at Headingley in 1963. It extends through Bobby Fulton in 1973 and Mal Meninga in 1982 and Brad Fittler in 1994 with others in between. And, in the present generation – on Sunday – it has now been extended to Johnathan Thurston and Greg Inglis and Cameron Smith: each now probably in the latter stages of his international career, but amongst the best to have ever played the game.

For the presentation of a series of sports blogs, that's not a bad place to stop. If only temporarily.[20]

www.anordinaryspectator/news-blog November 2016

Notes

An Echo at Rangers
1. The Rangers FC plc was liquidated at the end of the 2011-12 season. With a new corporate identity, the club entered the fourth tier of Scottish football. After three promotions in four years, Rangers returned to the top tier in 2016-17.

"It Makes Me Realise…"
2. The feedback on *An Ordinary Spectator* has continued since the publication of this blog, of course, much of it of considerable detail and length. Some of it has been from Leeds-based readers of the book, who recalled the memories of their own youth in and around the city: buying sports kit from the Arthur Clues or Sutcliffe's sports shops; collecting the autographs of Fred Trueman and Gary Sobers on the same day at Headingley; seeing Bev Risman land a touchline conversation in a howling gale at Odsal Stadium in Bradford…

    Other respondents have drawn on their recollections of watching sport in other locations: mid-week (Monday) football matches in Wrexham; standing on the terraces at Roker Park, Sunderland; watching the Tour de France pass through a French village… More generally – and poignantly – there have been additional reminiscences of father/son relationships, some of which have moved on to the next generation of grandfathers and grandsons.

    I have been struck, also, by the perceptive reflections that people have made with regard to their own sports spectating and its associated activities. Robert Broughton – a fellow graduate of Trinity College, Cambridge – referred to his own habit of hoarding the sports books and memorabilia that had come into his possession over the years. He drew my attention to the research done by Desmond Morris on the hunter-gatherers of primaeval times and suggested that the present-day fascination for collecting is the modern equivalent.

"Rough Play on Both Sides"
3. In the next edition of the *Rugby League Journal* (Spring 2014), it was stated that Malcolm Dixon, the former Featherstone Rovers captain and a reserve for Great Britain that day, had pointed out that it was Barry Muir, the Australian scrum-half, who threw a bucket of water into the crowd. (As noted, Muir had been sent off during the match).

Into The Valley
4. Charlton Athletic retained their Championship status at the end of the 2013-14 season. However, after climbing to 12th in 2014-15, the club was relegated to League 1 at the end of 2015-16.

Television Lines

5   This blog was included in a "Blog Hop" arranged by SilverWood Books and, as a result, generated the largest number of comments of all the *An Ordinary Spectator* blogs included in this volume. The feedback ranged from discussion of the great darts commentator Sid Waddell's comparison of the drama of his sport to that found in Shakespeare through to Sweden's equivalent of "They think it's all over...," which occurred with their success in the 1962 World Ice Hockey Championship.

   Some of the comments emphasised the compassion shown by a couple of the commentators at the moments of sporting drama and loss – notably those concerning Don Fox and Doug Sanders, as described by Eddie Waring and Henry Longhurst, respectively. I thought that this was a perceptive insight and, in one case, responded as follows: "The humanity of some of the commentators reflects their particular ability to reach beyond the chaos and ephemera of the immediate sporting action to our common experience of life's highs and lows."

A Polish Masterclass and "Our Club"

6   Bayern Munich won the 2013-14 *DFB-Pokal* Final 2-0 after extra time.

"Hard But Fair From Gun to Tape"

7   Westport GAA remained in Division 1B of the Mayo Senior Football League in 2015 and 2016. Hollymount/Carramore were promoted to Division 1A at the end of the 2014 season.

Casual Conversations of a Sports Tourist

8   Adam Lyth made his test match debut for England against New Zealand at Lord's in May 2015. By the end of 2016, he had played in 7 tests and scored one century.

Return to Scotstoun

9   Things did indeed look a little different in the spring. Notwithstanding their poor performance in the opening game at Scotstoun, Bath Rugby went on to win the group. They were beaten in the European Rugby Champions Cup quarter-final by Leinster.

Ruhleben

10 I received some interesting feedback to the references to the Ruhleben camp – in both *An Ordinary Spectator* and this subsequent blog – from people whose grandfathers or great grandfathers had also been interned there. The individual stories were both interesting and poignant. One respondent described how his great grandfather had been building a woollen mill in Germany in 1914 and, like Alfred Niblett, had not got out of the country in time; the historical artefact that had been handed down

(equivalent to my camp magazines) was an inscribed pipe. Another reported sadly that his grandfather had never really recovered from illness contracted in the camp and had died a few years after his release.

A Stramash in Paisley

11 Ryan Christie was transferred from Inverness Caledonia Thistle to Celtic for £500,000 in August 2015. He went on loan to Aberdeen in January 2017.

Stade Toulousain

12 As noted above, the qualifying group was won by Bath. Toulouse finished second but, despite winning their first four games, did not register sufficient points to qualify for the quarter-finals as one of the best-placed group runners-up. Glasgow Warriors finished third in the group.

Internazionale

13 Inter Milan won the second leg 1-0 a week later. In the next round, they were defeated 2-5 on aggregate by FC Wolfsburg.

The Clan and the Capitals

14 The Sheffield Steelers won the 2014-15 Elite Ice Hockey League by one point from the Braehead Clan; the Edinburgh Capitals finished ninth. The end-of-season play-offs, involving the top eight teams, were won by the Coventry Blaze (from sixth place).

The Spectacular and Thrilling "Boy Hero"

15 Roger Millward died in May 2016 at the age of 68. A blog I wrote in tribute to him at that time – not reproduced here – took the form of a lengthy extract from this article.

Allegiances

16 Airdrieonians finished fifth in the 2015-16 Ladbrokes League 1, one place out of the play-offs. Cowdenbeath finished ninth and were relegated after their play-off match with Queen's Park.

The View from the Milburn Stand

17 Newcastle United finished 18th in the 2015-16 Premier League and were relegated along with Norwich City and Aston Villa. Sunderland finished 17th.

The Bully Wee

18 Clyde beat Elgin City 5-1 on the semi-final play-off over two legs. However, they lost 2-3 on aggregate to Queen's Park in the final.

Eights

19 At the end of the 2016 Middle Eights competition, Leigh Centurions were promoted to the Super League at the expense of Hull KR.

Elite Sportsmen at the Top of Their Game

20 Australia defeated New Zealand in the 2016 Four Nations final by 34 points to 8.

Acknowledgements

In the acknowledgements of *An Ordinary Spectator: 50 Years of Watching Sport*, I noted that sports spectating is a communal activity and that my thanks were due to all those – administrators, officials, players and coaches, as well as fellow spectators – with whom I had shared the sporting events described in that book. The same sentiments must be expressed here in *Still An Ordinary Spectator: Five More Years of Watching Sport*. The opportunity to attend the events, large or small, covered in this volume has been dependent on the efforts of many other people.

The team at SilverWood Books has produced the book with great professionalism. Helen Hart has again consistently provided positive and constructive guidance. Annie Broomfield has overseen the publication with considerable care and skill and has been a diligent and reassuring point of contact. The SilverWood design team has produced a book cover that perfectly complements that used for *An Ordinary Spectator*.

Several acknowledgements are due in relation to the photographs used in this book. I am grateful to Harry Edgar, editor and publisher of the *Rugby League Journal*, and Mike Berry, editor and publisher of *Backpass* and *Backspin*, who very kindly gave their permissions to reproduce the covers of their magazines. The photograph of the author at the Stadion an der Alten Försterei in Berlin was taken by Llyr James. All the other photographs at sports stadiums were taken by or on behalf of the author and, in reproducing images of their various sporting institutions, I am grateful for the permissions given by Barrow RLFC, the Olympiastadion Berlin, Leeds Rhinos RLFC, Newcastle United FC and Yorkshire County Cricket Club. My thanks are again due to Trevor Graham of Trevor Graham Photography in Milngavie for his assistance in the overall presentation of the photographs.

All reasonable efforts have been made to contact copyright owners. If anyone feels that their copyright has been breached, I should be very happy to address that in any future reprint.

Finally, to Angela, Tom and Katherine, who have, at various times, provided valued feedback on the drafts of many of the blogs and articles that appear in this book, my grateful thanks. (Any errors that remain are entirely my responsibility.) More generally, they have continued to indulge me in my various interests and passions and (very occasional) rants. To them, I give my love.

John Rigg
Glasgow
May 2017

Bibliography

Books and Booklets

Sport

HG Bissinger, *Friday Night Lights*, Da Capo Press, 25th Anniversary Edition, 2015.
Mike Brearley, *The Art of Captaincy*, Hodder and Stoughton, 1985.
Tony Collins, *Rugby's Great Split: Class, Culture and the Origins and Rugby League Football*, Frank Cass Publishers, 1998.
Ken Dalby, *Headingley Test Cricket*, 1899-1975, Olicana Books Limited, 1976.
Harry Edgar, *Chocolate, Blue and Gold: 50 Years of Whitehaven Rugby League Football Club*, Edgar Publishing, 1998.
Ray French, *My Kind of Rugby: Union and League*, Faber and Faber Limited, 1979.
Gilbert Gaul, *Billion Dollar Ball: A Journey Through the Big-Money Culture of College Football*, Penguin Random House, 2015.
John Marshall, *Headingley*, Pelham Books, 1970.
John Rigg, *An Ordinary Spectator: 50 Years of Watching Sport*, SilverWood Books, 2012.
Saltaire Cricket Club 1869-1969, Courier Printers, 1969.
David Walsh, *Seven Deadly Sins: My Pursuit of Lance Armstrong*, Simon & Schuster, 2013.
Wisden Cricketers' Almanack, John Wisden & Co Ltd, 100th edition, 1963.
Windsors Rugby League Annual, 1962-63, compiled and edited by Ken J Adams, Windsors (Sporting Investments Ltd publisher, 1962.
Yorkshire County Cricket Club, *Annual Report*, The Yorkdale Press Ltd, 1976.

Other

Harold Fullard ed., *Philips' Modern School Atlas*, 65th edition, George Philip & Son Limited, 1967.
Clive James, *Unreliable Memoirs*, Picador, 1980.
Jonathan Meades, *Museums Without Walls*, Unbound, 2012.
Matthew Stibbe, *British civilian internees in Germany: the Ruhleben camp, 1914-1918*, Manchester University Press, 2008.

DVD

1962 and 1963 Ashes Tests. Rugby League, Open Rugby.

Film

Death of a Gentleman, (Directors: Sam Collins, Jarrod Kimber, Johnny Blank), Dartmouth Films/Two Chucks/Wellington Films, 2015.
The Private Life of Sherlock Holmes, (Director: Billy Wilder), Metro-Goldwyn-Mayer Studios Inc. & Phalanx productions, 1970.

Magazines

Sport
Backpass; Backspin; Rugby League News (Australia); Rugby Leaguer; The Rugby League Journal; Voice of the Valley (Charlton Athletic fanzine).

Other
Ruhleben Camp Magazine, Christmas 1916 and June 1917.

Newspapers (various editions)

Austin-American-Statesman; The Economist; Evening Standard; The Guardian; Mayo News; New Statesman; Sunday Herald (Scotland); The Sunday Times; The Times; USA Today; Yorkshire Post; Yorkshire Evening Post.

Radio

Test Match Special, BBC.

Records and Tapes

John Arlott: The Voice of Cricket, BBC Radio Collection, BBC Enterprises Ltd, 1990.
Max Boyce: 'Live' at Treorchy, EMI Records Ltd, 1974.

Websites

www.anordinaryspectator.com – John Rigg's website for *An Ordinary Spectator: 50 Years of Watching Sport*.

www.stats.cricketworld.com – Historical cricket statistics and scorecards.
http://ruhleben.tripod.com – Chris Paton's website on the First World War internment camp.

Index

Abbey, Ray   114
Aberdeen FC   267
Aberfan Disaster Fund   68
Agnew, Jonathan   106-7
Airdrieonians FC   218-9, 225, 267
Airds Moss, Battle of (1680)   47
Alamo Stadium, San Antonio   199-201, 205
Alamodome, San Antonio   136, 203-6
Albion Rovers FC   72
Allen, Dave   169
Alston, Blair   165
Alston, Rex   104-5
American Football   xiv, 76, 199-206
Anderson, James   242
Ansell, Danny   169
Ardrossan Academicals RFC   9
Arentoft, Preben   230
Arlott, John   81-3, 104-6
Armstrong, Neil   26
Armstrong, Lance   213-5
Arsenal FC   109, 164-5, 196-8, 203, 208
Ashes, The
    cricket   104, 116-7, 185, 188-9
    rugby league   54-8, 192, 263
Ashfield Stadium, Glasgow   181
Ashton, Eric   55, 144
Ashwin, Ravichandran   107
Askey, Arthur   70
Aston Villa FC   164, 267
Atherton, Michael   171
Atomic Kitten   28
Auchinleck (town)   46-7
Auchinleck Talbot FC   46-7, 88

Austin, Texas   205
Austin American-Statesman   206
Australia
    cricket   16-9, 34, 52, 81-3, 116-7, 173, 185, 190, 209, 214
    rugby league   xiii, 54-8, 169, 192, 262-3, 268

Backpass magazine   xii, 141
Backspin magazine   xi-xii, 141
Bairstow, Jonny   242
Ballance, Gary   36
Balderstone, Chris   259-60
Bangladesh (cricket)   17, 19
Bankfoot CC   177, 179
Bapty, John   56
Barnes, Simon   xiii
Barnes, Sydney   178
Barnes, Wayne   126
Barnett, Richie   8
Barrow/Barrow Raiders RLFC   xi, 40, 62, 168, 224-6
Bartram, Sam   60
Bath Rugby   111-2, 266-7
Batley Bulldogs   254
Bayern Munich – see FC Bayern München
Beechwood Park, Auchinleck   46
Belarus (football)   5
Belfrage, Anna   150
Belle Vue, Wakefield   145, 148
Benitez, Rafael   230
Bennett, Alan   37
Bennett, Mark   112, 220

273

Bennett, Phil   211
Berlin Cricket Club   79
Berliner FC Dynamo   80
Berrington, Richie   42
Berwick Bandits (speedway)   181
Best, Tino   90
Bet Butler Stadium, Dumbarton   22
Bevan, Brian   xii, 25-6, 51
Biabi, Botti   165
Big Fellas Stadium, Featherstone – see Post Office Road
Binks, Jimmy   11, 241-3
Bird, Dickie   93
Birmingham Bears – see Warwickshire CCC
Bishop, Tommy   238-9
Bissinger, HG   199, 201
Blackpool Borough RLFC   xii, 25-6, 51, 70
Blackpool Tower Company   70
Blakeney (racehorse)   77
Blank, Johnny   207
Bloomer, Steve   119-20
Board of Control for Cricket in India (BCCI)   208
Bogenschutz, Blake   204
Bolton, Dave   55-6, 58
Booth, Major   194
Borussia Dortmund   78, 80, 89
Botham, Ian   116-7
Bouhaddi, Sarah   6
Bow, Clara   191
Bowes, Stephen   167
Boyce, Max   212
Boycott, Geoff   11, 13, 14 48, 83, 104-6, 116-7, 173, 190, 241-2
Bradford and Bingley CC   178
Bradford Northern/Bradford Bulls RLFC   29, 192
Bradman, Don   13, 52-3, 81, 173
Braehead Clan (ice hockey)   150-2,
176, 181, 267
Brearley, Mike   xiii, 34, 90
Bresnan, Tim   242-4
Briers, Lee   56
Bristol Rugby   62
British Premier League (speedway)   181
Broadwood Stadium, Cumbernauld   233-5
Brooking, Sir Trevor   262
Brooks, Jack   243
Broomfield, Nick   208
Broughton, Robert   265
Brown, Freddie   104, 106
Brown, Gordon   64
Brunton Park, Carlisle   258, 261
Bryan, Lamont   44
Bryson, Craig   60
Buckley, Alan   55
Gordon Bulloch   9-10, 64
Bullock, Joe   225
Bundesliga   78-80, 89
Burgess, Sam   111
Burnett, Calvin   42
Burnett, JR   194
Burns, Scott   233
Bussaglia, Elise   6

Caddick, Andrew   53
Calcaveccia, Mark   249
Camden CC, Cambridge   180
Caplan, Phil   256-7
Cardiff Arms Park   49
Cardiff Devils (ice hockey)   150, 152
Cardiff RUFC   49
Cardigan Fields, Leeds   86
Carlisle (city)   258-9
Carlisle United FC   258-61
Carmichael, Sandy   64
Carmont, George   222
Carter, Andrew   48, 186
Carter, Dan   216

Castleford/Castleford Tigers RLFC   8, 55, 90-92, 101, 112, 128, 146, 190-2, 253
Catalan Dragons RLFC   8
Celtic FC   1, 22, 133-5, 156, 267
Chandos Park, Leeds   86
Channel 4
Chapel Allerton Primary School, Leeds   236, 257
Chappell, Ian   185
Chapple, Glen   41
Charlton Athletic FC   59-61, 88, 265
Chicago Bears   76
Christie, Ryan   122, 267
Clark, Frank   230
Clarke, Colin   238
Clarke, Giles   208-9
Clarke, Sylvester   48
Clarkson, Jeremy   30-32, 167
Clay, Cassius   237
Clay, Eric   56, 262
Clitheroe, Neil   207, 209, 248
Close, Brian   11, 242-4
Clough, Brian   59
Clyde FC   xi, 233-5, 267
Clydesdale Cricket Club   41
Coetzer, Gert, 146
Collier, Frank   55
Collins, Sam   207-8
Collins, Tony   xvi
Commonwealth Games (2014)   98-103, 161
Comrie, Craig   72
Connacht   84
Cook, Alastair (cricketer)   19, 52
Cooke, Alistair (broadcaster)   25
Cooper, Henry   146, 237
Corruption in sport   213-5
County Mayo   84
Coventry Blaze (ice hockey)   267
Cowan, Ed   207-9

Cowdenbeath FC   218, 233, 267
Cozier, Tony   74
Craig, David   230
Craven Park, Barrow   136, 224
Cricket
  bats   xii, 245-7
  County Championship   xv, 35-37, 90, 93, 172-3, 193-4, 196, 241
  future of Test Matches   16-21, 52, 159, 207-9
  on the radio   81-3, 104-7
  Twenty-20   90-1, 157-8, 171-2, 207-9, 246-7
  World Cup   157, 214
Cricket Australia   208
Croft, Steven   42
Cronje, Hansie   214
Crown Flatt, Dewsbury   174
Culloden, Battle of   259
Curtis, Ben   249
Cycling   213-5

Dalby, Ken   186
Daly, John   249
Danty, Jonathan   221
Darrell K Royal-Texas Memorial Stadium, Austin   205
Davies, Ben   152
Davies, DHT   146
Davies, Russell   76
Davies, Steven   36
Davis, George   185-7
Davison, Emily   187
Deedes, WF   xiii
DeFeitas, Philip   214
Delaney, Trevor   224
Derby County FC   59-60, 89
De Villiers, AB   157
Dewsbury/Dewsbury Rams RLFC   174-6
Dixon, Colin   70

275

Dixon, Malcolm   265
Dodd, Ken   70
D'Oliveira, Basil   105
Doncaster RLFC   255
Doussain, Jean-Marc   126
Drake, Ted   198
Drama
   in sport   102, 189, 193
   nano-dramas   xiii, 1, 13-5, 116-7, 189-92
Dravid, Rahul   53
Driver, Jeff   177, 179
Dumbarton (town)   23
Dumbarton FC   22-4
Dumfries Saints RFC   64-5
Dundee United FC   1-2
Dusautoir, Thierry   125
Duvall, Denise   150
Dynamo Berlin FC – see Berliner FC Dynamo
Dyson, John   116

East Fife FC   233
Eastmond, Kyle   112
Economist, The   205
Edgar, Harry   49, 167-9
Edgbaston cricket ground   49, 172
Edinburgh (rugby union)   124
Edinburgh Capitals (ice hockey)   150-2, 267
Edinburgh University Hockey Club   161-3
Edmonds, Phil   185
Edward VIII   96
Edwards, Derek   190
Edwards, Gareth   49, 77, 251, 263
Egypt (football)   5-6
Elgin City FC   235, 267
Elite Ice Hockey League (EIHL)   150, 152, 267
Elland Road Greyhound Stadium   49

Elland Road Stadium   57, 59, 263
Elliott, Maddison   99
Els, Ernie   248
Emirates Stadium   139, 196, 203
Enberg, Dick   76
England
   cricket   13-4, 16-9, 52-3, 104-6, 116-7, 185, 260, 266
   rugby league   262-3
   rugby union   86, 154-5, 220
England and Wales Cricket Board (ECB)   208
European Rugby Champions Cup   111-2, 126, 211, 216
European Union   71, 73
Eurovision Song Contest   27, 29
Evans, Ieuan   211
Evans, Laurie   91
Evans, Stephen   79
Evening Standard   60
Excelsoir Stadium, Airdrie   218-9
Eyre, Ken   146, 191

FA Cup   164
Facchetti, Giacinto   135
Faletau, Taulupe   221
Falkirk FC   22, 164
Farrell, Andy   xiii
Farrow, George   164-5
Fathers 4 Justice   187
FC Bayern München   78, 80, 89, 266
FC Internazionale Milano   133-5, 267
FC Union Berlin   78-80, 89, 96
FC Wolfsburg   267
Featherstone Rovers RLFC   7-8, 44, 55, 69, 128, 252, 254
Ferguson, Sir Alex   37, 122
Fédération Internationale de Football Association (FIFA)   165
Finch, Aaron   91
Finch, Brett   222

Finn, Liam   7, 44
Finn, Steven   93
Firmani, Eddie   59
Fittler, Brad   263
Fitzpatrick, Marc   218
Fletcher, Duncan   19
Foley, John   187
Ford, Mike   111-2
Forsyth, Bruce   70
Forthbank Stadium, Stirling   71-3
Forty-20 magazine   256
Four Nations Tournament (rugby league)   262-3, 268
Fox, Don   55, 57-8, 75, 148-9, 266
Fox, Neil   144-5
Foyles Bookshop, Bristol   62-4
Fragapane, Claudia   103
France (rugby union)   154, 221
France (women's football)   5-6
Freeman, Johnny   70
French, Ray   237-8
Friedrich, Caspar David   xiv
Frisby, Sons and Whipple Ltd of Leeds   67
Fulton, Bobby   263

Gabbitas, Brian   146
Gaelic Football   84-7
Gale, Andrew   36, 91, 243
Ganguly, Sourav   53
The Garden Gate, Hunslet   113-5, 256-7
Gasnier, Reg   57, 263
Gateshead Thunder RLFC   108-9
Gaul, Gilbert   205
Gavaskar, Sunil   107
Gelling, Anthony   222
George, Charlie   196
Gibbs, Herschelle   90, 214
Gibson, Alan   104-6
Giles, Ashley   53
Gilfedder, Laurie   239

Gillespie, Jason   243
Glasgow (city)   xiv, 98-101, 250-1
Glasgow Film Theatre   207, 248
Glasgow Tigers (speedway)   181-4
Glasgow Rugby/Warriors   xiii, 111-2, 124-6, 211-2, 216-7, 267
Goddard, Tom   177
Goldthorpe, Albert   114
Golf   75, 142, 248-51
Gonzales, General   200
Gooch, Graeme   117
Gordon, Craig   134
Gowers, Ken   56
Grainger, Danny   260
Grange Hockey Club   161-3
Grant, Peter   165
Grasmere   xiv, 225
Gray, Jonny   126
Great Britain (rugby league)   xiii, 54-8, 192, 223, 262-3
Greenidge, Gordon   33
Griffiths, John   145, 147
Groves, Perry   196-8
Guardian, The   55-6, 148, 238, 245
Guidetti, John   134
Gunney, Geoff   49, 67, 90-1, 114, 145-6, 149, 191
Gymnastics   101-3, 142

Haddock, Arthur   191, 238-9
Hadley, Tony   28
Haigh, Gideon   53, 208
Haigh, Schofield   178, 194
Halifax Dukes (speedway)   95
Halifax RLFC   90, 95-7, 174-5
Hall, Ryan   263
Hambly, Brian   56
Hamilton, Jim   65
Hamilton, Todd   249
Hampden Park   5, 164-5, 262
Hampshire CCC   194

277

Hampshire, John   194, 242
Hanley, Ellery   70
Hardaker, Zac   92
Hardisty, Alan   190
Hardy, Martin   230
Harinordoquy, Imanol   125
Harley, Robert   126
Hartlepool United FC   258-61
Hartley, Dennis   58, 146
Haughey, Tommy   44-5
Hawksworth, Dave   33-4
Haynes, Desmond   33
Haywood, Matt   152
Headingley (Carnegie) Cricket Ground
   general   xiv, 13-4, 35-7, 52-3, 81-2, 90-1, 93, 105, 116-7, 138-9, 171-2, 185, 190, 193, 214, 241, 246-7
   Western Terrace   33-4, 50, 172, 241, 244
Headingley (Carnegie) Stadium (rugby league)   xiii, 54, 56-7, 128, 138, 145-6, 192, 262
Headingley RUFC   49, 63, 86
Hear'Say   28
Hegazi, Ahmed   5-6
Heineken Cup   124-5, 211
Henderson, Carlos   204
Henson, Gavin   112
Herrera, Helenio   135
Hertha BSC   78, 89
Hiadlovsky, Tomas   151
Higgs, Ken   41, 91
Highbury Stadium   128, 237-8
Hignell, Alastair   62
Hilton, Malcolm   173
Hirst, George Herbert   194
Hobbs, Sir Jack   178
Hockey (field)   161-3
Hockey (ice) – see Ice Hockey
Hodd, Andrew   172, 243

Hodgson, Roy   135
Hogg, Stuart   153
Holden, Keith   55, 58
Holding, Michael   17, 74
Hollymount/Carramore (GAA)   84-6, 266
Homeless World Cup (2016)   xiv, 250-1
Horan, Neil   187
Horse Racing   77
Hough, Vic (uncle)   3, 11, 56, 128-9
Huddart, Dick   58
Huddersfield Town FC   260
Huddersfield/Huddersfield Giants RLFC   50, 144, 253
Hudson, Robert   104-6
Hull FC   112, 253
Hull Kingston Rovers RLFC   40, 60, 145, 192, 253, 268
Hunslet/Hunslet Hawks RLFC
   general   35, 38-39, 50, 54, 176, 220, 254, 256-7
   history   113-5
   matches   25-6, 30, 40, 44-5, 49, 51, 62, 91, 108-10, 128-9, 144-9, 167-9, 190-2, 224-6, 238, 255, 257
Hurst, Sir Geoff   75
Hutcheson, Ellie   162
Hutton, Sir Leonard   14-5, 81-2

Ibehre, Jabo   260
Ibrox Stadium   xiii, xv, 1-2, 133
Ice Hockey   142, 150-2, 266
Illingworth, Ray   3, 12, 242-4
Imperial Crown Hotel, Halifax   96
India (cricket)   16-19, 105-7
Indian Premier League (IPL)   16
Inglis, Greg   263
Inter Milan – see FC Internazionale Milano

Inter-City Fairs Cup   229-30
International Association of Athletics Federations (IAAF)   215
International Cricket Council (ICC)   208, 245
Inverness Caledonian Thistle FC   121-2, 130-3, 164, 169, 267
Ireland (rugby union)   153-5, 221

Jackman, Robin   48
James, CLR   xiii
James, Alex   198
James, Carwyn   211
James, Clive   57
James, Llyr   xiv, 76, 79
Jarvis, Peter   114-5
Jauzion, Yannick   124
Jayasuriya, Sanath   157
Jefferson Mustangs (high school American Football)   199-201
Jenkins, Roy   186
Jepson, Harry   50, 114, 240, 256-7
John, Barry   49
Johnson, Dustin   248
Johnston, Ben   95
Johnston, Brian   106
Johnstone, Jack   47
Jolie, Angelina   31, 167
Jones, Berwyn   146
Jones, Lewis   211
Jorgensen, Thomas   182
Joubert, Craig   65
Juventus FC   22

Kain, Andy   7, 44, 169
Kallicharran, Alvin   263
Karalius, Vince   55
Karmakar, Dipa   102
Katrina and the Waves   29
Keatings, Daniel   102
Keedy, Gary   194

Keighley/Keighley Cougars RLFC   7-8, 44, 253
Killeen, Len   239-40
"Killing Times," The   xiv, 47
Kilmarnock FC   216
Kilner, Roy   194
Kimber, Jarrod   207-8
King, Collis   17
Kirby, Kathy   70
Knott, Alan   185
Kobiashvili, Levan   79
Kohlmann, Patrick   80

Ladbrokes Coral Group plc   5, 130-1, 217
Laker, Jim   173, 177
Lancashire CCC/Lancashire Lightning   3, 10, 11, 41-2, 91, 241-3, 247
Lance Todd Trophy   75, 239-40
Langton, Billy   49, 113, 145, 147, 192
Larwood, Harold   177
Lascelles, James   231
Laurent, Josh   260
Leaming, Jack   242
Lee, Barry   191
Leeds/Leeds Rhinos RLFC
    general   109, 114, 240
    history   127
    matches   28, 50, 59, 75, 90-2, 101, 129, 146, 221-2, 252-4
Leeds RUFC   63, 86
Leeds United FC   xiii, 1-2, 39, 133
Lees, Alex   36, 242
Leicester City FC   255
Leicestershire CCC   260
Leigh/Leigh Centurions RLFC   254, 268
Lemonhaze   122
Leonard, Justin   249
Lewandowski, Robert   xiii, 78, 80
Lewis, Jonathan   36

Lillee, Dennis   116-7, 185
Lindwall, Ray   81-2
Lister, Jim   218-9
Liverpool FC   198
Livingstone, Liam   247
Llanelli RFC   211-2
Llanelli Scarlets   211-2
Lockwood, Dicky   174
London Broncos RLFC   254
London Stadium – see Olympic Stadium, London
Longhurst, Henry   75, 266
Lord's Cricket Ground   82, 247, 266
Louisiana Tech Bulldogs (American Football)   203-5
Love, Jim   10
Lyth, Adam   36, 91, 93, 241, 243-4, 247, 266

Malinga, Lasith   17
Mallett, Ashley   17
Mann, Simon   106
Manning, Dane   175
Mantle, John   239
Marsh, David   233
Marsh, Rodney   116-7
Marshall, John   14-5, 193, 195
Marshall, Malcolm   33
Martin, Jenny   62
The Masters (golf)   50
Match day programmes
    ice hockey   152
    football   46, 72
    rugby league   66-70, 140, 148
Mather, Harold   55-6, 148, 238-9
Matthews, Stanley   51
Maxwell, Glenn   171-2
Mayo News   86-7
Mayo Senior Football League (GAA)   85, 266
Mazzola, Sandro   135

McAllister, Gary   xiii, 1-2, 133-4
McAusland, Marc   122
McClune, David   72
McCollum Cowboys (high school American Football)   199-200
McConnell, Joe   162
McCullum, Brendon   157
McDermott, Brian   92
MacDonald, Jamie   165
Macdonald, Kieran   219
Macdonald, Malcolm   231
McEnroe, John   74
McFaul, Willie   230
McGillvary, Jermaine   263
McGilvray, Alan   104-5
McGuire, Danny   254
MacHale Park, Castlebar   84
McIlorum, Michael   222
McIlroy, Rory   248-50
McKay, Billy   130
McLaren, Steve   230
McLaughlin, Mark   234
McLennon, Gordon   179
McMahon, Jim   76
Meades, Jonathan   28
Medard, Maxime   221
Meekings, Josh   122
Memmson, Preston   42
Memorial Ground, Bristol   62-3
Meninga, Mal   263
Menzies, Luke   175
Mickelson, Phil   248, 250
Middlesex CCC   90, 93, 243
Milburn, Jackie   230
Miller, Shaun   260
Millward, Roger   190-2, 267
Milngavie and Bearsden Sports Club   161
Mitchell, Arthur   243
Mitrovic, Aleksanar   231
Modi, Lalit   208

Mohammed, Hanif   105
Montford, Arthur   122-3
Montrose FC   71-2, 89
Moore, Bobby   251, 262
Moore, Brian   74
Moore, Richard   44
Morgan, Cliff   76
Morley, Alan   62
Morrell, Cyril   129
Motherwell FC   1
Motor Sport   27-9
Mourinho, Jose   135
Moxon, Martyn   243
Moynihan, Lord (Colin)   118
Moynihan, Sir Berkeley (1st Baron)   118, 120
Muir, Barry   56, 265
Murphy, Alex   236, 239
Murrayfield Stadium   18, 28, 124, 128, 133
Myler, Frank   55

Naiyaravoro, Taqele   212
Nakarawa, Leone   112, 126
National Coal Board   69
National Covenant   47
Necib, Louisa   6
Nevin, Pat   123
New England Patriots   76
New Statesman   76
New Zealand
   cricket   17-19, 266
   rugby league   xiii, 263, 268
   rugby union   18, 133
Newcastle United FC   xiii, 229-31, 267
Niblett, Alfred (grandfather)   118-20, 266
Niblett, Charles (great grandfather)   118
Nicholson, Tony   242

Nicklaus, Jack   75, 263
Nijinsky (racehorse)   77
North, George   221
Norwich City FC   267
Nottinghamshire CCC/Nottinghamshire Outlaws   3, 171-2
Nyanga, Yannick   125

Offiah, Martin   13, 27-29, 190
Old Paulines CC   180
Old, Chris   185
Oldfield, Trenton   187
Olsen, Merlin   76
Olympic Games (2012)   5-6, 215, 262
Olympic Stadium
   Berlin   78-80, 137
   London   xi, 262
Open Championship (golf)   75, 161, 248-9, 251
The Original Oak, Headingley   128
Ortega, Jordan   200
O'Sullevan, Peter   77

Padgett, Doug   194, 242
Paisley (town)   121-3
Pakistan (cricket)   17-18
Palacio, Rodrigo   134
Park Avenue, Bradford   246
Parkside, Hunslet   26, 30, 32, 45, 49-51, 54, 108, 113-4, 145, 148, 167, 190-2, 220, 238, 254, 257
Partick Thistle FC   130-1, 133, 164
Patel, Jeetan   90-1
Patel, Samit   172
Paton, Chris   19
Patterson, Steve   243
Payton, Walter   76
Peden, Alexander   47
Peel, Dwayne   211
Perry, William   76
Peterhead FC   72

281

Pettigrew, Craig   47
Picamoles, Louis   125
Piece Hall, Halifax   96
Pietersen, Kevin   35, 37
Piggott, Lester   77
Pilling, Harry   41
Plisson, Jules   221
Plunkett, Liam   243
Plymouth Albion RFC   62
Poitrenaud, Clement   xiii, 124, 126
Pollard, Kieron   17
Pollock, Graeme   105
Ponting, Ricky   35, 52
Pope, George   26
Post Office Road, Featherstone   7, 44, 137, 52, 254
Potts, Gareth   175
Powell, Chris   60
Poynton, Harold   144
Preece, Alan   147, 149
Prince, Ashwell   42-3
Pringle, Derek   33
Prior, Bernard   146
Protests at sports events   186-8
Proud, Ben   98
Pullar, Geoff   41
Pullin, John   62
Puskas, Ferenc   134

Queen's Park FC   267
Queen's Park Rangers FC   89

Racing 92   216-7
Ramirez, Mike   200
Ramsey, Bill   146, 191
Rangers FC   xiii, 1-2, 133, 219, 265
Rashid, Adil   241, 243-4
Raynes, Michael   260
Recreation Ground, Whitehaven   30, 168-9
Reus, Marco   78

Rhodes, Wilfred   178
Richards, Sir Vivian   17, 246
Richards, Tom   62
Rigg, John (grandfather)   118-20
Rigg, Peggie (mother)   118-9, 121, 186-7
Rigg, Robert (great uncle)   118, 120
Rigg, William (father)   3, 11, 25-6, 28-30, 32-3, 50, 52-3, 56, 84, 108, 114, 116-7, 129, 144, 148, 190-1, 220, 224, 237
Roberts Park, Saltaire   177-80
Roberts, Ken   55
Robson, Sir Bobby   139
Rochdale Hornets RLFC   69
Root, Joe   16, 19, 52, 159-60, 242
Ropati, Tangi   8
Round, Gerry   144
Roundhay RUFC   63, 86, 169
Rowntree & Co Ltd   69
Rowson, Keith   114
Rugby League
    Championship/Championship 1   7, 44, 90, 108, 168, 174-6, 224, 252-5
    Super League   7, 39, 90, 146, 168, 210, 252-4
Rugby League Challenge Cup
    Finals   27-9, 50, 69, 75, 112, 114, 129, 174, 189-90, 192, 224, 236-40, 256
    General   144, 146-8, 169
    and Hunslet RLFC   114, 129, 145-6, 148, 236, 238
Rugby League Journal   xi, xiii, 49, 55, 66, 70, 141, 167, 265
Rugby Leaguer   66-8
Rugby Park, Kilmarnock   216
Ruhleben internment camp, Berlin   xiv, 118-20, 266
Rutherford, Rachel   121
Ryder Cup   161, 189

Saad, Saadeldin 5-6
Salah, Mohammed 5-6
Salford/Salford Red Devils RLFC 253
Salt, Sir Titus 177
Saltaire CC 177-80
San Antonio, Texas xiv-xvi, 199, 201, 203
San Marino Grand Prix (1994) 28, 50
Sanders, Doug 75, 266
Saracens FC xiii
Saxton, Tommy 95
Sayer, Bill 239
Scarborough cricket ground xi, 3, 93, 246
Scarlets – see Llanelli Scarlets
Schofield, Garry 256
Scotland
    cricket 10, 41-2
    politics 73, 98
    religious wars of 1680s – see "Killing Times"
    rugby league 263
    rugby union 18, 133, 154, 220
Scotstoun Stadium xi, 111-2, 124, 211-2, 216
Scottish Cricket Union 41
Scottish Cup (football) 46, 88, 130-2, 164-5, 169
Scottish Junior Cup (football) 46
Scottish National Party 73
Scottish Professional Football League (SPFL) 71, 233
Scunthorpe United FC 131
Seed, Jimmy 60
Sellers, Brian 243
Selvey, Mike 106, 245, 247
Senna, Ayrton 27-29, 50
Shakespeare, William xi, 149
Shankly, Bob 46
Shaqiri, Xherdan 134
Sharpe, Phil 104, 173, 242

Shaw, John 65
The Shay, Halifax 95-6
Shearer, Alan 231
Sheffield Steelers (ice hockey) 150, 152, 159, 267
Shelton, Geoff 58, 145-6, 220, 223
Sidebottom, Ryan 244
SilverWood Books 62, 64, 266
Simpson, Tommy 213
Simpson, Wallis 96
Sinfield, Kevin 56, 91-3, 146
Singh, VJ 109
Sissoko, Moussa 231
Six Day War (1967) 105
Six Nations Championship (rugby union) xii, 64-5, 153-5, 220-1
Skids, The 60
Smales, Tommy 50, 55
Smith, Cameron 263
Smith, Ed 106
Smith, Geoff 55-7
Smith, Graeme 35
Smith, Harvey 211
Snowden, Alan 113
Sobers, Sir Garfield 3
Soldier Field, Chicago 49
Somes, Mr 236, 239, 257
South Africa (cricket) 13-14, 16-19, 42
South Leeds Stadium xi, 39, 44, 108, 255
Southend United FC 166
Speedway 95, 181-4
Sport on television 74-7, 150, 154-5
Sport on the radio 81-3, 104-7
Spry, Richard 179
Sri Lanka (cricket) 17-19, 106
Srinivasan, Narayanaswami 203
SSE Hydro, Glasgow 101-2
St Cuthbert Wanderers FC 46-7, 88
St George RLFC 49

St Helens RLFC   29, 109, 236-40
St James' Park, Newcastle   136, 139, 229
St Mirren FC   121-2, 130, 176
St Paul's Church, Milngavie   121
Stade Toulousian   112, 124-6, 267
Stadion an der Alten Försterei, Berlin   xiv, 79, 96, 143
Statham, Brian   12, 41
Steele, David   185
Stenson, Henrik   251
Stevens, Brian   3
Stewart, Payne   13
Stibbe, Matthew   119
Stirling Albion FC   71-2, 89, 233-4
Stoke City FC   51
Stott, Bryan   194
Stopford, John   56-7
Stranraer FC   88
Strauss, Josh   126
Sturm, Dalton   204
Sullivan, Brian   70
Sullivan, Clive   70
Summons, Arthur   55
Sunday Herald, The   23
Sunday Times, The   31-32, 167, 215, 230
Sunderland FC   267
Super League (rugby league)   7, 39, 90, 146, 168, 210, 252-4
Super Rugby (rugby union)   210-1
Surrey CCC   35-6, 52
Sussex CCC   193-4
Sutcliffe, Liam   254
Swann, Graeme   106
Swansea City AFC   229, 231
Swanton. EW   104-6
Sweden (women's football)   5
Swimming   98-100
Swinton RLFC   54-5
Sydney Cricket Ground   49

Tait, Alan   27
Tansey, Greg   130
Taylor, James   172
Taylor, Ken   104, 242
Taylor, Lyle   131
Technological progress in sport   xii, 245-7
Temlett, Leslie   145
Tendulkar, Sachin   52-3, 251
Tennessee Titans   203
Test Match Special   82-3, 104-7
Tetley's Stadium, Dewsbury   174-5
Texas   199-206
Thomas Jefferson High School, San Antonio   201
Thomas, Michael   198
Thomson, Jeff   17, 185
Thrum Hall, Halifax   95, 97
Thurston, Johnathan   263
Times, The   55-7
Todd, Peter   50, 113-4
Toivonen, Henri   51
Tollcross International Swimming Centre, Glasgow   98
Tompkins, Sam   222
Topliss, David   128, 148
Tottenham Hotspur FC   51
Toulouse (rugby union) – see Stade Toulousain
Tour de France   158, 213-5
Townsend, Andros   231
Traill, Ken   144
Tremaco, Carl   165
Tremlett, Chris   36
Trevino, Lee   75
Troon golf course   248-51
Trott, Albert   247
Trueman, Fred   104, 106, 241-4
TSV 1860 München   78-80, 89, 96
Turner, Derek   144
Twickenham Stadium   154
Tyler, Bonnie   27, 29

UEFA Europa League   133
University of Texas at Austin Longhorns (American Football)   205
University of Texas at San Antonio (UTSA) Roadrunners (American Football)   203-5
USA Today   205

Vakatawa, Virimi   221
The Valley, Charlton Athletic FC   59-61
Verity, Hedley   194-5
Verity, Sir Gary   158
Vincent, James   122, 165
Voce, Bill   177

Wacuba, Ann   99
Waddell, Sid   266
Wakefield Trinity/Wakefield Trinity Wildcats RLFC   75, 91, 128-9, 144-9, 153-5, 210, 221-2, 253
Wales (rugby union)   86
Walkington, Jack   14
Wallace, Daniel   99
Walsh, David   213-5
Walsh, Ian   55
Ward, Fred   146-7
Ward, Jamie   59
Ward, Johnny   55, 57
Waring, Eddie   75, 266
Waring, John   241-3
Warner, David   209
Warrington RLFC   26
Warwickshire CCC/Birmingham Bears   90-1, 93, 158, 172
Washbrook, Cyril   14, 81
Washington Redskins   203
Waters, Chris   172
Watkins, Kallum   254
Watkins, Marley   130, 132, 164-5
Watson, Anthony   112

Watson, Bubba   xiii, 248-9
Watson, Cliff   56, 262
Watson, Paul   72
Waugh, Steve   214
Week, The   258
Wembley Stadium   27-9, 54, 192, 236-40
Wenger, Arsene   197
West Indies (cricket)   16-19, 260
West of Scotland FC   9-10, 64-5
Western Wildcats Hockey Club   161-3
Westport St Patrick's (GAA)   84-7, 266
Whitehaven RLFC   30, 49, 62, 90, 95-6, 167-9
Whitehead, Keith   145
Whitlock, Max   102
Widdop, Gareth   263
Widnes/Widnes Vikings RLFC   129, 253
Wigan/Wigan Warriors RLFC   28, 112, 144, 221-2, 236-40, 253
Wijnaldum, Georginio   231
Wikipedia   23, 46, 62, 72, 80, 82, 105-6, 135, 150, 205, 225, 233, 250
Wilder, Billy   62
Wilkes, Oliver   225
Wilkinson, Jack   144
Williamson, Kane   91
Willis, Bob   116-7
Wilson, Don   3-4, 241-3, 246
Wilson, Harold   236
Wilson, Ryan   126
Wilson, Vic   50
Winfrey, Oprah   214
Wisden Cricketers' Almanack   178
Wojtkowiak, Grzegorz   79
Wolstenholme, Kenneth   74
Wood, Garry   72
Woods, Tiger   109

Woolf, Lord   208
Woolley, Frank   178
Worcestershire CCC   243
Workington Town RLFC   167
Wotherspoon, Tom   219
Wyatt, Chris   211
Wycombe Wanderers FC   166
Yardley, Norman   13, 104-6
Yorkshire CCC/Yorkshire Vikings
    general   19, 40, 50, 104, 156-60, 246, 260
    history   139, 193-5, 241-4
    matches   3, 10-11, 35-7, 48, 52, 90, 93, 171-3, 241, 243, 247
    Members' Forum   20, 33-34, 207

Yorkshire Cup (rugby league)   54, 144-5, 190-2
Yorkshire Evening Post   56, 115, 148, 191, 238
Yorkshire Post   96, 146, 172
Young, Julian   179

Zanetti, Javier   135
Zimbabwe (cricket)   17, 19

www.ingramcontent.com/pod-product-compliance
Lightning Source LLC
Chambersburg PA
CBHW081920180426
43200CB00032B/2860